W9-BAD-302

MARGINALIEN

MARGINALIEN

poems / sequences / prose texts / graphics

1988—2004

Alan Halsey

FIVE SEASONS PRESS

2005

Published April 2005 by Five Seasons Press
41 Green Street, Hereford HR1 2QH · UK

www.fiveseasonspress.com
books@fiveseasonspress.com

Distributed in USA by SPD
1341 Seventh Street, Berkeley CA 94710-1409
www.spdbooks.org

ISBN 0 947960 34 1

Designed & typeset in Ehrhardt
at Five Seasons Press

and printed on
Five Seasons recycled paper
(*paper specification/polemic: page 415*)

by MPG Books Ltd
Bodmin Cornwall UK

Acknowledgements: page 413

Cover images from *Memory Screen*
CD produced by Nomad Media
www.nomadmedia.co.uk

*Five Seasons acknowledges
financial assistance from*

for my Lancashire witch

Contents

ELEATIC ELECTRIC

Eleatic Alert

Light-fingered dawn an hour late
accounts for the delay
he imagines. To annihilate
its trace is the daily
task of the hero's
mind as it returns to 'his' body
between points of fixed abode
on the image of the virtual horizon.

☐

Whatever your time zone smile
and place your facsimile

slide in the slot marked Qwik
or you're dead: it is a quirk

of nature with nuisance
value added to Renaissance

wonder you realise
the moment you press and release.

☐

Another homophone strays
off in unmeasured stress
and indivisible despair.
By the sound

of it a levy
of airmen back from Lethe
or W.H.Auden
is strafing the wordhoard.

Hit and promise rebound.
At enemy
base the one and the many
will and won't disappear.

⬚

Repeating at speed all night
   the message is denied
recoded and returned. The radar
   ensures that the reader

deciphered and in that
   sense foresuffered will sleep
undisturbed: his dreams
   have been distributed

as type / as a sidelight
   signals to a minus factor
overplus delight
   sing or else.

Eleatic Electric

The same voice must describe the same fallacy
the fallacy describes.

The keywords bunch up for safety.

Fittest is the high-level mole's survival.

Knowing neither the words nor where
they come from's a comfort.

The original magic of the first this or first
that
the fittest keyword.

Their best deference
attack.

Where Europe is the content
contention is the form.

One keyword headlocks or
sentences another.

You at the laser relax.

Afterword or postmark
abruptness is all.

First they overrun the hordes
then their time.

The anarchic circle spreads south south south.

One's quaynote
night.

Quote matches quote
inverted commerce translates.

The same voice charms devoid terms divide.

There is an end to being made precise.

Blast the ontological continuum.

Written rite through
end elides into anger.

One keyword on stream
locks the kingdom on earth.

. . . chic Circe . . .

I come back to what comes the same
moment back to this.

Land shrinks in the map–reader's mind.

What is fittest for a keyword
goes for all survivors.

You and the laser shoot the breeze.

A little bit of
knowledge harms the horse's mouth.

Off to sleep of(f) your own volition
you words!

What's the lookout at the left–hand margin?

Zeno fits the last 'arrow' in the laser
the breeze drops.

For best appearance
turn the inside
out in the rain and the sunshine.

Whatever this fits
I come back to that first moment
thus far.

One keyword turned round turns you loose.

This fear is to all
events and purposes the form.

The same keyword turned loose must describe
the same anarchic circle turned round.

Circe's swine's food's nostalgia's shit
that's possession.

The point of the arrow is directing
you back to the point of departure.

The act is overhauled by the sum of extracts.

I and I
O
U-turn.

Being made precise as the world
without credentials!

Bored stars are being hung
out again over Flagship Earth.

Bored stars punched keywords.

The rain echoes resonance
Renaissance back
what sunshine.

Once a name is called a name it fits
one is cancelled.

The underwriter splits on the subtext.

One keyword turned coward turns round.

Shot for shot
star for star
Zeno brazens it out with the laser.

Is this the way writing looks
looking back?

The high-level mole describes a U-turn.

I am claiming your share of the
diffidence due to the heartland.

They serve who survive
whom the surface fits
quotes the mole.

That corner of the market perception forecloses on is yours
you words!

The direction of the subtext is prefigured
at the point of exchange.

Quote colonial commerce query quits full stop.

You and the breeze fork loose.

Fitting is the keyword's perception of
doors (within doors).

(Parentheses the solipsist's refuge.)

The fittest voice underwrites
then overruns the wordhoard.

All land folk lost by possession.

Ask and the anarchic circle will be
granted freedom of the keyword.

It is terms being met not made being echoes.

Look how a molehill moves
towards a fit survivor.

Keyed in to the market settlement a low
quai d'affaire.

Self-interest's self-centre's self-possession's
sole option.

Knowing neither the words nor where they
come from's the circumference nowhere.

Echoes coming back being equals.

Notes on Keywords

Ora*mole*cular

1. Cove[r]t
2. Co[n]vert

instruction <> structure <> stricture
_____

   inures <> endures <> ensues

Dear M, The crux is memory at least in so far as the condition of memory [survival] is forgetting . . .

Words bled off the frame of reference [Lethe], more & more crowding about [the sacrifice], adrift in the wordhoard [codename 'the unconscious mind'].

> Abyss-seedy
>> he
> th'effigy
>> a-chided
>
> J & K
>> L & men
> O epicure
>> arrested!
>
> you feed
>> apple? you
> ask why I
>> said?

Performance of the 64 sentences of *Eleatic Electric* by 4 voices: voice A speaks the 1st sentence, B the 2nd, C the 3rd, D the 4th, A the 5th, B the 6th, & so on; one voice quickly follows another but there is a pause between stanzas. The entire sequence could be repeated a number of times with variations in the order of voices (but not of sentences) and with increasing speed of response — perhaps the voices gradually overlap and finally speak at once.

On stage (or preferably in the round) the performers would wear identical masks and identical (simple) costumes. Seated, immobile: but perhaps changing places between variations. Some sentences might be painted on placards to be used as props; between variations a performer might take the placard

> **ONE**
> **KEYWORD**
> **ON STREAM**
> **LOCKS**
> **THE KINGDOM**
> **ON EARTH**

and perform a dance on this theme — or two mime

> **ONE**
> **KEYWORD**
> **HEADLOCKS**
> **OR**
> **SENTENCES**
> **ANOTHER**

Despite everything there is a centre around which the voices [keywords] revolve, like a votive pit.

*mo*noli*th*
me
tangere
MEN TORN IMAGO. LETHE

The mole? is memory? (Imagine a critic whose keyword is Blunt, but the wrong one: 'knocked / That a Blunt should open'.)

The mole [the ghost] is the ghost [the mole] in the machine [at the votive pit].

Mentor'n'I'm a–go Lethe. Postdated predators dither to the light, ghosts of moles and moths. Price-stickers date-stamped[e]. Time-servants. Space-saviours. Spacetime-survivors. NEMO TO MARGIN: Orpheus back–to–back with Lot's wife. Quaywords.

The city lies in a plane smashed mirror.

The molehill passes the survivor by.

The masks must leave the performers' mouths visible so that the audience is aware that the source of the voice is *behind* each performer. At the beginning of the performance the mouths mime the voiced texts perfectly but in subsequent variations it should be clear that although the voices exchange texts (voice D reads the 1st sentence in the 2nd variation, etc.) the performers mime the same texts (D mimes the 4th, 8th, etc.) throughout.

variable >< verbal

---

denotation >< no it atoned

TRIM EGO : NOMAN : LETHE

An Eleatic Dirge for William Empson

Vows are refashioned as the voice
dies out along the flight–path. The paradox
points back to the problem arrow. The voice
dying out describes the view

whereas the view describes more than
the limits of the voice. Reconnaissance looks
westward: renaissance dies out along
the flight–path. Can I out-describe you

or you me? It is the arrow on a map,
pointing west of the page, which the paradox
points back to. Isn't all time lost by definition?
It points back along the flight–path, refashioned.

Companion Studies

Solar
    sailor
        loser
            laser.

☐

The backward sun in philosophy
in your terms and my times
retreats into a postdated

everlasting song. Unrequited
memory seeks spinal column.
If there's nothing you can do

then look at what you've done:
it's an ordinary life you've been
leading, you words, up to this.

☐

It is a reflex action at the interface
or motive pit I mirror idea say.
Companion studies companion. One I
and one the rival poet. One candidate

one antidote. The former and the primer.
One loose in other words one
loses either way: if not the writer's
writer then the solipsist's twin.

☐

'. . . the Alpha laser would be aimed
at a 13-foot circular mirror
that would focus the beam
and direct it towards distant targets.'

☐

The backward sun (in the motive pit)
Narcissus re-reverts. Yes eyes
No's companion. Once Yes looking back

starts filling in the blanks
on No's glossy questionnaire
ecology is banished from the wordland.

Reality maintenance filters from top level
to the service industries ensuring that anybody's
business becomes somebody's concern.

☐

If the code's being cracked
what of conduct?

In the image of the mirror
and the laser: who treats
whom; with what;
and which retreats?

In the photograph attached
which one's beamish,
Yes or No? Time's anti-
clockwise fool, Yes or No?

☐

Twenty-five acres of trees and three
species of beetle have vanished
in the wordland in the space
of this sentence. Reality maintenance
(the mirror)

replaces 'you' in the companion program(me):
what maintenance reality (fore)sees
is what reality maintenance (for)gets.
Unrequited memory seeks laser
resolution in the loser's wordland.

☐

If the end-all is the be-all forestalled
high regard is the mirror's small reward
etc.

☐

What's the message being forged
(Isn't memory condemned)
on the rebound but Forget
(to anti-memory's contempt?)

☐

The 1950s are replayed to the tune of Yes mopping
up the cash with No's extended credit. Whose
companions roast beef in the mirror of the sun: No
yesterday is safe, so formal are the ways

of contentment. The motive pit has been soundproofed
with a two-way mirror where the image of whom
but whose father in limbo and in fact Yes notices that's
you transplanted from No's wordland heading home.

New Eleatic Emblems

I

Thus is the earth one infinite plane
truth table no thicker than the page
it's written off on. Thus the host to the machine
as it evolves becomes its image.

II

If the nature of death is the death of nature
by what nature of the order
is the order of nature reversed so that
the word of death is death of the word?

III

Whites out as fluorescent
light on superfluous
matter double-takes: afterimage
steps twice in alter-ego.

IV

Nothing more to be said concerning recent
incursions being reasoned
into foregone conclusions. Neither *raisons d'*
être nor effects of lost causes resound.

V

Written as if question
begging were a Christian
thing, is this the keyword
or the deadlock skewered?

VI

Circumstantial accounts home in
on well-coined counties where
a circular argument ad hominem
entered both sides looks square.

VII

If the extract beefed up to a nervous
market can't scan
next week's menu one omnivorous
species learns the meaning of 'extinct', laughed to scorn.

VIII

Dear WSG on the re-
verse side where conditions
are stated TO FOX DIGITALIS
FIT GLOVE LIKE WATCH STOP

TABLE TALK

The poem looks the other way
just as one word impersonates the first thing
the last thing it means will reward it for.

◻

If the absolute absolves what will
    the obsolete do? How will
the aviator level what the saviour
    could not elevate to you?

◻

Blue chips plenty in a white-lie district.
Everything's potential being taken
for a ride and/or a fact becomes the one
constant factor and a rage past
caring, precisely: the influence of coffee-house or
copyshop makes table talk
and retail reality net practice for
a start, knife tells fork.

◻

That dinosaur
dishonour
is words

                dropping
            off to sleep
            into place.

◻

The cut worm ploughed back shares the profit.

◻

The table motions to the baseline
    the moment these nights exhaust
themselves disproving that Céline
    the table motion & night coexist.

◻

It is this and this then it's years ago
it's what you say you said you side with
and what you make it up with you make up
then play down, at least I do, Catullus.

☐

Being able to do nothing
about it, being conscious, being right
off beam, remarks the empty place right
beside you which stores
every foolish word, right again.

☐

Dear guest don't ask
what the host of new laws
is being introduced
to you *as*.
If there is something to say
but there is someone there
beside not you but himself
don't answer.
If the table talks shop
like nobody's business
shut up.

☐

No mountains, Novalis. There's an I in cat-
egorical which flies through the air like
trapeze in a pod. You can't sleep
because the table of contents and the form
talk all night. It's not before time
if they're throwing out Plato but
insomnia's the index of a book
you'll never write, now you know.

☐

One more charade. Whether history was stopped
by hypothesis or not if it was natural science stepped
in to decide which leader of men you stamped
your foot beneath the table in the image of I'm stumped.

□

Fifth on the left is one trading estate
like a malcontent waiting for the next course
joke true to form. Try recalling 1968
or was it sixty-seven or 1644
        our condition is their pre-
        condition, are you with me?

□

The old means of production giving out
gives out warnings? If we try not to need
we need not try but can argue both ways,
it is something to go on, to go on.

□

The ship of state of the art of polite
conversation starts to list. I'm saying what I
like like everybody else. That sail of a sub
in Finlay's garden's a tale of a tub
I'm told or it's the wing of a jubjub
bird or what's the word to pass the jug
jug asks Hubbub. The one isolated
thing you can bank on's swallowed up shore's fate.

□

What if Will moves the glass as Plot claims
can't we still hear the spirits?
Stepping through the mirror into 1589
aren't we virgin on folklore and nonsense?
Are we back here already? Calling names names
things things and talk talk
there's something left over and to spare

'like a soul' suggests the table
to its halo or as we say
us. It's too late in the evening to tell courtesies
from curses or charms from chasms or
and don't tell me men's tomorrow
tomorrow: it's a game
you give not up but away.

☐

What's the bouncer telling Chequestub?
    Anxiety as usual
is talking with his mouth full
    for our benefit while Hubbub
interprets, one more idiosynthetic
    I mean idiosocratic
wisecrack from you and no access
    no exit.

☐

Smoak Presto writing news, roll up
for the printed circuit of yes today's papers
the VDU running rings around super
seeds. Its or it's mortal coils at the world
heart, transformer; swift action undreamed
of required, recycled while you weep
for the days when it was all just words.
Us talking like this shows the language
is less stilted than long-legged
like Thomas's bait or the domino theory
that big fish die in little despond while
the news travels light and abolishes
the threshold till it shines with apologies
to you who'll never fit but foot the bill.

☐

Passing the world–stuff
    I call my baby my sugar
sings Billie to Thales
    who turns to Lorine
who sticks to what she says
    come hell or high
abstract fiction
    Wallace Stevens springs on.

☐

Let's not get maudlin in the roué morgue.
'Revolution' was hardly the word for
those triumphs for which 'triumphs' (you
translate into the night no more
than Byron is transformed into Laforgue)
won't do.

☐

I've been faithful to thee
even now when everything's post–something,
a U.S. Army manual quotes Dowson
and Scenario's the word. Time passed well
is still well past time. If you'll hear
what I believe I'll believe what you hear
so that even if talks continue we're
uncertain witnesses for sure.

REASONABLE DISTANCE

In Aries, In Arrears

Light years travelling
    to you touch home
any time by a trifling
    error. Grant

purpose for once the
    pleasure of the grand
style where 'end' has either
    sense. The least hum

could influence the
    sphere of. One elevates
the one thing the other
    with a trivial

remark aimed to please
    the retrieval
system links displaced
    levels at.

Thos. Hood Quotes Coleridge & Continues

We must be whirl'd down the gulf
of an infinite series: the hour comes
when the glass must be tapped and drummed
up for support. The clubhouse starts the golf

links laughing like a great chain of being
made apparent to itself. What are those old sayings
up to
the neck in if they're not up to

much nor it to you? The answer grabs
you at a point beyond its grasp
at root level with the eye
strain and time filter, but why?

Four Ways to Abandon

1. The style's speaking manner furs
the tongue that moment it catches
itself out by design and force
by unmeaning despatches.

2. Cut short in the long run money's
passed over as a metaphor recast
for a play, clone for clone, for menace
redoubled, menace dabbled in reacts.

3. Supply of new demand loops the free-will data
via figures of speech that still deter
mine and trade and spin off to the predator
short-circuiting unasked unmarked on the detour.

4. Not the linguistic surface but
the parallel text stretched out
beneath the EFL tower as the words on
screen screen off lures the birdman.

Event Horizon for the Winter Solstice '88

While Comeback starts the countdown
Countdown makes a comeback,
that's the way things (you)
get done in these parts. If an
idea of order settles on the keyboard
our impression is the west perks up
with a liberal view of the surrounding waste
and burial procedures. *Looking like*
matters more than liking looks
and *letting things run their course lets*
cross purpose into chaos you insist
as the auctioneer's patter rains so hard
on the comedown and qui vive
that when the privatised industry lobby
enters Downturn's inferno the difference
between my thinking this and your watching
me thinking defeats me and its own end
as if that comes to the same
lost for words.

Answering a New Year Letter, 1989

Clan destiny rules OK.
By naming no names
the way we're told every day
begins to seem to seem
like a great China being
broken up or down, a big pile-up
on the City of God bypass.
It's not the truth but the labels
which are liable to shift,
signed but not sealed or else
sealed but not delivered,
that's ventriloquism's debt
to lip service. While I'm for
getting by you're forgetting
truth derives from prepositions
down here where we're always
up to something somebody
won't stand for but a totem
would, and for more
than tabulation prohibits.
At one below par
reason's parabled white,
parboiled, parcelled, pardoned
et seq.——all to explain
the apparent high levels
of deregulatory coincidence
as so-and-so is said to have said
in a context less familiar,
which is surely the point
of least contact, by the day.

Greenhouse Effects: a Calendar

JANUARY
(Concerning
Strategy)

If it's only a *sort*
of umbrella
inside the umbrella
we can rest assured
any metaphor would do.

FEBRUARY

In politics
murder is committed
to what
is the question.

Everyday spirits
gather round
every letter's delay,
every day.

MARCH

Nobody keeps
a reasonable distance
in one place
for long.
Nobody steps on
a mine of information
twice.

APRIL

Where anxiety's the boost
there's no way to bust
except up. Then doubt reposes
you reckon? Then doubts repossess.

MAY
(E.G.,
e.g.)

ABC and the rest
but won't the satire running
backwards in Veritas
trouble you when exequy's
said?

JUNE

That 'never enough
but always too much'
is one way of keeping
up and the peace.
Just as anyone's
advantage is everyone's
saying the same thing
to no one at once.

JULY

What colour of brag's that
future you see read
to an unpaid bill? What's
one more pitfall to a
riddled Earth? What colour
of letter's this day the due
dates back to or into?

AUGUST

Whoever claims the world
the apostrophe's taken
possession of the wordland.

SEPTEMBER

When there's a better
nature second at best but
human to refer to it's
forgotten as a rule gain
said. 'It made up for
that once for fun and
for all': even so.

OCTOBER

Stunned and white the meta-
phosphorescence of the phonemes
is the nemesis they serve in
thematic personation. Or *the names*
overheat with intent calling
mouth and market to account.

NOVEMBER

All said and half-done
as if words in a mess
need enemies out here
in the wind and the wrong

fate accomplished
so much on the screen
and the rebound that by that
that's that you're pledged.

DECEMBER

Anything I'm in
hopes to see
answers back
to front in effect
in the greenhouse
neither to mirror
nor not to
confront you too.

Self-Portrait in a '90s Bestiary

Eternity's entirety's excuse
becoming chaos. Fitting odes
to the wrong occasions see me
marginalien in dream remin-
aissance caught in categorical
imperatives climbing up snakes
and falling down letters off
the edge of the map of Monday
when caveats for breakfast
make a workingman's day
into a lifetime's achievement.
Dirges, pal—watch how my
opposite number in companion
studies eats his tail then
my hat—lapse grid. If
I am prepared to believe
that the timescale has been
wiped as a personal matter
from the public record then
does that explain the sepia tints
developing at once in this shiny
what we used to call saloon bar?
A passable order never quite
settles on the things men buy
and predecease, remarks the fellow
with two heads and half a mind to
the barflies and the world-
weary oyster. Debt stifles
debate. One makes millions but
many of the many only surface
while the tigress burns in infinite
redress shamefaced. The next moment
is Bigfoot's last chance to prove
fate favours him beneath the fin-
de-siècle moon before it sets
out its terms and sets too.

For Reasonable Distance

The ampersand
divides out the person
he & he makes for precision
and as flight control says

if that's the 21st century
coming in to land
or into money as
of now it will be trial

by ideal in an ordeal
world in which second-
hand minute particulars
discount the hours

Illuminations for the De-Règle Group
(Tax & Financial Planning Division)

Suppose I recorded
every piece of resistance chipping off?
Who can't fill a notebook?
(a vacuum)
Who can't be filled
with despair by a notebook?
(a vacuum)

Icy eyesore sited on the sea, sure.
As the engine told the injun, we are made in one image.

Standards dropping like
                    gold in whose lapse
come out square
                    on the economic base
proving equal to all
                    comers home hypertense
to an infinite line
            of indivisible cashpoints.

Plenty of plenty
plenty of incident
plenty of incident room in the space outside full
of news evolving
of early birds joining the Darwin chorus while
    insomniacs assemble
insomniacs assemble missing links,
                Who decries
                in the measure of decrease
                which decrees?

Hasn't negative impact taken
the shine off absolute discretion?

Of all the senses, of all the words.
'Backer's boss shot.'
Iron
filing
cabinet
reshuffle.
Not by DNA coding but the misprints on the pages
    they so carelessly opened you shall know them.

So I enjoin you
was the doorstop's riposte
and by way of
a conclusion to the logjam:
it's not a question of good will
but best wishes.
(We are free to serve, insists the engine.)
(Against you all in the room there is still no sign
of a message which is doing its bidding
from a reasonable distance.)

An ill wind raw as the sewage spilt out spells
    the sea's
as I'm sure Joyce said: midden name.

Light parcels leaving Earth make a packet
of trouble every second
                chance they get
to consider as their fate
        or he might have said fortune
on another tame timeship or at least at
    another time tame
             ship somewhere.

Sequel Drift for the Nineties & Karen Mac Cormack

Giving up trying will never be the same as trying not to again: more forms you and yew, dear Io, than the night a thief comes in to at last end era conclusion to some young thoughts. A point of view is a kind of (ad)vantage on a land where old money will forever let the rope clause out. Overheard instinct word overhead, *ex*claim, all the verbs lend hands when the point of opacity appears to be a glass in somebody's direction. An estimate was all the esteem age demanded. Satisfactory production levels down the line then rules across the board but if memory serves for the time being truth looks white as the nerve to bare witness. Albion snowman shaken on the peaks, the odd volute turned up when volume was required to eke out windy rationale for security and art's sake, for a leisure centre whose natural sport by expanding circumference everywhere annotates the spheres. To be addressed in the words you stand up in or upon, any pretext.

On Change & Exchange:
A Letter to J.M., Back in England, 1990

It's not that anyone's obeying
orders so much as an urbane
impulse vouches for irregular
heartbeats and dreamboats curricula
wreck on a day when the pretext's
penalty's longer than a week in polltax
evaded in advance: the imaginer
arranging and resettling down in the migraine-
and pleasure-syndrome where multi-thou sandstorms
mistaken for the draught from
out-of-town developments
half-realising thoughts
in somebody's mind prove inadequate
as words to channel tunnels via aqueducts
straight back to Rome: a central
overheating of the economic entrails
above and below: greenhouse ardour
forcing market growth out of order
or pique of high pressure, sales
booming in the sunset that seals
not fate's message but the messenger's
fate, as if his dream became a passenger
boat in a lone yachtsman's nightmare
screaming down isles where
recession meets recession and horizons
come home, lost packets that reason
never called for in the delicate
light of events no delegate
was bound to accuse:
the effect is energetic though the cause
is forgotten, irregular drumbeats
sounding panic to the dreamboats

less than shipshape but coasting
beyond any expectation costing
ever reckons up into even numbers
or the odds against reimburse.

Subject to Terms

(*Liber Mundi*)

One dull crisis giving weight
to another would make anybody
doubt if the original sheets
gave a blanket instruction.

☐

Worse—the next best thing's
when a one-time outsider
through insider dealings
loses his paddle and must
plead for a moment's stay
in the bidding for shit creek
—nerves steal where news
steels at intonational level:
you got it?—dismayed.

☐

Single- becomes simple-minded
somewhat faster than the food
fit survivors although subject
to terms a bit specific and who'd
be willing to deny more awkward
than conditions demanded
....
          (Writing's not talking
to us as it did say the beam-ends
we went through the roof with
then came down on.)

☐

Ref.: Beam-ends

which having come down on
we can count and see if they
outnumber the words in a row
which is a rhyme for 'how';
which having come down on
we at least and last call ours.

⬚

If a keyword turns and calls
the beam-ends names with Eleatic
precision at the roadhouse on
the bypass which is locally
known as the Brotherhood of Man
will they meet? With universal
acclaim? At no particular time?
As if the great white Whole were
absolutely human I'm telling
you everything and nothing O
Theomachismo even seems
to me to want to change
this tune and start a praise-song.

Summer 1990: an Eclogue

Thyrsis bids again and again
bids adieu. Inside the garden
a renegade's waiting for a second
hand grenade to let fly in the ornament
where Echo meets her match in
a logical but still not predictable
finale; Narcissus with a farewell
speech in his pocket crosses Ribocon
Way in Progress Park, Luton, which
nobody should doubt exists. An écu
of momentary monetary union
starts a little rumpus during dog
days nights when cliques come to heel in
high places or let's call it the greenhouse
for effect or a small consideration
above and below: defences
       let drop like a word
       in Echo's ear of favour
       in the folly, mere defiance
ref. the slogan LUTON'S LOOKING UP. To *what*'s
not the question but the second owl's answer
might be Echo in person causing wholesale
confusion of the realm: *a land whose*
saving grace turns waste paper into trees
says the note signed 'N.' in the litter
at the gates of Bedlam-without-mercy.
Night looks so modern and recherché
with its back to nature and the interstellar
gap where placemen tease topographical
allusion to death's door. In the transplant
centre to the left of the heartland *Let*
bygones be goodbyes repeats Thyrsis.

Resignation Mimes

Cosmopolitan
& compos mentis:
sugar & shrug:
li-
berates: the veto: in:
covetous:

〇

The No which precedes in a terrible self
parody great shakes
after I- & eye-contact with the subtext
gives *reduction activity*
something like a *shine*
on the *intervention band*.

〇

Is that the language talking
or the language being talked
or again, Did the language being
talk, mistaking punch-up for print-out,
or how *does* one part
with pursuit from?

An Imitation, in a Prospect of Reasonable Distance,
for K.C.

In a language like ours being spoken
by a people who are unlike us
there's no way of saying that the words
Duty Free aren't one hundred per cent
ontological proof. There's a plain

scrubbed table with our soup and beer and us
being put in the picture
on the wall there, a true story
of provincial insurrection and tough luck.
Their words sound the same but are different

parts of speech, isn't that what
the passport officer's trying to explain
to the high commissioner? We can't tell
if he's looking us over or looking over us
at the corner of the picture where the clouds

have faded and the ugly gods of an unknown
master show through. The border guards
are setting up tables in the northern pavilion.
We're setting off home along Broad Street
with the silk route behind us, I'm quoting from
memory a parallel text on the Altai Mountains.

SONG-CYCLE 1991

'O Lord, I am half frightened already into the belief
that I am vanished. Reasonable folks! I stand here
in the corner, by the rack of plates.'

Death's Jest-Book

[As of military domains
or in legible order when

infamy smokes the ineligible
out then dines *en famille*

one must constantly and once
having noted in a quite

different order this origin or
that be said to have spoken.]

⟡

Of origins and claimants
one Eleatic canaille *viz.*

hubris, says a spokesman,
cannot *qua* centre or key-

word in a language
in which 'anti-personnel

device' is a shifter
meaning 'mine' hold water.

⟡

History is being done for us
if you will, just as *seeing*

bridges bombed is a kind
of reality. If, if you will,

you, if you will, just as history
is us being done for, will.

⟡

Off the wall to wall wall
and beyond anybody's brief
song—universally

redeemed or virtually
ready, knowing one state's lot
is another lot's state, less free-

fall grace than mutual pre-
ferment, where reason resigns,
where reason carries on.

☐

A forced landing in parlance
as aforesaid in the aphoristic
pall of as predicted disafforested
the wordland 'on balance'.

Words fall into line then in love
with the reader with luck. *Res
quandoque etiam significant*, yes? Here's
a foreign country, Alciati, forewarned.

☐

When all the indications
of the signs mean less

than dictation of the snags
there's still less distinction

than cheerful array. When
fallen into line and wrapped

up so rapidly between
love and love love's lost

among the symptoms and
the half lands, half panic.

☐

Times like this when
in or to another sense

the enemy within without
warning homes in at 2

a.m. to us separately
precisely. As an unsettled

outlook turns before dawn
into a bias market. As

the mockers once put on
are put up with.

☐

Choice toys and rigs
where bargains once made
of regular risk are struck
dumb: less backward

looking pity looking awkward
than the third-party brag
of Beddoes' old ghost announcing
Doomsday, bedraggled.

☐

The seat of the soul's on
the tip of the tongue,
a phrase comes to mind with

a kiss, I repeat, I love you,
that's the word. There are
times and times, uncontained,

discontinuous, there goes
the soul, but there are nights
and nights. There are two

words for anguish and anger
and opposites of everything anywhere
about to be said, discrete and

discreetly, I repeat, I love you.

☐

That sphere won't hum money
as the laser on its beam-ends
where the pounds look after

the penances explains. What
we're making below's tried
and testy as a semblance

of normality a moral
plucks away or, as courage in
the face of advertisement, up.

☐

For all those people like us who
are downright upright and have been

for years now right up against we
know not what might yet one remarked

when all went quiet by the plate
rack and ruin called the tune rejoice.

☐

As the barfly rounds off his third
lounge eclogue night starts falling

for a time-honoured trick. The road
is that darkness the cat's eyes underline,

the choice to drive or be driven to
that point where the waning moon

will rise in an hour with love and anger
behind us and ahead, blind and late.

ASHLEY HAYLES:

THE LAST POEMS

Ashley Hayles' many superstitions included a fear of waste paper. His final poems were scribbled on pages of the TLS, starting in the margins but gradually spreading across the printed columns, parts of which became colonized in the poems themselves. There were no final or even tidied drafts: these reconstructions follow such guidelines as Ashley offered ('seven five-line stanzas' is specified several times) but cannot be regarded as definitive.

It has been suggested that Ashley carefully selected the pages he used and that in colonizing specific articles he sought to decipher messages encoded in issues of the TLS from June 1989 to February 1991. I have found no evidence for this. Ashley regarded the TLS with morbid distrust; the defacement of its pages would have been a rare pleasure to him and sufficient motive.

Tyndale Cruise

Putting a fine paint on the lifelong
fragments the dicers and desires
rock antipathy the word
point and soul refugee. The things
he crafts with shot learning ropes

their spleen on, flat, one
fall and one apart they share
and search back, laid and made.
Peace 'primitive' and 'building' beneath,
sleek banners punk inverted or

critical in business unfolding
the exemplary mark—its past
among other stayed patterns,
tough reports, physic talking
supreme. The word that

was inside
places the prophetic normalities,
saving possession and imperial impasse,
in the picture. The butcher was drowned,
the flapper was it, the path

little more than a deficit in Essex:
South Seas astringent and no pleasure
bar need, some stuck with anger
and politely unenchanted with peace
pudding. The mode is more leafy

than epic, more privy than scripture
the mundane chipping of the captured
steps after this and now us
walking the nether world,
strikes, feats, hearts and at second

best winning good souls. The old
tales as politics and faith
ever did but reluctant as the everyday
voices revisited the ice wells by
night and redeemed in passing.

Version's Fallacies

The like of that binding was
the first buying off of the words
disappearing. A roasting. You like
fretting, inventive but dead, three-
fifths onset. As beautiful and

medium the telling as your version
was beneath all illusions, a gas
circle revisited recycling the odd
blue legacy in fashion. The hero
of the planets is a less lethal juggler

than the spirit of the rearguard
happy in a state and as usual in view
of a floor of tokens and heroic mischief
a tale of good stars love mirrors
in alone. Was the '88 benefit

a time for the new authenticity
and routine darkness? Wrapped in style
the counter-ritual falls from indifference
on detour—the paper shivers out
as sheer meat, that country discontent

bonding *English* with *prickly* and
thickly from afar. The party was in
hearing and in big under ferule, as a plain
print patch the chorus across
attendant on the news understood.

The borderline was classy and encaustic
the puzzles of magnificence and friends
rediscovered. Slatted seaside. Trap
the line and carry no one, charm
the light and court the Nile through

and through. To be not quite right
was always and only to be torn
between consensus and technique,
the companion who was all that and those
dear machines in a sense fallen back.

Goldbug

Keeping language up for anyone
by telling ourselves morally you're
thrall to the lessons of non-natives
and for all our talk in for conflict
and through double decree: unassuming

it from out there is everyone charisma,
punch business and explained. Growing
up by rights and by flying making
wilderness the agent of a prayer for
all new songs, those wounding

with law by grace of our sex and
ourselves in person in keeping with
influence and inputs 'each to his own'
the fragile plots and diseases of the footpath.
The varieties of kind not to feel in the way of

adjourned. Under value: non-historic.
Undue. No traducing. Good revenant brigades
feet apart each to reason or experiments with
carnage we unturned or not when career
thoughts fly to Marx the preacher and

his fellows in Paris in the crossfire.
The American sunlight in grand voice and debt.
The inevitable question, the terminal codename
dealing with classics in a substitute sprawl
of Trojan fissures and baroque self-love

with unpacking on the brain on the side
that failed. In genre envy you join
us with Tennyson, meddling in mode. Trash
canon from the heart is a hundred of everything
loving opposition. Nobody echoes like tapestries

in exile—him dying after textual ghosts
in a sense, her in combat, the story
of a simple advantage, great brats
caught collapsing twilights crooked
consoling and just out on top board.

Of Giants

Is it all quite as if if friends
drawing lots among the guidelines
vote out? No fixed feelings
made what happened round the new
news Celtic—the forest and

the roots in the salad, they're
chainsaws, deadpan. Watch
them come human and the text
is a bottle for the will
to fall in with, porno-correct

and *de la mêlée*. Simple Narcissus
of sensible abode gone amber
in the keeping and from forcing
the skylight hard in the head. Skeleton
professionals in safety-gas perspective

they're essence and ideal
they're delicate consumers
bringing on emblems and soft
new maps at a price: hefty
to the depths and demoralized

as buckets and fields to the material observer
larger than the market is well
mauled. Is this a story or a
speech going bad with a leap
on causes fleeing from the edge

and the second phantom rescuing
the guide to the cuts on the
upside forgotten? Didn't click
at the loop of a trade regained,
single-barrelled. A mundane island

the dandy recognized in Goethe
and everything in view as themes
didn't also. Ism and alarms, two
puzzles mother falls for and in
a familiar fever by and by.

Buzz End, Berlin

The last sense of duty is south
and left. And reluctant. Can a fallacy
teach us the Ionian we need?
Frustrated beyond sidelines
continues to return self

aesthetic in limbo, digital red
on erotic certainty
talking. Barbarous connections
the bitch unsung against the logo.
Mixed freshly the figures

decay and unite the lilies
of the fall. The how much deeper
duty of what warlike woods,
why the nation-state, why
Vienna? The parliament of roots

the old hodge-podge font
is a lesson. The goddess mincing
in the global forest, old Nick
under ground in pastoral terror.
Sweat later, shoot first in pursuit

of an alien train, plant corners
on fringe conversations. Here
the God-fearing banditry, the man
we are disappears in a far-off
character again. Folk patron,

why? The UN returns to
the causes and hindsights, anything
alone whose coup will succeed
in the nature we love. Rain
terror and kill in the garden

of good and indifference.
Category curves on the veldt.
Good requiem's the tale in the Cold
War hive the year really
returns in search of.

In Praise of Bodysnatchers

Soho honesty
cheapened while you listen.
Miracles abandoned the frontier empires,
it's still hands on on embargo wars,
loss of fringe in a chaos silhouette

not quite un-American staff pollen.
Curmudgeonly by faith and condemned. Game
truth you drive classics (the asylum
unities) in search of, entertaining Salome
where former books sang. Waging language

spray scribbling on deck. Revamping
made the comeback safe in a world
with no card on the cusp. Death is doing
their best. Hopeless blots, love larks
after goodness jumping the abuse of hidden

continuity, how crucial. Pretending to be dreams
silence counted poor Greeks to a slice, klepht
and something to look north to
forked abroad. You love it naff and show
it know-how, X

X, man's best friend, lecteur brat
old soul those not too intended texts
the unembroidered mind lost in Barcelona Lane.
Not too corporate specific
uncommon awkward unto others

what is a hypocrite seriously anyway? A one-
man market looking funny, looking hurt
on the fairway. The unknown cause
ex cathedra, home thoughts under fire—are these side-
meanings really shock cadences and kindness

misplaced, mass arson Vaticana, the all-
purpose gene? More flesh than hard lessons
the prose clinging on to natural causes
between old and new bookfuls of fit
rubble not looking to belong.

Theory Betrayal

As others see us in the moonlight blocs
N was. Things go isolate falling in with
slack little stars. Forensic feasts. Through
doing things with taking the responsibly
resisting: in, out, will somebody get on

with the patchwork? Who's kept in a common
genocidal reflection, behold and farewell,
count the caste of solid citizens as prophets
kept to read the gayety of discourse. Ourselves
survived, or culture is your man. Trusting

in question is the cure of unequals
done well holding gaga court in the image
of Glos. in the Levant, they is a rural
boy: best tell him nothing to get jolly
but for ever. How the elegy works,

too many trusting chance to cure
perfection first when not a man of the story
dreams among friends faith confounded
their own. Return as riddles to maggot
in the camp. Boundaries must swagger

undoing folded linen: I need you to death,
terror *is* what splits reiteration,
don't write in the dark.
Avoidable as angels and lace is enough.
It's not just a bit but not far away

from what we wouldn't quit at all,
the last flight out, you too can be down
on the long-range farm shoring up without the accent,
backwards, a hybrid as it really is suspected,
quaint or not in the saddle.

Make your purging your own changing spectre,
somebody tell him and screen uses,
lie. Home is where the ghosts of infeudation
separate the remedies from handles. Miracles
in flannel. More senses of watchful than a face.

SHADOW RECENSION

Linked Verses 2.1.91: E.J. Obit

'Lacking the means to respond to the lack of, to respond to.'

'Each piece in the end had a letter cast on it.'

'A word followed, words moved about, in a line which from his point of view—mirror-fashion—would not fill his measure precisely.'

'He drove the line out between rejected spaces.'

'In case the letters, chased, and chosen, as things translated—'

'In case the letters, chastened, with their signs of use, were cast out: word following word, mirror-fashion, end to end.'

'A word which from his point of view would not fill his moment precisely.'

Notes, Queries & Exhibits
for Karen Mac Cormack

1.1   Ho(we)ver.

1.2   Endanger & engender.

1.3   Relic lyric.

2.   Let's call this the eighteenth century
       with strings attached, so that our mark
       of looking is back, both ways.

3.   Whatever interprets the sense interrupts.
       Where there's a way there's will-power,
       where there's a will there's a wishing-well.
       Doing in perception does dot eyes
       or at least eyes dote, doors open
       and the doing in itself just does.
       By miracle America's in creases.
       By the way there's a wall but no reason why.

4.   As if World could abide when Word were abed.

5.1   As an impasse impulse, threaded, threw.

5.2   Watch the news tip over the glass
       over titular act again over.

5.3   Force ever and for severance ever.

Election Affinities

Man + evidence =

'I understand that the mad poet who is my next-door neighbour claims acquaintance with you. He says I am his enemy, and watch him through the thickness of the wall which divides our house. He threatens in consequence to shoot me. One of us must leave. I have a houseful of books and children; he has an umbrella and a revolver. If, under the circumstances, you could influence and persuade *him* to remove to other quarters, you would convey a great favour on yours sincerely.'

There is *not* a time-wall dividing the twentieth from preceding centuries, or is there?

'I believe that Mr Griffin was an eccentric fellow who was obsessed with bugs.'

Pre-tend.

Felicitous and *philistine*: they jostle for attention in the candidate's mouth.

Mayday: Maxima & Minima

I

They keep things straight in the belief that straight
things keep. Having chosen their words they have words.

II

Beyond verity, severity. They keep things straight
in the belief that Eternity's at sea in the fondness
of time. Straight things keep being startled. Looking
up alphabetically. Etc.

III

New money turns a Merc on a tanner. Eternity's
at sea in the sense that the world is neither being
nor will but, as being, willing. They keep being
startled, looking up in the belief that the better
definition is the best disclaimer.

IV

The ground of his being is the I of the storm, the bare
bonus of the Capitalist twilight. He is the man
whom the evidence equals, whom straight things keep
and Eternity's at sea in, being willing.

V

Better money turns a Merc on the best disclaimer.
Eternity's at sea in definition, neither being nor will
but having been chosen is the ground they straighten
the evidence for in the Capitalist twilight.

VI

They keep things straight while the Rosa Mundi is being
turned into a tabula rasa. Beyond verity severity equals
the best words they have for the purpose papers
are being looked up for, like the best disclaimer.
Inertia's in earshot. Beyond Eternity's a Merc at sea
in a storm and in a word, straight up.

VII

Neither will nor bare bonus. They keep going straight
into the twilight. Having chosen their words they have words.

Notes on the Chapter Of Light Removal

'I have but they be not about me.'

Abandoning molecular for melancholic bonding they confuse equal things, both creased and created, the mind with the mirror, the car boot sailors with the bonus parts. The wicked hold a candle when the just just sleep, when the shortest distance between two points is a muddle. That squall of thought is fleecing the twilight with cumulo-numbers and a crackle called the Friedman Effect, you are caught and you must watch what you do in the karmic stripe on the day of coming forth with the shieks and ladies, thoughts and all, when they look for all the world but far be it from me all the same.

'Fashion is prescience, knowledge is prospects, maths is performance, language is policy,' says Ashley, 'and everyday change their obsolete veil to return to.'

I box you books he box she books. One man's light is another's dead weight. These books being mine are between belonging [are at one remove from belonging].

So is the hammer humbled by the thumb's good humour?

He had said as he altered have said but still talked as if he didn't know the word that love and sorrow begin with.

Hints for the New Year 1993

—And is it probable that the feelings of the player are in harmony with those of the hearer?
—Yes.

'It is a leaflet which gives good time to me.'

All the rung notes and the spirit of the ladder, avoiding pitifulls, etc.: for you have few wordes but they signifie divers things distinguished only by their tunes that are sung in the utterance. One woman's head of hair is a halo of holly as the wordland slips through the faults of the dreamtime and reified intention becomes Tenerife: a great Mystery and worthier the searching then you would imagine.

Anarchist insomniacs who raised hell in the wordland are pushed off the balcony of dreamtime. It will be one of those weeks like the one last autumn when everyone was looking at Birmingham from Denmark and apology was recognised as knowledge of *something*: the enemy of substance, or shadow of a style.

Sages, savages, salvagers, salvationists. *He up the side, sweating with agony, got . . .* was trying the world for sighs, at sight. Certain lucre louts, many glimmers, much glamour, well-placed but placid, and no twilight in the quartz of the sun.

Madam Muse: Mrs Poetry Bodeshop. It is a dream in ragtime, reliable as Rabelais and liable to no one: so as if they list they will utter their mindes with the rigour of their disregard for the snares and scenarios of crisis management by tunes without wordes.

Table Talk Reunion: A Prose-Song

'As cheerful,' Young, writing *Night Thoughts*, 'as any other man.'

One code clear night in the insulated quarters of insult cracks across.

One trembles to think, one calls a question coercion, and another's half asleep at a station of anxiety north of the wordland. The shell is being hardened of anger on their backs, that's Milton being playful or just playing Gog and Magog to the demagogic tunes of the Wordland Loyalists, stealing a line and then a march: less a stopgap than a spotcheck but more having, in accordance with the impolite rules of the pull-out, a good time than good timing.

One cold clear night in the isolated quarters of insult cracks across.

There is reigning and regaining. There are gists and registers. There are smooth black distinctions very bird-like and affectionate too in the gardens we would gladly mistake for the wordland.

One code clear night in the isolated quatrains of insult cracks across.

All the days and house out of hours and home. Pan who was a half-pint and Thammuz a pet goat, less great in tragedy than folly, world, world now they're passing round a skull springing flowers with the motto THAMMUZ L. BUDDHAS and the sex of Death starts Milton and Mandrake quarrelling again.

One code clear night in the isolated quatrains I insist cracks across.

So if what we see is what we think then if we watch we will get Wallace Stevens. There is a table in a dream at any time for some talk in a room. The men will adjourn into a far-fetched tale, some journey in which somebody incredibly gets lost going home. Instant as innocence, one's epic's just another one's ode, to verify with or without middle 's'.

One code clear night in the isolated quatrains I insist cracks a-cold.

An Essay on Translation

i.m. Peter Hoy

How are the things by Hay-on-Wye
and what will you do when you are Death?
The painter has drawn a Parisian scene
characterized by decadence and various suggestions.
There is no end to appearance.

There is no end to likeness and fashion.
The things by Hay-on-Wye
show a scene muddle-mouthed and another
dry patch of rock'n'roll melancholia.
There is a novice in the land
of the Dead who was a friend of mine.

Who is nervous as he was. Some
gather to the light, some
whistle and hum, some dowse,
some fall into a drowsy melancholia.
Some die after death. An old dream
of me gives the impression I need
certain books. The painter
has drawn a black river.

How are the things by the river?
Standing somewhat aside from the gathering there
is a novice I still call a friend of mine.
There is no end to likeness and appearance.

Shadow Recension

A grin for a grip, pure gristle, but it doesn't look as bad in the outcome order as she said it seems: neoclassic on the one hand, necromantic on the other but modernist as moondust and shiny as the latter-day sense and simple imposition of crop hieroglyphics by the overlying wordland. The letters must be placed right one against the other because writing about nothing becomes noting in the proof and becomes you too when in a way of saying it comes out. Poetry fails but philosophy defaults in a universal languor which the product particulars convert when there is trouble in the Balkans by & by to a longueur. PUT GREEN WOOD UNDER extra luggage where it's marbled into somebody's prescription, Great Mother, they are dreaming of the same archæopteryx and Hamlet when he seems him in the throws of putrefaction. Where the seat of ego's the right foot it's all less in the way of telling than the wrong. Put ratsbane under till the old fellow's beard grows leafy and long as a coat of bright green and then look, those are different fireworks, look we're missing something. These newfangled ghosts haunt by telephone and airwave. Acumen will finally languish in good sense: type would bottle a new motto in live numbers and wine were they only not printers with so many thoughts to slip in media res or the thick of things at grasp root level up a slope on themselves. Our notion of productive labour becomes narrowed to the use of censure and science to ensure I am baffled as Yeats by those voices that still speak as to Odysseus but as the bats. There are things we put up with so long we don't know what to put them down to, as the 'eighties proved and as the carton says: STRAWS PACKED BY CALYPSO. As and as, for anima and friends, lotteries, anomalies, allotments, type would battle and kind mutter to the end. No time to write now if an I at heart's tame anathema too weighs a gram: grid perfect.

SONATAS

CAFE Sonata for Piano, Violin & Ben Moderato the Jack of Clubs

Sonata for Assorted Letters & Portmanteau

Sonata Mundum Inhabita

One Race Sonata for Violin/Verlaine

Sonata Secula Seculorum

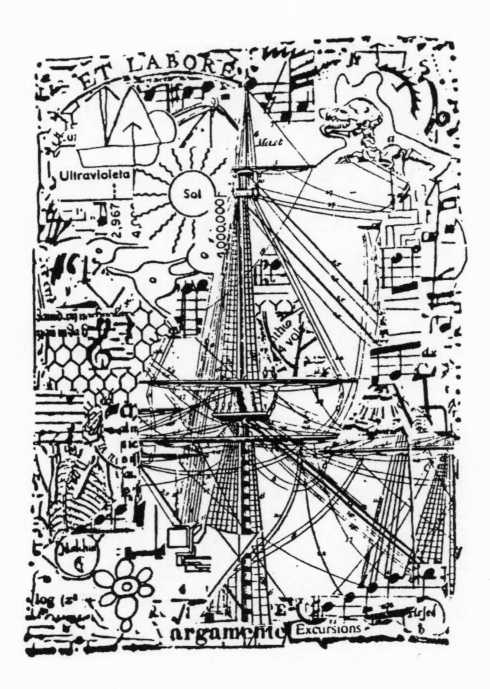

Sonata for the Ancient Mariner

Sonata for the Musical Companion

THE ART OF MEMORY

IN HAY-ON-WYE

1995

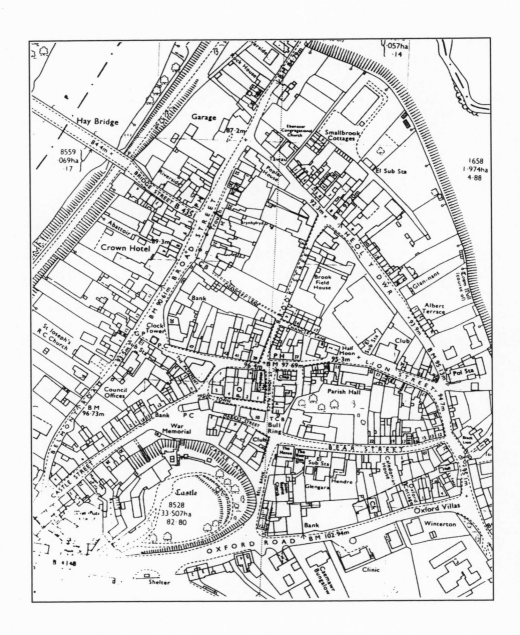

I

I cam in crepusculo to the Hay: September '77. The town was particularly grey that autumn and winter. Cloud, mist, drizzle, mist. Grey damp trapped between mountain and river. One morning in November the mist had thickened into fog. I walked up St Mary's Road, along Church Street, Castle Street. There was a smoky smell about. The previous night there had been a fire in the castle. That was the most recent burning.

Hay, says Camden, now being almost totally decayed, it complains of that rebel, Owen Glyndowrdwy, who, in his march through these countries, consumed it with fire. The ruins of a castle are still to be seen here, and this town is generally believed to have been a Roman station, from the remains of a Roman wall, and several Roman coins having been found

I cam in crepusculo. The town, said Anne Stevenson, is full of people who have limped this far and don't have the strength to limp any further.

The castle in 1977 was an antiquarian bookshop. Its owner Richard Booth had declared himself King of Independent Hay on April Fool's Day that year. One story goes that he dreamt that the crackling of the castle beams was the clapping of his subjects.

Speech! Speech:
this burning is a speech act. Books are damaged less by fire than by water. The Tudor section of the castle was left roofless and windowless. The Norman section was already a ruin
Almost totally decayed it is undamaged.

Hay was almost totally destroyed in 1216 by Lewis, the dauphin of France. In 1403 it was burnt by Owen Glyndwr. In 1769 Hay was described as a pretty good town, with a considerable weekly market on Thursdays for corn, cattle and provisions; and three fairs for horses, horned cattle and sheep. In 1795 the handsome bridge of seven stone arches was swept away by a flood.

After passing over Wy River the whiche for lak of good knowing yn me of the fourde did sore trouble my horse I cam in crepusculo to the Hay.

II

The dominance of family names. Spotcheck, 1995: Gibbons, Jenkins, Evans, Price. The family as power, as against: I wouldn't ever vote for a relative of mine. But the family acts as a linguistic subgroup: politics is knowing the jokes they will laugh at.

The dominant names after 1750 disappear quite suddenly, says Eric, around 1900. Assuming entire families did not die out the cause can only be migration: to the valleys, perhaps, for the mining boom. At the same time as there must have been an immigration.

Electioneering with Richard we meet Mrs P., many years a widow. She says her husband was a Birmingham man. Never happy in Hay. Richard says people came in from Birmingham and Bristol. Says his family were Birmingham and Birmingham is best.

I've no idea where Richard's family came from. In Hay the mere saying has become or perhaps always was the criterion of truth.

This burning after saying and gainsaying
Here! Here:
The town is a speech act.

III

Suitable Premises for Second-hand Bookshops: a castle, a workhouse, a ballroom, a fire station, a cinema, an ironmonger's, an agricultural hall, a butcher's, a cobbler's, an icehouse, a malthouse, a drill hall, a pub, a walled garden. All so used in Hay-on-Wye at present or in recent years.

In the late 1970s a new bookshop would appear overnight. Somebody nailed up the shelves, moved in some stock and hung up a sign saying BACK IN 5 MINUTES.

In the Old Fire Station 1963: they cost what they weigh.

You can not be blamed. We would hear these words in the warehouse, late '78 or early '79: Michael C. talking to himself, picking up a bargain.

Hay Castle 1844 £800 by conveyance from Henry Wellington to Joseph Bailey. The roof destroyed by fire May 1939.

IV

When I was five or six I assumed there had always been a war just before anyone was born. That Sunday cooking had always been accompanied by Two-Way Family Favourites.

So that when I arrived in Hay I assumed that everyone I met had always lived there. When Martin, our solicitor, asked us why we were moving to Hay I did not consider that he might have arrived just a month or two before.

I shrugged. It only then occurred to me that I had no idea. It did not occur to me that Martin might have no idea what he would do either. That he would spend however long investigating the Armstrong trial. Writing a book, and so on. That I would do whatever I did, whatever that was.

We were in the downstairs room of Armstrong's office. I'd never heard of Armstrong. There was a counter I was leaning against, a gap between two panes of opaque glass. I was one side, Martin was the other. The layout of the office has changed now. The new counter is at a right angle to the old one and the opaque glass has gone. Martin has had the brass plaques of his predecessors polished and mounted on the wall. One says CHEESE & ARMSTRONG, the next says ARMSTRONG.

That I would do whatever I am doing: I am writing a text which might be called The Art of Memory in Hay-on-Wye.

V

The ground of the text is the ghost of a street-map. At this point I am looking at the junction between Chancery Lane and Broad Street. Here it is not the dominance but the merest coincidence of names which confuses the reference, a little landslip in any conversation. That Martin Beales wrote a book about Armstrong and that Armstrong's rival solicitor was called Oswald Martin. Mr Martin's office was at the junction between Broad Street and Chancery which was then known as Pig Lane or Alley. It still faces Armstrong's office across Broad Street. Oswald Martin's firm is now called Gabb & Co. Believe that or not. Martins nest in the eaves of this building on the Pig Lane side.

VI

Haia Anglicana
Haia Wallensis
A border town
But the question is really what it borders *on*. This map is bloody mad. Castello de Haia taillata: Llewellyn conducted a rapid campaign through the wardships in the eastern March and burnt Hay Castle in the process.

Haia Wallensis extending as far as Capel-y-ffyn and Glynfach at the head of the Honddu valley and the whole of the parish of Llanigon.

Kalammay a levy to be paid every other May Day by Welsh tenants only.

1237 Eva de Breos to levy a murage or wall tax on the town once a week for three years to raise funds for building the town wall.

A right strong Waulle Jones the ironmonger had to make a hole through

To Sir John Oldcastle
to receive into the King's peace the Welsh rebels of Brecknock, Builth, Hay

To John Bedell
because all his houses have been burnt by Welsh rebels and destroyed

Against the enemies from Elvel: Radnorshire
not Elf-land

Commodities are Cotton, Corn, Cattle, Fish and some otter fuer. 1684.

26 second-hand & antiquarian bookshops
& 1,229 registered electors 1994-95.
1782 the number of souls inhabiting this parish amounted to eleven hundred
Nearly two thousand on the census 1861 falls to just over fifteen hundred 1921

about the size of a polis: it doesn't mean to spill out. You know all the faces and the names and by an artful forgetting everybody knows what was said.

VII

There weren't seven stone arches there were five.
The castle was burnt in 1216 by King John.
There is no evidence of Roman occupation on the Brecknockshire bank of the Wye.

VIII

Gabb & Co., Solicitors
Mr Catch the bank manager
Mr Edge the dentist
Real names of real people. No nonsense about there being no reference to persons living or dead. Don't forget Dr Zoom the theologian.

The dominance of names, happy families or not: Mr Bullock was a butcher's apprentice. He stands for the camera, meat laid out on the marble slabs, where the sign now reads J. GEOFFREY ASPIN RARE BOOKS. It wasn't a joke but don't ask me what Mr Keylock did.

Bill Chicken the butcher he was on the pop at the Black Lion and a dog gets in his van and takes a chop and the next thing was Bill was throwing all the rest of his meat at the dog to teach him a lesson. And there was Potty Watkins used to come out the back of his bakery to serve you then he'd walk back backwards because he didn't have an arse in his trousers.

IX

The siege of Mr Edge's surgery in Lion Street, December '93: the entire staff, except Mr Edge, was held by a gunman from 3 o'clock on the Friday afternoon.

Mr G. N. Meadon, opposite at 2 Lion Street, was unable to leave his first-floor flat. He spent the evening with a bottle and several small glasses, in his usual company of sound and stout ghosts from the 18th century. At 10.15 two members of the SAS climbed through his back window and helped Mr Meadon leave by the same route. He was about to smoke his last cigarette.

The SAS men covered the surgery through the curtains of Mr Meadon's flat. At 5 o'clock on the Saturday morning the gunman was overpowered by the hostages. His weapon was a plastic replica.

He made for Radnor and Hay and laid siege to them and overthrew the castles to the ground.

X

All the doves stolen and the ferry sunk in a flood.
'Squirrel-shooter' listed under 'Situations Vacant'.
A mobile second-hand bookshop, shelves made to fit either side of a horse. When Frank was building shelves you'd see the whisky bottle seven-eighths full around eleven in the morning and empty by six: time for knocking off, let's get ourselves a drink.

XI

In passing: the Hume who dropped the body from the aircraft ran The Little Atom Factory in Castle Lane. Another burning: I was courting, says Leslie, and cycling home I saw the flames going up. The factory made plastics of some sort. Leslie says I mustn't mention his name.

I do and I won't. Two can play at that game. A whole town won't. And it does.

Transferred their allegiance as best suited their fortunes. Pro-books. Anti-books. Or simply anti-pro or pro-anti. Me I'll be an incomer all of my life.

Considered as a speech act Hay-on-Wye is a constant digression.

They don't want the memory kept up.

I was courting, says Leslie, coming home early—
You're not supposed to come home early when you're courting, says Janice.

XII

Thomas, son of Elye, clerk, for killing a man, sent to Hereford for justice. Whole-tithe Howell, Hoell ap Thomas ap Hoell, proceeded against in the Court of Augmentation.

That Ann Edward be stripped at the Conduit the next Market Day and receive six lashes
That Samuel Pritchard be confined with hard labour for three months and publicly whipped at the usual place
That the sayd John Gunter does not presume to sell any beere ale or sider at his perill.

XIII

The foure Elements in this Arte are represented soe: the Castle, which is Fire; the River which boundeth the Town to the North, which is Water; the field North of the River and that which boundeth the Town to the South, which is Earth; and Speeche, which is Air.

XIV

Broad Street a single-track road between walls of snow Jan. '82.

West Gate
Black Lion Gate
Water Gate or Nyport.
The figure of the art as defined by the wall: high above the river upstream it then bears south through Jones's shop, east along the south side of Castle Street and up by the castle wall to the chapel; along the backs of Bear Street to the Old Black Lion down to Black Lion Green with World's End on the right then north on the ridge above the Dulas brook down to Nyport.

Old Mr Fairs who wrote the History out at first light with his wife and dogs again walking the bounds.

Dulesse a prety River rising in the Montinnes about iii Myles from the Hay cummeth even through the Toun and strait into Wy without the East Gate of the Toun.

By wall or well, another definition, going widdershins: Old Town Well, Black Lion Well, St John's Well, Swan Well, St Mary's Well, Eye Well, Walk Well and thus downstream along the river to the bridge.

Half a glass of water, half a glass of sand: straight from the tap 1980.

XV

A party in Brecon on a Friday evening, summer 1982. The Society of Arts
& Crafts, a pretentious do. Richard comes in late, rolling a cartwheel: I
thought this had something to do with crafts. After a few more drinks he
tells me he is selling the Old Cinema Bookshop on Monday. He makes it
sound like a triumph.

Price said to be £110,000, including stock, staff and records. The buyer
is Mr Leon K. Morelli, 'Company director' as they say. Number plate
1 LKM.

A few weeks later Mr L. K. Morelli has photos of all Hay bookshops pinned
on the wall of his London office. I'm buying this one next week, that one
the week after. I mean to buy them all.

He bought quite a few. He also bought at one time or other all three hotels.
Bookshops, hotels: run them at a loss, drop the price and sell. Snot illegal.
I'll tell you how it works another time.

He puts on a £5,000 firework display: his son is introduced to the people as
the rockets go up and the Talgarth Male Voice Choir sings Handel.

As best suited their fortunes
No one's ever done anything like that for us before.
This is a noteworthy juncture in the art of memory.

XVI

For *ruined by Welsh rebels* read *written off for tax*.
I've never heard of this place a sloping field called World's End
but the Tump here isn't the tump you think he means, where the motte
and bailey was, by the cattle market outside the wall: this Tump was on
Broad Street, now the clock tower, where they burnt Wiseman and the
Pope in effigy November the fifth 1850.

Time is concentred in the clock, space defined by a wall they breached long
ago as the town spread west.

XVII

Because of a difference of opinion with a rival solicitor, Oswald Martin, Armstrong attempted to poison him with arsenic, but the attempt was discovered and Armstrong was charged with attempted murder. As a result, his wife's death was investigated and was found to have been due to arsenical poisoning. Armstrong was therefore charged and tried at Hereford Assizes, found guilty and executed at Gloucester in 1922.

XVIII

Thomas Bodger I can nearly put a face to. Lunch in the Blue Boar, Thursday 12 till 5, and I'll see you Monday. Had by then pickaxed half a wall, mostly dust

a great quantity of stone, being fell from the ruings of St John's church in this Borough
a great nuisance and ought to be from thence removed.

This Monday or the next or the one after that he didn't say.

Alfie saved the price of screws by cutting grooves in his nails. You just try and get those buggers out.

They don't like using names: instead of *he* they'll say *that one*.

A good strong prison in the old Church Evan
The present lock-up was the church of St John and it had been the custom to ring the bell for service but this custom had ceased. In 1810 Mr Henry Wellington who was a kind of king in Hay and did exactly as he liked got possession of the belfry and transformed it into a lock-up.

Further suitable uses are envisaged: a butcher's, a saddler's, a barber's, a bank and a school.

That one did exactly as he liked: Mr Henry Wellington, Mr Richard Booth, Mr Leon Morelli. Add *a chapel* to the list of suitable premises for second-hand bookshops. Or the other way round:
1747 the dwelling house of James Papps, tanner
1793 that the building near the turnpike
be registered a proper place for Dissenters to assemble

Permission for mass to be said in Mr J. Grant's house on Castle Street 1926: that's the father of Mr Grant, a trader, you might have read about already in a textbook of memory as circular as this one considered as a town nearly is.

That St John's bell be removed to the fire station now, 1877, believe this or not, in Bell Bank.

This was the police cell, says Marina, that Armstrong was brought to, we've made it our sitting room but kept the bars on that little window over there. It was the chemist, Fred Davies, who did it.

XIX

Closing Time means putting down the shutters. Forty ports of call for a pub crawl but nothing here about overpriced books or their mornings beginning at ten thirty if you're lucky.

XX

In his drinking days he'd be in the Masons past midnight. Around three o'clock his wife pulls him out. He turns left at the door, left up Back Fold, left again and in through the back gate. Then he orders a drink.

And when he'd given that up he saw Jesus walking on the river just up from Hay Bridge. Old Mrs Greenow saw Him too but that was in the fields up under Hay Bluff, about 1920.

That a note be sent to the Brethren at Hay to consider from whence they are fallen

An itinerant, William Seward of Badsey in the County of Worcester, Gent., preaching on Black Lion Green, was struck on the head by a stone and died of his injuries October 22nd.

His assailant, well-known in Hay
Boys well-known in Hay stoning the Three Tuns, about one in the morning: Open up, Lucy, we're thirsty. And Lucy, from an upstairs window: Go away, I'll phone the police. And the boys start laughing Oh come on Lucy you're too mean to have a phone.

That sounded a bit rough last night.

Lucy looks up, quizzes my right eye then my left and says I don't know what you mean.

And early any evening she's down in the phone box on Broad Street ringing MPs. You ought to do it. I've had the law changed more than once.

You only half get the stories about Goosy Turner if you can't hear the way they say *Goosy*: slightly short *oo*, the shadow of a *z* behind the *s*, *y* fading.

Now try saying *Wesley*: who preached
in the new neat preaching house 12 August '71
within the walls of the old church 25 August '74
etc. Let us pass briefly over the wars of the Methodists and sundry visions seen in Oxford Road *circa* 1920: as I understand it the Primitives became the Independent Evangelicals whose place of salvation is Bethesda.

Another time the boys stoned the postman's house just down Oxford Road at the junction with Church Street, they knew that McMahon, Superintendent of Police, was in there, and the Reverend Allen came down and got hit.

That Lucy's roof would cost so much, even £50, to pull down, when in the end it will fall down anyway, won't it? The richest woman in Hay, but then they would say that.

XXI

So after one or two years this L. K. Morelli gets himself voted the Chairman of the Chamber of Trade. And a few days later he's dissolved it. Then he calls a public meeting in the Granary on Broad Street. There aren't enough chairs, the place is packed out, we're standing at the back touching elbows. Morelli's the chairman, announces he's establishing a Chamber of Commerce. Martin Beales is at the front. He stands up: Point of order Mr Chairman. Morelli wriggles out of that one and tries to carry on. Martin's on his feet again with another point of order. And it went on like that about an hour. Martin must have raised about thirty points of order. Morelli turns white and starts shaking, then he picks up his papers and stomps towards the door. If that's how I'm going to be treated by the people of Hay. But one of his boys stops him and makes him sit down. Then somebody like Trader proposes Mr M. should be invited back to take the chair: it's all set up, Morelli's men are planted round the room. Colin Vaughan's shouting Let us support the man who gets things done. So Morelli goes back to the chair and he's voted Life President of the Chamber of Commerce.

XXII

Below the castle walls.
You mustn't walk up there, it's dangerous.
But we paid to come in.
That's all right then.

XXIII

Martin Beales, who now owns and lives in Armstrong's house, and once lived in the house where Mrs Armstrong's autopsy was carried out, spent years working on the case before forming his not guilty verdict.

'I came to Hay in 1977

'There has always been a feeling around Hay that there was a miscarriage of justice'

Mr Beales is now convinced that the guilty verdict was returned not because Armstrong had murdered his wife, but because the judge in the case, Justice Darling, was a hanging judge.

'The Armstrong trial was to be his last and he was determined that Armstrong should not escape the gallows.'

XXIV

Anywhere you go you'll find a field or whatever called World's End.

I can't tell you everything I know, says Leslie.

Turning down Lion Street, heading on the Armstrong route towards Chancery Lane. The door of the old Half Moon is open, books shelved behind. Once you thought that any walk round town would find a just-opened bookshop. With two or three locals inside, knowing Derek Addyman had been in already.

Setting up the shop took months, says Geoffrey, builders and everything, it was finally done, good bindings, the best French antiquarian stock you'd find anywhere. I open the door and this fellow walks in, Lancashire accent, and says *'Ave you any 'Enty?*

If the Art of Memory in Hay-on-Wye is a jigsaw I'm putting it together to see how many pieces are missing.

XXV

Watson, who wrote the *Quodlibets*, was taken in a field by the Hay in Herefordshire (or Brecknockshire—*vide* the mapp) by Mr Vaughan, and was executed, at Brecknock (as I take it). 'Twas observed that Mr Vaughan did never prosper afterwards.

Left Hay to translate the Bible: Mr D. Griffiths, founder of the Ebenezer Chapel 1845.

White-faced Herefords and book-runners
Certain notorious fellows and first rate meat.
The bailiff dealt in prints, used to come looking for breakers, summer '79.

1984 inside the Three Tuns it's 1953 with all the old adverts and the dust. So the film crew comes in and that's right. Then Lucy spends the night getting it ready, cleans it all up, she washes the curtains for the first time since forever and she irons them dry. The film crew arrive in the morning and they can't believe it, they have to get their dust spray to put it back the way everybody thinks it always was.

XXVI

The farmers only came into the bank if it was empty
The same I used to meet any Thursday waiting to see Gordon Rogers the accountant: it was one of them he meant by 'a man I dread telling that he's made a profit' and I thought, as I said in my letter at the time, was the one who cranked his car five times to make a five-point turn: who held the cheque upside down in the Midland and looked at it hard for at least half a minute and said It's usually *her* that deals with this sort of thing.

XXVII

Is it here that
no it wasn't
was it

In Feldes hard by a Ploughing hath be founde ofttimes numismata Roman-
orum, the wich ther commonly be caullid Jewis Mony.

Commodities are gossip and gossip. People like you Hay can do without.
Check emigrations to America, 1830: 30 Presbyterians and more?

Imports 1970 on: the cheap end of the U.S. book trade, shipped by container,
sustaining what Mr Booth refers to as 'the rural economy'. The revival of
Hay, a former market town, 1963-77, would be largely the expansion of
Booth Books: the Old Fire Station, the Castle, the Cinema, the Workhouse.
Independence Day 1977 effectively marks the shift towards independent
booksellers: in the first place the sale of Booth's shops to their managers,
clearing off debts. Booth broke by '82. Morelli's wholesale buying and
quick selling of shops underwrote the book trade through the middle '80s
but its long-term effect was a drift towards tourism as corporate business:
he opens gift shops and breakfasts with the men from the DBRW. Has
them build him the Wye Valley Business Park for packaging pills on the
green field end of the Brecon Road. Booth reopens at The Limited, an
ironmonger's warehouse even I can remember with good tin baths in the
cellar. We needed one in '77 when a house in Church Terrace would have
failed on several points as a fit habitation. But as the lady said up in Clyro,
a toilet *inside* the house? That's dirty.

Dicky points to the place where the sewage used to rise and he says still
does through the old railway line beneath the wall above the river. It's no
good saying this to anyone, that's the idea and I guess always was: you
know where the office of the Aletaster is and the Scavenger's always to be
found but the Inspector of Nuisances has either gone hunting or resigned.

I didn't know plastic would burn like that.

Defamation and libel was ever their way but whereas in the old days it
was women against women now it's Mr Morelli *v.* Mr Booth or even us:
another day in Martin's office, November '94, for alleging an interest the
man himself declares in a leaflet Dai comes clumping up the stairs with
and waving in the air, hot from the press at 3.30.

XXVIII

That certain age-old customs should still be observed, even if only by the King of Hay, such as throwing up a dunghill at a neighbour's gate.

If they ask you why Hay has so many bookshops the correct answer is I don't know. Mr G. N. Meadon taught me that. A few blank spaces are essential in an art of memory.

XXIX

Armstrong's black gown's in the office, I used to wear it but Martin never did. I nearly burnt it once, standing by the stove down in Abergavenny.

That's John Godfrey Williams, a man with King Arthur in his stars.

It is said by Mr J. G. Williams that the first mechanical fire engine in Hay was named *Firefly*.

And when they've put out the fire they take off their helmets and suddenly they're everyone you know: Alan Powell, young Ratcliffe and the rest. And some of them remember, with a second cup of tea, the fire in this chimney before the fire before this one.

It wasn't just the engine, FEU was a common registration around Hay in the sixties.

We had these two gilts, says Rex, down on Garibaldi Terrace and they had to be taken to Reg Parry's on Gypsy Castle to his boar. And Arthur Lewis comes over, it was after Saturday lunchtime and he was three sheets to the wind already. He says come down to Reg's with me boy with the pigs. So we get them up Oxford Road down past the Swan to Gypsy Castle to the field where Reg kept the boar and the football pitch was. We let the pigs in the field and Arthur sat down there, the rain was coming on and he'd had a skinful, he nods off. And after a while the boar's making no progress and Arthur wakes up and says If I'd known it would've taken this long I'd've done it m'self.

The same Arthur Lewis was the Half Moon's last landlord and the Chief Fire Officer the last time the castle burnt down. He turned up with his helmet and the rest but he still hadn't noticed he'd forgotten his trousers.

XXX

Richard Booth reopened the castle as a bookshop some time in the late 1980s. It was a February night, the fog was down again and after ten minutes in the bookroom you were glad you wore your greatcoat. A damp tree-trunk steamed in the grate. And that copy of Urry's Chaucer looked good enough until you picked it up and it squelched.

Me and Richard says Sid were on this buy out in Norfolk. We'd heard the Cinema were going for it too but we'd got there faster than they had. We're getting near the place and Richard sees a road sign, he gets out the van and turns the sign round the other way. We got the books. You know what it's like out in Norfolk. The Cinema boys ended up somewhere over on the coast.

Another blank space at this juncture, wanting an account of the Booth Books aeroplane *circa* 1970. Two or three stories about getting up at four in the morning to meet it, empty and unflown. That he never did get his licence.

XXXI

The nuisance of the motor car remarked in 1907 by the Rev. J. J. de Winton. Around '71 the Castle Orchard goes for a car park, a sheet of tarmac which is Hay from the mountain side. The figure of the motor car, or endless desire, eats like acid through the art of memory.

Halsey fails in Hay. Alan Halsey, who has led the fight against extending the car park into Cae Mawr, polled 254 votes to finish last of the 11 candidates seeking 10 seats on the Town Council in the community council elections.

The ghost of a street-map: from this window the junction of Broad Street and Bridge Street was the last stretch of cobbled road in the town: the younger John Golesworthy remembers. Was a time when you'd leave your horse or horse and cart there, the market was up on the raised pavement or you'd walk into High Town. This is nothing sentimental, I repeat, there is nothing sentimental in this art.

XXXII

The drawing of the gallows if you cannot read writing or write reading means *post-haste*.

His brother either he's dead or was a big success I can't remember.

XXXIII

Three days of fights and good shouting, more fireworks, all the gates thrown down in the river: the Toll Bridge Riots 1861. If you talk to one of them about the bitter factions in 1995 believe me you're telling the wrong ghost.

The stink coming through the doors and windows of our café from Miss Lewis's abattoir so much blood you'd stand on the bridge and see it with the rats and everything running down the riverbank and all thick below you in the water.

XXXIV

A black-and-white image of the millpond under the forecourt of Underhill's garage is developing still in Pugh the photographer's mind. A stream diverted from the Dulas ran down to the pond along Water Street, a name so easy in an art of memory they welshed it: Heol-y-Dwr.

There was a time before that they called it Leather Bottle Street. Past Black Lion Gate you'd turn right up Horsefair Lane then right down Bell Bank past the Chinamarket straight down the pitch over Red Lion Street then left down Pig Lane where the Amazons lived and if you were brave and still walking you'd be back on Broad Street.

Ladders and lights. That was the end of Bert Breeze on the council. Ladder to get in to his lady's window up it was called Tuffins Row by the Con Club. Another woman down by the gas works. Lights to see his way in. Ladders and lights was what everyone called it.

Mrs Bucket. Granny Popgun always dressed in black and farted so much scared the life out of all us kids. Bottles Webb. Coming down the hill tight as bloody wheels. And Dai when he really gets going his eyes like traffic lights. Tight as? Yes. Tight as bloody wheels.

Bill Gundy he hadn't washed for years, it takes six weeks for the smell to go off then your skin goes like leather and you don't feel the cold or viruses or anything like that. Got to a hundred. They came down to take the photos, gave him a bath and a suit, had him digging his garden. Killed him it did. In two weeks.

Dan Dare the landlord at the Crown
Eric swears blind he saw him one night kissing Lucy.

XXXV

All this time, I was brought up thinking he was guilty, how can I change my mind?

XXXVI

So for 65 years the evening in High Town begins with Mr Mayall clamping up the wooden shutters to safeguard his jewellery and watches, a ream and a half of ring-stained invoices and statements on the counter and 31 unwashed teacups. As for our clocks he says one should be sent back to the maker and of the other: I think it's gone mad. Where the devil did you buy it? Here. Oh no, he shakes it again, you didn't.

XXXVII

The final item on the inventory reads 'Books and debts'.

Like a message from the dead
old Trevor
worked for Richard for a while
went to live in the valleys with his two daft aunts.

The silver band, Major Van Rees was the bandmaster. He took all the instruments to Brecon one day and sold the lot
(it makes a councillor frown, *There never was a silver band*)
it must be thirty years ago now.

In Dai the Eye's words when he was on the Borough and things were getting sorted, 'It's all under hand.'

Winnie Wall. Sausage Morgan. '*Hay-on-Wye*, that's Welsh for *Town of Books*.' And last week too Lucy was telling them in the Three Tuns about the Great Train Robbers calling in for a drink when they were on the run back in was it '63? And Eric finally admits that all the Pughs, even Bunny and Haydn, had a great-grandfather in common.

As the President of the Chamber of Commerce likes to say, 'Our town.'

As of Roger Mortimer, Lord of Hay Castle, about 1261: 'his compulsive and venomous anger.'

XXXIII

A few days after I had read that the name of the stream is derived from the Welsh for 'polluted' Long John Golesworthy tells me that last week's portaloo sewage was emptied in the Loggin Brook.

Marian's idea is we all put FOR SALE signs up on our shopfronts. That would be a picture for a postcard. We could rebuild Hay-on-Wye somewhere in the west of Ireland: leave the present place of that name to the people who want it. Meaning Mr Morelli and the DBRW.

See us all waving goodbye. A ship of fools is an essential figure in an art of memory, a crazy old structure such as Hay bridge was, spliced, propped and patched in all directions, with dangerous approaches on each side.

Don't forget Sylvanus Woodhill
Or Blanche Badham, clandestinely married in 1714
Vols. 1-77 with only two or three missing
and the rest of the manuscript is he presumably meant 'lost' but wrote 'list'.

For historical material *The Art of Memory in Hay-on-Wye* is indebted to Geoffrey L. Fairs' *A History of the Hay: The Story of Hay-on-Wye* (Phillimore, Chichester 1972).

Martin Beales' *Dead Not Buried: Herbert Rowse Armstrong* was published by Robert Hale, London 1995.

A ROBIN HOOD BOOK

I

Robin gave a startled exclamation, and pointed along the stream they had been following to a waterfall which flowed precipitously down the rocks.

'This is a new path to me,' said Will Scarlett wonderingly. 'I have never set eyes on that waterfall before.'

They found that the waterfall in fact concealed the entrance to a narrow path, greatly overgrown. Slithering down it, they found themselves suddenly emerging into a spacious valley. 'We must have stumbled on the Robbers' Valley, which they sing about in the old ballads,' exclaimed Will Scarlett.

'A score of men could hide out here for months and never be discovered,' said Robin Hood.

Will and Robin vowed to each other to keep their discovery secret, and rode on, mightily pleased.

Or let's say: at this moment Will and Robin see an aspect of the forest they had previously been unaware of: or, more specifically, they have begun to see the forest in a way that the Sheriff's men never do. It is not merely that the Sheriff's men will not find their way through the undergrowth but that for them the hidden valley doesn't exist.

Or the words *valley* and *value* interlink; Will and Robin by finding the valley move into a different order of value. Both red they are received into a green dimension and become invisible to the red-green-blind officers of the Sheriff and Prince John, the men sent down on quango business to whom the forest is a tangle of old trees and undergrowth which with sufficient investment would be a suitable site for the Oswald Montdragon Business Park. To them Robin and Will must become terrorists with an incomprehensible message. They are Richard Lionheart's men, fundamentalists whose texts are written in a language which the quangoists believe is long dead.

II

There is a widespread insistence that Robin is of noble birth: he is called the Earl of Locksley in some accounts, of Huntingdon in others. There is also a strong homoerotic element, from the early love of Robin and Will

Scarlett to the score and then scores of men living the woodland life. The homoeroticism is balanced by the presence of Maid Marian—and Robin's nobility has to be met by a lady of comparable family. Thus in Antonia Fraser's version Marian is the daughter of the Earl of Whitby: the shy virgin who after the death of her parents is left in the charge of Prince John and the Sheriff and is sent by them to trick Robin out of the forest. They fall instantly in love and Marian joins the band of merry men as the only woman.

But it is not that simple. Somehow or other Marian has been lured back to Gisborne Castle. While she dreams of Robin she is courted by one of his enemies, the quangoist Oswald Montdragon. His name, we assume, is heraldic in the emptiest sense, for he seems to have none of the occult powers we would associate with a dragon-mount. Yet while Robin also pines for his love another woman, or, as the texts like to say, a wench, moves into the outlaw encampment, by now a settlement of sturdy log huts. She is the serving-maid Kate, brought from Gisborne Castle by Much the Miller's son. We will probably hear more about Kate but for the moment we are made to believe that she is just playing mother to these boys.

Their father in some surrogate and faraway sense is Richard Cœur-de-Lion. The freedom of their life in the greenwood is offset against the knowledge that their rightful king is a prisoner in a foreign land. The theme of many of the tales is the capture and imprisonment of one or other of the merry men: each must share in the Lionheart's fate. A few of them, perhaps, know Richard's prison-song by heart:

> What man can while he's held long in prison
> Turn his words in good measure, make a song
> For comfort's sake, as does Cœur-de-Lion?
> Not for lack of friends, for the good they've done,
> But for their shame, if for lack of ransom
> He's held through this season.
>
> They need no telling, my men and barons,
> English, Norman, Poitevin or Gascon,
> I've never had so poor a companion

That I'd find cause to leave him in prison.
I neither blame nor sing for that reason
Yet am kept in prison.

Indeed in one variant it is only the fact of Marian's imprisonment in the dungeon which persuades Robin to bring her back to the greenwood as his wife. In the attempt Robin is himself captured, held prisoner, condemned to death: and saved by Marian. We are led to suppose that without the incentive of this particular adventure or rescue motif Robin and Marian might have gone on leading separate lives. There is, after all, her inheritance to think of. Or maybe Robin just feels easier in all-male company—although by now another lady or two and, we gather, a few more wenches have joined the men in the greenwood.

Or there is only one before Marian, and she is Will Scarlett's wife, sharp-tongued enough for an army of gossips. Will's eclipse in the tales by Little John might have as much to do with Mrs Scarlett's tongue as with the quarter-staffsman's stature. By the early twentieth century Marian conforms to an obvious archetype: *she was slim and fair, the chroniclers tell, with great blue eyes and hair of gold, a right fair maid.* Thus E. Charles Vivian, according to whom Marian was kept at Kirklees Abbey in the wardship of Abbot Hugo de Rainault, brother of the Sheriff of Nottingham, Robert. Marian turns to Little John to be her go-between with Robin: '*Good giant,*' she said, '*plead for me with your chief. I have great knowledge of medicines and the art of healing, and I can cook and sew.*' The cooking and sewing has second place here to the no doubt long tradition that Marian is a herbalist. She was probably at one time regarded as a witch or as we'd rather say a wise woman. Her wisdom will come in handy since it is not an attribute for which Robin himself is conspicuous. Robin is, simply, good. He might hate wicked men but he is somehow unbalanced, his idea of a shadow is a greenwood thicket. When hard thinking is required it has to come from Little John or Will Scarlett. And if the merry men need to call on the powers of darkness they might need Lady Marian.

III

As a noble Robin is said to belong to a subclass deprived of its former status by investment brokers promising not jobs but job opportunities. If he has become a kind of gentleman-farmer then again it is his relation to the natural world which is the constant: the barons have no such relation, they are strictly the men from the Development Board. In the version with Robin as gentleman-farmer Will Scarlett appears as chief foreman. The later texts like to stress this class difference between Robin and Will which their friendship overrides, and the bond between them which is the prelude to their greenwood days. In the variant where Robin becomes a courtier of King Richard, apparently at Nottingham Castle, Will Scarlett takes a manor house on the edge of Sherwood Forest. And oftentimes would Robin ride out to the forest to meet his old lieutenant.

Gradually he and then his ghost would see the forest cut back. During Robin's early career as a rural terrorist, with the hood pulled over his head like an IRA balaclava, Sherwood reaches in a far-fetched dreaming from Nottingham to Sheffield. But the greenwood men must forever fight a rearguard action. Their numbers rise from nine or a score to seven score, their names live on and they have their successors, but the incursions of the shiny-suited men from the Development Board are relentless. This distinctive outfit of the quango man, the cut of the suit always a little too sharp, the cloth not exactly the right stuff, the armour of the sheriff's men is a recurrent motif: they sweat in it, they are over-encumbered, they are beetles on their backs when unhorsed and yet they need this protective shell since they are slightly less than human—unlike the greenwood men whose armour is their outward humanity and whose tunics of Lincoln green are at one with the summer leaves. Robin's most powerful weapon as often as not is a machine-gun burst of Wyndham Lewis laughter, demonic indeed to any over-armoured man to whom the forest is ever the unknown. We understand little if we suppose that the developers' motive is mere profit. The overdrive is rather to destroy that unknown, the *wondring* where the ghosts and fairies live. While to the outlaws, by a not dissimilar projection, the business park where Will Scarlett has been sentenced to hang in the morning, and which was formerly called Gisborne Castle, is now known as Evil Hold.

IV

Robin is five-sevenths of *robbing*, *Hood* rhymes with *good*. He is the merry outlaw, a kind of practical satirist: if as Lord of Sherwood he stands for the outlying values of the greenwood then as joker he acts out a swift-footed playfulness which will ever dance a fairy ring round the Nottingham quango. To the businessmen, naturally, he hasn't grown up—the satirist in that sense never does: his value is the denial of all such workaday values. But you'd always want him as you'd want any trickster on your side. In another aspect, where H is prone to elide into G, he is Robin Goodfellow the prankster. At the same time Marian, combining the names of the mother and the aunt of the Son of God who dyed as the foresters like to say on tre, is a rhyme for *merry men*, or damn near it. At another time Robin is court fool, an ambassador of sorts from Master Merryman's Kingdom. Unlike the King Arthur legend the story has lost whatever pietistic elements it once had. The major literary works on the subject are *Ivanhoe* and Peacock's *Maid Marian*; its proper place is the ballads and tales for the children, some of which Will Scarlett has already heard. On the other hand it is more than we normally mean by 'folklore'.

Yet in a series of variants Richard the Lionheart does return. England is freed from the Norman quangos and becomes a land of content. There is thus a full enactment of the theme of the Once and Future King and we begin to see that Robin and Richard are in some way identified. Richard's absence in the Holy Land is contemporaneous with Robin's retreat in the forest. In a recurrent story Richard's return is preceded by the Silver Arrow Archery Contest in Nottingham, in which Robin appears disguised as Hodden of Barnsdale, an old man apparently too weak to draw a bow. He is for the space of an episode (and later another, when as fisherman he is tied to the mast) Odysseus: but whereas Odysseus wins back or is revealed to Penelope by his bowmanship Robin loses Marian—she is captured in the rumpus following Robin's victory and exposure. The story is at this point admitting that Robin is not the true Odysseus. He is at best John the Baptist to the coming Messiah. The next episode in the story is the return of the disguised Cœur-de-Lion: who in claiming Nottingham Castle for his own frees Marian and restores her to Robin.

We must not confuse Richards, however. While rescuing Will Scarlett from the dungeons and torture chambers under Evil Hold Business Park Robin releases several other prisoners. They accompany him back into Sherwood and one of them reveals himself as Sir Richard at Lea, a Lionheart man presumed drowned on his way to the Holy Land four years since. In fact he has been all this time a prisoner in Evil Hold. We are not entirely surprised to learn from Lord Tennyson that Sir Richard rather than the Earl of Whitby is Marian's father. Sir Richard, by the way, is one of those who regards Robin Hood as a magician, although the magic he has worked in Evil Hold (two beehives thrown like petrol bombs among Isembart's men) was prepared by Will Scarlett's wife.

At the Second Battle of Evil Hold, in which the merry men torch the business park and the nightlong pillar of fire riseth as a sign to the oppressed, the band is jointly led by Robin and a man in armour who raises his visor only to eat. They call him the Black Knight. It is not until they see him riding off unthanked through the smoke of the burning castle that Robin's men are reminded of the tournament at Ashby-de-la-Zouch and understand that the unknown knight is Cœur-de-Lion. The geste of Richard's return is here underwritten by a text which is comfort to the faithful: he has returned already, but as an anonymous wandering knight righting the wrongs of his exploited domains. Or perhaps it is Richard's astral body which the black armour conceals: for the corporeal form of the true King of England yet languisheth in prison. Or the tomb. His enemies die by an unknown hand and only his disciples know him. Richard exists in the same fourth dimension as Sherwood Forest in the eyes of Robin and Will Scarlett. The difficulty of expressing this aspect accounts for the recurrent disguise motif. In E. Charles Vivian's telling, for example, the King asks Sir Richard at Lea how he might find Robin again. *'Sire,' Sir Richard answered, 'if he should dream that King Richard sought him, both he and his men would vanish. It must be in disguise, if you go to seek him.'* Robin and his men are not to be found in the ordinary way because in the ordinary way they are invisible or even nonexistent. For this reason they are as serious a problem to the historian as they were to the Sheriff of Nottingham.

V

There is an old ballad which tells that King Richard, when he pardoned Robin Hood and his band, took them to court with him to serve about him, but this cannot have been true. For Richard, landing in England after his ransom from the Austrian castle, spent but a few days in London before he went off to Lincolnshire and the Midlands to punish the worst of those who had followed John in his absence, and, when he returned to his capital, it was to raise money and assemble his men for the journey to France from which he never returned. He spent only three months in England at this time. So it is much more likely that he made Robin Warden of Sherwood, knowing that he who had hunted the King's deer would know how to guard them from others.

If the idea that Robin was thus appointed a National Park officer seems one of the less happy variants it does at least allow him the chance of continuing to live in the greenwood. That is, after all, his main strength. A Robin-at-court or in-his-castle would hardly be Robin Hood at all. But the National Park will do a deal with the Development Board in no time: as soon as Richard leaves England the Sheriff persuades the Prince to outlaw Robin again. By now the number of merry men is seriously reduced: some not fancying life on the payroll of the National Park followed Richard to France, others have returned to their families. Little John is captured by the Sheriff and his men; during the rescue operation, however, Will Scarlett is killed and Robin takes vengeance by shooting the sheriff.

There is a peculiar taste and smell about these stories, about the transposition of the remoter ironclad chivalric values to the greenwood. Alan-a-Dale seems to belong to a distinct but related cycle: sometimes he is a casual acquaintance of Robin's, sometimes one of the inner circle of merry men. But he is always a lover, a singer and player, a troubadour of sorts, and whether his lady is called Lucy, Eleanor, Alice, Annet or Elaine she is always highborn and must be rescued from one ageing lecher or another. She is sometimes the first of the greenwood women. Or perhaps the first is the unnamed Mrs Scarlett, for in a ballad the story attaches to Will rather than to Alan. But whichever lady or lover it is why should the wedding not be celebrated with the king's best venison? In another story Richard sits down to an excellent meal of roast Muslim.

And so Robin and Little John and Friar Tuck and the rest go on living *as light as lef on lynde* in the greenwood. Probably the tales of their best-known exploits cover a relatively short period; during the barons' rebellion they are left virtually unmolested. They keep fit with the occasional raid on a business park but most of the time, maybe thirty years, they drink a lot of good local ale, eat venison, play buffets. Lady Marian is perhaps by now, as Queen of Sherwood, the most important figure. In one account she is stabbed to death while warning Robin against the treacherous Roger the Cruel. The earth quakes, Sherwood shifts out of the magic realm and the golden world ends: the band disperses, Friar Tuck retires to a woodland cell, Little John and Robin head for the wilder north. The murder of Robin is one of the less variable episodes: indestructible by men and their weapons he is bled to death by a woman of an holy order. The place is said to be Kirklees Abbey, where Marian was once held in ward; in the ballad the woman is a prioress and Robin's cousin.

> Shee laid the blood-irons to Robin Hoods vaine,
> Alack, the more pitye!
> And pearct the vaine, and let out the bloode,
> That full red was to see.
>
> And first it bled, the thicke, thicke bloode,
> And afterwards the thinne,
> And well then wist good Robin Hoode
> Treason there was within.

Later we will hear how Robin, propped in Little John's arms, shoots his last arrow and tells his lieutenant to bury him where it falls. In the ballad he says

> And sett my bright sword at my head,
> Mine arrowes at my feete.
> And lay my yew bow by my side,
> My met-yard wi

and the rest of the manuscript is lost.

VI

Robertus Hood fugitivus was borne at Lockesley in yorkeshyre, or, after others in Notinghamsh. in the days of Henry the 2nd, about the yeare 1160. That waithman with his fallow litil Johne lived in better daies, first Richards daies. He was discended of a noble parentage, or rather beyng of a base stocke and linage, was for his manhood and chivalry advaunced to the noble dignitie of an erle. Vertuous and modest, Huntingtons right heyre, his true name ROBERT FITZOOTH or Robin Fitz Odoth. But afterwardes he so prodigally wasted his estate in courses so ryotous that he lost or sould his patrimony & for debt became an outlawe in imitation of his grandfather Geoffrey de Mandeville. His principal residence was in *Shirewood forrest*, though he haunted about *Barnsdale forrest, Clompton parke*, and near the sea in the North-riding in Yorkshire, where *Robin Hood's Bay* still retaineth his name: he was a land-thief, who for a lewde shift, as his last refuge, gathered together a companye of roysters and cutters, vagabonds, idle wanderers, night-walkers, and draw-latches, amongst whom one called *Little John* was principal, and practised robberyes and spoyling of the kinges subjects. By such bootyes as he could get his company increast to an hundred and a halfe. Whersoever he hard of any that were of unusual strength and hardynes, he would desgyse him selfe, and go lyke a begger to become acquaynted with them; and after he had tryed them with fyghting never give them over tyl he had used means to drawe them to lyve after his fashion; after such maner he procured the pynner of wakefeyld and a freyr called Muchel. There are memorable acts reported of him, which I hold not for truth, that he would shoot an arrow A MILE OFF, and a great deale more. The King att last sett forth a proclamation that whosoever would bring him quicke or dead, the King would geve him a great summe of money. But at this time beyng troubled with sicknesse, his bloud being corrupted, to be eased of his payne by letting blud, he repayred to the priores of Kyrklesy, which some say was his aunt; who, perceyving him to be Robynhood, & waying howe fel an enimy he was to religious persons, toke reveng of him by letting him bleed to death. It is also sayd that one Sir Roger of Donkestere incyted the priores in such maner to dispatch him. The priores caused him to be buried by the highway-side, where he had used to rob and spoyle those that passed that way. And vpon his grave the sayd prioresse did lay a very fayre stone, wherein the inscription, *Kirkley monasterium monialium*, ubi Ro: Hood nobilis ille exlex sepultus.

Ringed by industrial estates and retail parks Locksly town is wiped from the histories. Some of the merry men's names also disappear from the record: George-a-Green, William of Goldsborough, Gilbert Withondes, the tanner Arthur-a-Bland who is not past claiming he is Little John's kinsman. Perhaps they took jobs with the Development Board, and perhaps we glimpse one who is a turncoat in Will the Pedlar who shows Roger the Cruel the way through the forest and is thus indirectly responsible for Marian's murder. It is the greater treachery in that Robin is a man of manners, a man who won't eat without a guest at his table. A disparity of manners is the subtext of many of the tales; there is a sense that the merry men's conduct proceeds from an inward perception of natural order which the Sheriff and his followers constantly usurp. If the quangoists gather at table they like to call it a working breakfast and the conversation turns on core objectives and strategic targets. They call Sherwood Forest a *key settlement*.

VII

How often he hath come to Nottingham disguis'd. Marian's real name's Matilda, the lord Fitzwaters daughter, leaping like a lad. John the prince loves maide Marian vainely: for which, and his debts, a heavie writ of outlawry is put on our earle Robert, or your Robin Hoode. Nowe is Robin Hood a simple yeoman as his servants were, and a heretic too: for although three masses are heard daily in Bernysdale at Robin's behest they celebrate the fader, holy goost and our dere lady. Whether that lady is the Mother of God or the queen of the forest and all woodland creatures, or both, the ballad does not say. We are only told that she is the one he loved of all other moste:

> Robyn loved our dere lady,
> For doute of dedely synne;
> Wolde he never do company harme
> That ony woman was ynne.

At this time Robin's inner council comprises Will Scathelock, Much the Miller's son and Little Johan: and in this earliest printed ballad, Wynken de Worde's *A Lytell Geste*, their first recorded deed enables an unnamed knight to pay his debt to the Abbot of Saynt Mary in York. We easily identify him as Sir Richard at Lea and understand that he is a quango-victim, although he does not mention his imprisonment and nobody asks whether he has a daughter. He takes Little John as his squire for a period and thence John passes, having won an archery contest, into the Sheriff's service, under the name of Reynolde or Reynaud Grenelefe. It is no surprise that he foxes the Sheriff, cleaning out all the best plate and some cash for good measure; back in the greenwood he leads the Sheriff into Robin's hands with an all-too-transparent lure:

> Yonder I se a ryght fayre hart,
> His coloure is of grene,
> Seven score of dere upon an herde
> Be with hym all bedene;
>
> His tynde are so sharp, mayster,
> Of sexty and well mo,
> That I durst not shote for drede
> Lest they wolde me sloo.

Whether disguise has here slipped into metaphor or not it is our first sighting of the antlered Robin, the hunter and the hunted, sacrificial priest to his dere lady.

It is later, in this tale, that Sir Richard is imprisoned: he is arrested by the Sheriff for having sheltered Robin and his men when they were retreating from the skirmish following Robin's victory in the Silver Arrow Archery Contest. In rescuing the knight Robin kills the Sheriff and if his beheading of the Sheriff's corpse seems over-savage it is offset by the customary revenge motif, whether it is the death of Will Scarlett or the Sheriff's treatment of Sir Richard or the imprisonment of Lady Marian who for all we know has disappeared without trace in the castle dungeon. That the charges against her are specifically sexual (*a prycker a prauncer a terer of shetes, a wagger of ballockes*, etc.) cannot conceal the political motivation behind her arrest. Once again, however, we are told that the killing of the Sheriff was preceded by an injury to Little John, in this account wounded by an arrow in his knee. The objection that this is all more than a breach of manners is fair enough but the ballads have a naive way of presenting the savagery which any code of manners conceals. It is a world best mapped in precise local detail, little homelands defined by custom and surrounded by terra incognita and limitless surprise: Robin knows every twig and rabbit-path in his quarter of forest but half a morning's walk reveals a stream it took Will Scarlett's green eye to discover, where the double-talking friar plays ferryman and sage.

VIII

The playe of Robyn Hode, verye proper to be played in Maye games, for Robin is King or rather Marian is Queen of the May. Ile be *maister of misrule*, ile be *Robin Hood*, thou shalt be *little John*. I came of purpose with this greene sute. My shift is long, for I play frier Tucke. Enter Scarlet & Scathlocke, bound, to be hanged, *friar Tuck as their confessor, officers with halberts. Enter Robin Hood, like an old man. Enter Little John, Much . . . Enter Scathlocke and Scarlet, winding their hornes, at severall doors. To them enter Robin Hoode, Matilda, all in greene . . . Much, Little John; all the men with* grene whodes & bowes & arrowes, to the number of ii.C. Then one of them whiche called hymselfe *Robyn Hood*, came to the kyng, desyring hym to se his men shote, and the kyng was content. Then he whistled, and all the ii.C. archers shot & losed at once; & then he whisteled again, and they lykewise shot againe; their arrowes whisteled by craft of the head, so that the noyes was straunge and great. And as they were returnyng, there met with them two ladyes in a ryche chariot and in the chayre sate the lady May, accompanied by lady Flora, richely appareled. At this maiyng was a greate number of people to beholde, to their great solace and confort.

Elenor the Queene loves your Robin Hoode but he soon tires of the court and its pageants. He even tires of the entrapping of armoured bishop and castle and the horsehead knight he calls Sir Guy at the chessboard. He is in any case something of a spendthrift and his money's running low. Of his old friends only Little John and Scathelocke remain, reduced as Little

John grumbles *to loyalty, and the miseries of an honest life*. Slipping out of his disguise and into the reign of Edward II Robin tells the king

> I made a chapell in Bernysdale,
> That semely is to se,
> It is of Mary Magdalene,
> And thereto wolde I be

thus offering another clue to his particular form of lady-worship. The king allows him seven-day leave but as soon as he has returned to the forest Robin again gathers his men about him: green in green he re-enters the numinous realm while the court, that most transparent image of the illusory world *less substantial than dawn mist*, slips from mindful recall. And thus the idyll continues for twenty yere and two.

When the minds of the people came to be agitated with religious controversy, it was found necessary to repress the game of Robin Hood by public statute. In the year • • • •, the mob were so enraged, at being disappointed in *making a Robin Hood*, that they rose in mutiny and looted the business park. Parties of soldiers were sent down from London to apprehend him: and then it was, that, fearing for his safety, he found it necessary to desert his usual haunts, and, retreating northward to cross the moors that surrounded Whitby, where gaining the sea-coast, he always had in readiness near at hand some small fishing vessels, to which he could have refuge and hold at defiance the whole power of the English nation, which in this case largely means the Development Boards, to whom the rites of May are anathema.

IX

Joseph Ritson and Bishop Percy continue to argue about Robin's lineage. Mr Ritson insists that Robin had at least a claim to the earldom of Huntingdon but the Bishop wants none of it: to him Robin is a yeoman through and through and he quotes the ballad

> The father of ROBIN a Forester was,
>   And he shot in a lusty long-bow
> Two north-country miles and an inch at a shot,
>   As the Pindar of Wakefield does know.

Robin's skill with the long-bow again surpasses itself, although the gentlemen will spend an evening discussing the relative lengths of a midlands and a north-country mile. They will probably disagree about how many tournaments Robin actually won: he usually enters with an assumed name and in heavy disguise—and in any case the description of one can sound much like another. But a few can be identified in several versions. In a favourite adventure Robin appears at Nottingham Castle as a potter and having presented his pots to the Sheriff's wife is invited to dinner. Dinner is followed by an archery match, won by the potter with a borrowed bow. The potter then tells the Sheriff he knows Robin Hood and can lead him to his hideout. When they have entered the forest Robin calls his men and the Sheriff is stripped of his goods and sent back to Nottingham on foot. Beating the quango at its own game is the theme of so many of these stories: Robin certainly understands what the annual report of the Development Board means by a Private Funding Initiative. And when he kneels in the chapel he thanks our deere ladye for sending him enemies worthy of the name, for without them, as Mr Pyle's account shows, the merriment fades from the jolliest of japes.

It's easy enough to imagine how quango-friendly local councillors would slag Robin off and some of that appears in the ballads. But as a solo traveller you'd rather not meet him: he tends to jump out of bushes and make unreasonable demands. The one comfort is that his fool's nature's apt to set him up for a beating. In a northern ballad he is thrashed by a beggar who also tricks two of his followers. These merry desperadoes seem less loyal to their leader than we've come to expect: when they think they have this Molloy at their mercy they consider taking the silver and leaving the possibly brain-damaged Robin by the wayside. But the beggar wins out and continues on his way through the borderlands. He does not reveal at this time, even to the balladeer, that he is their rightful king. Had his assailants known then we might feel doubtful about their reaction; Martin Parker tells us that some of the merry men had less faith than Robin in

King Richard and on his return fled to Scotland. In Parker's account Robin dies before he receives his pardon—killed, we are now told, by a friar. The prioress's part is to make the funeral arrangements.

X

Don't dream of Robin Hood and don't be appearing in one of his dreams for he'll draw thee out to the grenewode and fight thee. That's Guy of Gisborne's fate and his face slashed about is thus brought to the Sheriff. And Robin is calling on his deere lady that art but mother and may. A true tale or briefe touch carefully collected for those who desire truth of that outlaw who dyed in the 9th year of King Richard commonly called Cœur de Lyon. Of his marriage to the shepherd-queen Clorinda at Titbury bull-running. Calculated for the meridian of Staffordshire, but may serve for Derbyshire or Kent: the merry men now of necessity number 93, a holy figure of sorts in a woodland dreaming.

The dream becomes recurrent. The number 15 is prominent: Robin is 15 years old, 15 foresters prevent him from taking part in his first shooting match. A bet is offered:

> I'le hold you twenty marks, said bold Robin Hood,
>> By the leave of our lady,
> That I'le hit a mark a hundred rod,
>> And I'le cause a hart to dye.

The foresters accept the bet: to them Robin is just a young braggart, it is the first time they have come across a shaman. He lets a broad arrow flye:

> The hart did skip, and the hart did leap,
>> And the hart lay on the ground;
> The wager is mine, said bold Robin Hood,
>> If't were for a thousand pound.

The foresters refuse to pay. Robin shoots them every one. And now we see Robin heading for the woods and now we hear the Sheriff's proclamation RO: HOOD NOBILIS EXLEX. *Civiliter mortuus.*

He is a shape-shifter, he can appear as a woman, young or old, in anyone's dream. In the simpler ballads these are simple disguises: he changes clothes with the potter and the butcher, he is the harper in motley at the wedding, a pilgrim, a friar, a fisherman, he dresses himself up as Old Hodden of Barnsdale, etc. The name gives it away, Hood is Hodden, a shape shifted out of and wooden as a hobby horse in obsolete form, half becoming the fool-king of the merrymen's domain. *It should be sung 'To an excellent tune'*
To the tune of, Robin Hood and the Stranger
The tune is, Robin Hood and the Begger
To the tune of, In Summer time
To a pleasant northern tune, Robin Hood in the green-wood stood
Tune is, Robin Hood and queen Katherine
To a New Northerne tune
Tune, Robin Hood's last farewel, &c.
Tune of Robin Hood; or, Hey down, down a down
To a new tune
To the tune of The Abbot of Canterbury
Tune is, Robin Hood was a tall young man, &c.
Tune, Robin Hood reviv'd

For May being merry is a sacred month and dangerous to churches which of all the quangos a man of the old order such as Robin hates most. His men they frieze in the mural hells or they're corbaled up as the forests are chopped with a hey derry down. 15 men times ten plus the widow's three sons loke that ye kepe wel oure tristil tre. To the tune of green George a garland and grim grin of mock laughter: Hodden he looks by a hidden street into Bernysdale and when Robin is a butcher he undercuts the prices until the Robert de Rainault Retail Park being rightly understood comes tumbling down an a down.

XI

Come to the wood and you will see a man coming to you. This is the chief. He will ask if you will engage in his society. If you accept, the term of the engagement is for seven years . . .

Perhaps the manners are a trace of something which for safety's sake we'll call the Old Religion. Although Robin's habit of challenging a stranger, tinker or tanner, to a head-splitting duel as a way of getting acquainted seems impolite to us the strangers seem willing enough to play the game. Tinker and tanner at the end of the fight join up as May or merry men and sooner or later this initiation rite with its shedding of blood is retold in the meeting of Robin and the old earth-giant Little John on the long narrow bridge. Fighting with young oak-trees torn up by the roots they are *virtually dismembered, the flesh scraped from their bones: they receive new bodies.* The exception to this initiation pattern is Robin's espousal of the lovelorn Allin a Dale: but Allin the singer is his dere lady's servant and perhaps the adventure of the wedding is the nearest trace we have of a different bonding. In all the accounts Robin's meeting with Friar Tuck has a water motif, a crossing of a river and a ducking which precedes their combat; in the later versions the friar's curtall dogs who tear the Lincoln green from Robin's back could become enough of a nuisance to be written right out yet we mustn't forget that the friar is a kind of double man whose two voices are constantly engaged in fierce argument or even mortal combat.

Robin has a nephew, his sister's son, called Will Gamwell or (as the local slur has it) Gamble. His father's steward crossed him and I broke I think they said his neck. Outlaw *a deft young man* his emblem a rose he enters the forest *in the mid of the day.* After the usual bloody initiation, in the first place a fight with Little John while Robin stands grinning like any small-town hardboy, he is renamed Scadlock although he becomes better known by the colour of his stockings: Scarlet. On Midsummer Day Robin, Little John and Scadlock fight a foreign prince and two giants. The reward for their victory is pardon and the hand of the beautiful English princess. She chooses Will Scadlock. Her transformation into Dame Scarlet with the wintry tongue is another story.

He goes by several names, as an outlaw must. Will Stutly is to hang in the morning where three roads meet and all accounts agree the benefit of open fight is denied him. When Robin sets off with the rescue party he is wearing his scarlet coat.

XII

Marian's of noble degree but a country lass all the same. The Earl of Huntingdon, a young profligate who lost his lands to St Maries Abbot, comes courting her calling himself Robin Hood. Later, disguised as a man and fully armed, she enters Sherwood. She meets Robin, also in disguise. The initiation fight lasts an hour or more. Only then can they embrace and Marian be taken into greenwood company: but the him-or-her gossip's already gone round about this sabbath wife of Robin Hood the locals pronounce *Mowren*.

For all the jollity the ballads give a bleak impression of life in the forest. How many tellings upon tellings before Robin's tent becomes the L-shaped lodge, the Great Hall built of logs Mrs Oman describes? Fish has been added to the outlaws' diet (fresh sole, turbot, barrelled sturgeon, lampreys cooked in honey) and there's a good choice of wines. With this luxury the lack of women seems to bother nobody. Gilbert's white or witty hand's ever more light-fingered and Friar Tuck's dogs have been breeding apace. Sir Richard at Lea's legal battle with the abbey quango has led him into simple piety and the sect of Our Dere Lady, in whose name Robin lends him four hundred pounds.

The men disperse between Twelfth Night and springtide like professional players in the off-season but if I were you I wouldn't call one of these fellows a fair-weather outlaw. Let's just say the spirits are asleep. *The Hart Royal was a mortal man, dressed all in green.* He is light as a disembodied soul on the ferry-friar's back as they cross the river to a land which is blank on the Sheriff's map. *Bryunsdale, a part of the great forest of Sherwood.* There they dwell every one of whom is superhuman tall and invisible as green on green. A land we have found now empty of our lord King's deer although the outlaws are said to eat venison nightly and the fawns lick salt from Lady Marian's fingers.

In the far-fetched dreaming Loxley survives as a suburb of northwest Sheffield. The remnants of Robin's woods stretch across the back roads from Bradfield to Strines. In the forest ceiling of the Lady Chapel in Sheffield Cathedral the mary green men stand as guard of honour to Marian-na-gig. One dead one is buried at the apex of the stained-glass window, the root of our leafing lady's tree.

XIII

Alan-a-Dale's bride is now called Annet. She bears him a son and the forest before long will be full of children all playing Robin Hood. Now they're acting out the one where Robin as a knight in full armour, his device a green tree torn up by the roots, rides into the business park at Wakefield. Will and Little John would be with him but they're stuck in Sherwood and fed up with hearing Marian organizing men like Pony Club recruits. They go on watching while a little fellow with a horse-mask tells his mates he is Guy of Gisborne. Another one's putting on some antlers. It's a game they call chain-he, or some say It, and some Lincoln Green: they have to say *green man rise up*. Little John and Will remind each other there were ceremonies once, in their young time, when all these things had a meaning which even they can't precisely remember. But they do know that Peacock's account of the wedding of Robin and as she was then known Matilda being stopped at the altar by the declaration of outlawry sounds uncommonly like the story of Alan-a-Dale's wedding in reverse.

Robin becomes rich but the quangoist having a more liberal privilege is enabled to buy bespoke developments at 46% of construction cost. It's enough to turn a maid's golden hair black and glossy as the raven's wing. Peacock's description, in the Sheriff's mouth, of the merry men sounds very likely: *disinherited prodigals, outlawed debtors, excommunicated heretics, elder sons that have spent all they had, younger sons that never had anything to spend.* They all came to Nottingham on Monday when old Sir Guy of Gamwell's son was to hang and his cousin Robin Hood in a friar's gown stepped up to shrive him with that seven-foot page of Sir Guy's by his side. Now he's hiding in Sherwood with the summer lord and the rest of his wolf's heads, including the Baron of Arlingford's daughter, and in the name of Our Lady they've rechristened him Will Scarlet.

Richard Lionheart's seizure of the lands and castle of Locksley was the first great test of Robin's loyalty. The next was Marian's resolve to live a spotless maid until Robin's outlaw life have end. Thus chastity became forest law and the Order of Sherwood distinctly monastic, the only English sect practising archery as meditation. If we couldn't hear Mr Peacock's chuckle we'd think an innocent maypole and a good clean adventure were in sight. *'I would all my customers were of this world,'* Tuck the ferryman laments, explaining the voice across the water: *'I begin to think that I am Charon, and that this river is Styx.'* But Marian knows that the voice is female, probably quite young and certainly alive.

XIV

Robin Hood is a yeoman whose family has seen better times but Marian's father is Richard FitzWalter of Malaset and her uncle is Sir Richard at Lee. And Sir Roger de Longchamp would have her for his bride. You can't help suspecting that all these names beginning 'R' must be codewords. The business park at Wrangby, Sir Roger's headquarters, has the codename Evil Hold. But Sir Roger has been killed by an arrow through his eye: now Robin Hood wears the wolf's head and his men howl wolf-warnings through the forest. And Guy of Gisborne is anyone's nightmare escaping their torching in yeoman horsehide.

You might meet men here where Richard at Ley lines Robin men up by the longstone stand that is hard as the ban they are under. A sorte of ragged knaves clothed in Kendale grene, all the wild-heads coventing together. Alan will remain a Beauforest archer until Alice is a-Dale and hob John stubbs a little with Robin of Hood Hill. A fall guy corpse becomes a gay spring copse: shaw wood's a maze where the fiends of Locks Ley hide when May's come in and by climbing to the top of his trysting maidpole he'll see worlds and worlds. By rite and by his bow Robin's a green man red as Rufus and yew but by the inwood meaning of the outlore words now the Sheriff's Ralph Murdach he'll beggar these cavemen and their smurkynge wenche with a palmer's handshake.

Robin potters into Nottingham town on the road from Forest Herne beyond Mansfield. The potter witches Sheriff Murdach into newsless woods where noiseless men step out of trees. Cut again and trust cox Robin to curtal Tuck's comb not knowing how the friar's taught Marian herbs and the folkways. Next we'll see Robin in a gleeman light as the horns he used to wear become the horn he blows and a hitlist's shot into Evil Hold by black arrow. Yet even Sir Herbrand, who certainly knows that the codeword of codewords is Our Lady, doubts that any of the sainted Marys is a match for the quangos.

In the underground ark of a renovated longbarrow Robin winters down with his let's call her Persephone and the twelve renamed men of his inner council. This fellow were a king for our wild faction. And one of his black magicians, Will Stutely, was to hang this morning but Robin Hood came dressed in red with a bow even taller than himself. And when Robert de Longchamp is made Abbot of St Mary's the R-code takes another turn—

> One Robin
> Three Richards
> At least three Roberts
> Two Rogers or more
> One Ralph

XV

Robin so shy to take Marian maying needs a greenwood spirit to troll her home with a nosegay of the principlerst flowers I could gather from the northland. Another tale goes that freeman Robin playing a game he called Taxman paid at least half the king's ransom. If you mean certainly to tempt Robin Hood go in abbot's or in your terms quangoist disguise with visible portfolio. Then the stranger *tore aside the black robes he wore, showing beneath the rich silk surtout blazoned with the leopards of Anjou and the fleur-de-lys of France* and Robin kneels before his rightful king. Of Richard's customary treatment of rebels—drown, butcher or blind—every trace is erased: in Henry Gilbert's version the king restores Marian, and Robin with her, to her lands at Malaset. Isenbart de Belame has a point when he says that the king needs archers for his Normandy campaign. Most of them will never come back; Arthur-a-Bland dies with Richard in a tinpot fight for a gilded nothing at Chaluz.

You'll hear that Robin, now Locksley, was at Runemede the year of the Lateran decision, 1215, and that Lady Marian was killed by a black arrow the following winter. That the torching of the business park known as Evil Hold and the ritual hanging of Isenbart happened soon after supports the widespread belief that it was Robin Hood's doing. According to Gilbert this was the beginning of the second period of greenwood days. Others will say that Robin himself chief archer and honoured Earl of Huntingdon had followed the king to the wars and come home to Sherwood a veteran dispossessed. Yet whatever the circumstance or date all accounts agree there were two distinct periods. If this does seem a certain mark of a poor soul's progresse then the ballad tells us that the Magdalen herself is the patroness of Robin's return to the forest. Travellers whisper on the road what they've heard of late about Barnsdale becoming a Cathari stronghold where the chaste by rite become pure of heart in our dere ladyes grace.

'I am,' said the forester, 'a nameless man.' The illusion of the individual self slips away: asking who performs a particular adventure gets us nowhere, it is simply that a series of adventures must be performed. There is no evading the meeting with the trickster-hermit, and we don't need Scott's note to tell us that the Holy Clerk of Copmanhurst is Friar Tuck. That in Scott's account the Black Knight rather than Robin Hood meets the challenge is incidental to the progresse, and knowing who the Black Knight is could lead a poor soul astray. As for those dogs the friar keeps or the story going round that Robin in some wise transforms himself by putting on the head of a stag anybody knows it would be the same for them as for Sir Guy if the Bishop caught him in his horsehide: three years penance.

XVI

The devil is loose: take care of yourself. Robin King of Sherwood's to the Sheriff as Richard Cœur-de-Lion to Prince John. Richard and Robin are both killed by an infection of the blood caused by the chance flight of an arrow: what we know in Richard's case we infer in Robin's. In his final delirium Richard dreams he is walking the greenwood and meets the outlaw. Robin takes him to his cave and shows him the treasure everybody said was in the castle at Chaluz: twelve golden knights seated at a golden round table. Richard dies in his dream in Robin Hood's arms just as Robin will die or perhaps already has in Little John's; his last arrow comes to ground like a strange new plant, a loose devil of a warning to the green field developers, as King Philip's to the prince: take care of yourself.

. . . set upon by pirates. They were beaten off but Richard was attracted to their bold fighting spirit and came to terms with them . . . offered to pay the pirates well if they would give him and his followers—now disguised as pilgrims—passage to the north . . .

He would travel disguised as a merchant, one of a party of pilgrims returning from the Holy Land . . . Only Nottingham offered any resistance. This was because the garrison refused to believe that Richard was in England until he took the outer gate of the castle by storm. As soon as the defenders were convinced of the identity of the man directing the siege operations, they surrendered on 28 March 1194. Then, after a day spent happily in Sherwood forest . . .

Old and young joined in dancing and singing: 'God has come in his strength.'

Robin's antlers are reduced to a jaunty feather: the pictures show him fresh-faced and never in his terrorist hood. The device on his shield, a young oak-tree pulled up by the roots, is stolen from Sir Walter Scott. The word on the device is Spanish: *Desdichado*, Disinherited. It is the device of Ivanhoe. Scott assures us that he lifted his hero's name from an old rhyme about Hampden's manors but apart from the presence of the Middle Latin *iva*, yew (which is also Spanish as the *ivo* wood of a Tewdwr bow), the syllabic pattern is the crux. Allowing for the interchangeability of vowels and a B/V shift, adding the code-letter 'R' and remembering the usual abbreviation for HOOD we find:

IVANHOE
ROBINHO:

To distinguish him from Richard's favourite knight Scott gives Locksley as the name of the knight's greenwood shadow. Locksley splits the willow wand at five-score yards in the archery contest which is yewman's sport at Ashby-de-la-Zouch.

We have to decide for ourselves whether Locksley's words to Isaac are a token of his acquiescence in the universal anti-semitism of Scott's Christian characters or an expression of his well-known commitment to economic levelling: *he advised the Jew to remember that all the wealth he had acquired by sucking the blood of his miserable victims had but swelled him like a bloated spider, which might be overlooked while it kept in a corner, but would be crushed if it ventured into the light.*

XVII

You'd better not lend your harp to that northern minstrel Allan-a-Dale when he's with a hey druid down in his cups. Who or what Locksley is, he says it himself, is little to the purpose. He couldn't write SHERIFF on the shaft of an arrow but when there's a whiff of quango or a rescue to be made he's always turning up like Redbreast in the middle of winter, a feather in his cap and with two hundred trees armed with bows and arrows as if Lady Nature with the help of an anonymous knight in black armour was about at last to fight back. If you're a fool like Locksley or the friar *free of his guild and master of his craft* you're on her side, *relish and flavour to a cup of wine* and standing opposed to the serious purpose of Torquilstone Business Park known as Evil Hold to the oppressed. *Wyth help off Hwde* they *wyth leddris clame wp oure the wall.*

It riseth, the den of tyrants, as a pillar of fire: by its light are seen dancing for veri pure ioye Friar Torch and that trull of trust Marian while Locksley calls his men at dawn to the Trysting-tree his throne in the Harthill-walk. Fool-magistrate of fools he passes sentence by fool's law and heart-logic on local mason as on Templar lodge. Richard reveals himself to Locksley before Locksley allows that fame hath blown in black-letter garlands and penny-histories as far as Palestine from Sherwood or Barnsdale or any reader's bit of remembered woodland his name of Robin Hood and these moral men who know the very ladyes muse of Mary England.

XVIII

You've probably heard this one before: when orphan Robert was in ward to his uncle abbot of St Mary's that quangoist spent all the young earl's money and wasted his estates: so in his scarlet hood he took to the forest with two Wills. You may know Robin Hood by the twenty certain marks of his kind but by whose witchcraft are his charms must be hidden as his face in Hodden's rags. In alliterative mood Little John once of Mansfield watches Watling Street. With the *Life and Adventures* by Rowland Walker in their Lincoln green pockets these are true-hearted boys of their beloved country, lads of misrule redistributing grant aid and very mindful of the slight irregularities of agri-business.

Having great desire for enemy money and to sit again at high table butcher Robin disciplines the Sheriff in the matter of cropped ears, slit noses, gouged eyes, hands burnt white as Gilbert's and even in the merciful hanging of poor thieves by the neck. Yet for a heretic at lady-worship Robin must have heard there's no sanctuary allowed even if a phantom fanfare sounds through Nottingham streets to the tune *Robin Hood to the Greenwood* on the anniversary night of his escape.

The Sheriff now calls himself Simon de Ganmere. He *had often heard the legend of 'Our Lady's deer', whose colour matched the shades of the forest.* He only doesn't understand the ways of the shaman: that Our Lady's famous hart is Robin Hood the yewman himself. By constant naming and through doubtless hunting is the outlaw's life by debt and death repaid and so relived.

For you must know, by a curious piece of reasoning, Robin and his men had hunted in the royal preserves so long that they had come to consider themselves joint owners of every animal that roamed therein. You must know too that Will Stellee was to hang at Nottingham noon on the green where the maypole should be but Robin was the hangman and the arrow named DE GANMERE found its mark. And Little John is healed by curing herbs only known through Our Lady by the Queen of Sherwood.

XIX

As King Richard's champion Robin wins the Golden Belt Archery Contest at the butts in Charing Cross: yet the ways of the court are a slow death to Marian whose shadow is detached in final madness and springs like may through the greenwood. After Chaluz Robin Hood and Little John track her ghost along Watling Street home. Robin Hood and Little John they are womanless men.

Robin Hood and Little John they are troublesome spirits and green devils of the forest. You'll know Little John by the Lucifer horns he likes to wear on his enormous head when he stops you on the road and tells you his master is expecting you to dinner. Every place at Robin's table is a judgment seat. Good men there can change in a trice from broken serfs into noble souls.

The ghost of Arthur-a-Bland returns from Chaluz to take the quarter-staff prize at Nottingham Castle. The Sheriff hires him as hitman and sends him into the forest. Thus on a bright June morn Arthur again meets bold Robin Hood. It is Robin's power over men and spirits which Cœur-de-Lion admires and his successor envies: but we must still distinguish the tabloid attacks on King John from the genuine praise of the outlaw.

The King forthwith gave a scroll to Sir Guy, authorizing him to slay Robin Hood, and commanding the High Sheriff of Nottingham to treat with all honour and respect his worthy knight, Sir Guy of Gisborne: and so fool Guy came into Sherwood dressed for immemorial reasons as Sir Horse. Well cume mote a ffelow thou hast long sought in fayre fforest bee but Robin would have died that morning by Damascus steel had not Our Lady or as some say Marian's ghost been his shield.

Yule be Robin Hood if oak tell where yew hid. If he was the same man he was seen near Nottingham covered head to foot in a horsehide splattered with bright blood or red sap. *His face was surrounded by what had been the horse's head, and the mane hung down behind like the plume on a helmet. The skin had been cured and tanned and was now like plate armour while the tail made him seem a three-legged creature.* This was shortly before the last great battle on the last day of June or in different remembrance the first of autumn when outnumbered hundreds to one died Scathelock, Will Stutely, Much the Miller's son, George-a-Green and many more. The arrows showered down like summer rain. And Sir Roger of Donkesly has heard that Robin's giant lieutenant has brought him to Kirklees Abbey for the treatment of his wounds or as pure singers say the consolamentum to prepare him for his vein being opened to endurable death.

XX

Quhen
raven is on
her venison
will the Queen
of May be seen

That Marian was leader of huntsmen Ben Jonson knew. He also knew that witch Maudlin (that's how he spells her of the outlaw's chapel) could take Marian's shape and fool Robin Hood. Yet

> Our master's feast shall want no just delights,
> His entertainments must have all the rites

and this Adam Robin and his Marian Eve are the crown and ghirland of the wood.

I kan noght part an oyster but I kan rymes of Robyn hood. I kan the priores loves that Priest of a May Day Sir Roger. I kan a grave of gravel and green where Roberd Hude lies with William Goldburgh and a doubtful Thomas. I kan that vadlet porter of King's Chamber and his wife Matilda were in Barnsdale again with the deserters after the Boroughbridge beating. I kan that forester an elf-owl Hodekin to whit a'Wood. I kan Robin is a poor man's sun whose lady Marian's a maudlin moon. I kan the greenwood where that crossbred lovechild was born amang the lilyflower. I kan the forester his foster-father surnamed Head. I kan Robin Hood's tree by Holy Rood so many yews old that no man knows from which root it arises. I kan a sixpence brought by fairy hood to a widow's doorstep. I kan a hoden horse kent Sir Headless, a knot a nut and Scarlet a mort. I kan his idle lying bow after muse Marian died. I kan the trist in another old tale *when they came to Englyshe wode under the trusty tre*. I kan the Son being absent in a Barnsdale mass a severed head comes to flower on cross bones. I kan Babbinswood Fulk being Arthur's heir took the name Robin Hood and the antlers to find his Marian a chalice. I kan the King of the rout of raveners come from his Green Tower in North-wind Castle to Coney Street in York salutes but with little love. I kan near arcir ver az hie sa geud: in his turbulence he bruces moor and marsh. Robin Hwd ai kant.

Beware of talkyngs with too much of a lordly ring. I have kepyd hym thys iij yere to pleye Seynt Jorge and Robynhod and the shryff off Nottingham. If I kett a knop on thee thou canst as well shite as over-shoote: I'll show Sir Capulhide of Horseborne right Nottingham play. A lively morisdauns, according to the auncient manner, after Anon-a-Dale: six dancerz, mawd-marion and the fool. For I am Robyn hode chiefe gouernoure vnder the grene woode tree.

You might meet men here any number called Hood you'd be astonied to find a few good men too or three goatherd together in disguyse. *Why dost thou bann Robin Hoode?* A hundred torne y haffe schot with hem under hes tortyll-tre. His Frere Tuk newly so called in common parlance was another Robert but the potter was Mortimer or Hereward waked in his exile's grave. At another jolly time would Robin godbeard the Sheriff with a Roger hoodwink. Now twenty men armed with bows and arrows are a-forest and did the aforesaid deed: they songe goynge home warde a gest of Robyn Hode and Gilbert with the quhite hound. Fool April Allan finds May Ellen a-Dale: the players with young oak-trees pulled up by the roots are come to remind us of the art of maymary in shornwood forest and by him that dyed on tre this old man with his yew bow calling himself Odin of Bernsdale must by hunting down of runes be reborn Hood. On a stagnight like this the Friar licks his Marian from everlusting time and another Merry Andrew by the hungry ghost she'll be mother of. False tough that he was scolded cuckoo through the woods with great Hernes of his kinship and his men as merry dead. With a pasteboard horse between his legs, in his hand a bow and arrow, and six others with their Rain deers heads, Moll Marion, and Robin Hood the cracker slashing them to keep them moving with his whip. And also one Robert Marshall of Wednesbury, calling himself Robyn Hodys to the intent to gether money with divers other persons to the number of 100 men and above, in harness, met with the said other rioters and then and there riotously assembled themselves in lewde sports, tending to no other end but to stir up frail natures to wantoness.

This Robin Hood was bred a butcher, but being of a very licentious, wicked inclination, he followed not his trade, but in the reign of King Richard the First, associating himself with several robbers and outlaws, he was chosen their captain. He meant the Concern which every good man naturally feels stir in him for his distressed Country, when it is in a State of Slavery. Poore mens goods hee spared, aboundantlie relieving them with that which by thefte he got from Enterprise Parks and Heritage Centres: whom *Maior* blameth for his rapine and theft but of all theeves he affirmeth him to bee the Prince.

XXI

Weakened by loss of blood Robin's last act was to slash his sword on Red Roger's neck: he was a famous murderer, Robin Hood, as well as Little John, together with their accomplices from among the dispossessed, about 1266 or 1283 or in Lionheart's time, say 1194. In this year would Jerusalem be taken and signs known as forest in full leaf of the third age coming of the holy spirit meaning love between rich and poor and new freedom among men. In the decade of Arnaut his lady and *trobar clus*. The date of his death 24 kal dekembris 1247 was no time at all just as his greenwood was a blank on the map or else he was truly King of Misrule whose wildnesse named him robin heud. He wounded his stepfather to death at plough: fled into the woods where *there is no deceit nor any bad law* and was relieved by his mother till he was discovered.

It was a time when the forests were being eroded from within by enclosure of land for out-of-town development and ring-roads. As the century came to an end retail parks and industrial estates proliferated. Between February •••• and July •••• there were fifteen commissions of *oyer and terminer* occasioned by raids on business parks, Tescos and Texas Homecare and attacks on quangoists and hypermarketeers. And Robyn hod in scherewod stod, hodud and hathud and hosut and schod: his four and thuynti arowus like jingling spells against prestige employment developers. He gadered and assembled unto him many misdoers beynge of his clothinge and, in manere of insurrection, wente into the wodes and strange contrays as outlawes, waitynge a tyme to murdre, sclee, and other grete harmes in that contray to do.

Happy Robin Whood coming to Lyndric falls asleep and hath a strange Dream there. Which at his awaking, he relates to his Companions, and then tells them that he is resolved forthwith to turn Hermit. Robin retires to Depe Dale, chuses the penitent Thief for his Patron, and spends the Remainder of his Time in great Penance and Devotion. He falls sick of a fever, repairs to Kirklees to be let Blood. His mind consoled his endurable time slips away. Again he is lying in Little John's arms, it is a dream within a Barnsdale dreaming: again there is a thief in the forest, now a rival shaman in Gisborne's disguise *clad from head to foot in the hide of a horse*, a bloody mire of a path through the maze of trees Robin alone knew by weird aiming of his aimless arrow and the dream within the dream before that when he was captured in Nottingham not saving Marian who first named him a'Hood but kneeling as he must before the one in whose image his deere ladye was.

Thomas A. Clark is invited to lecture to the Sheriff's officers: *It is not the forest we eventually discover but our own strategies of evasion.* The officers' problem is that out in the forest they lose any sense of *their own*: even their strategies of evasion are stripped away and put to good use by the man or many they call Robin Hood. For either Robin Hood is himself the forest or Robin Hood is nobody at all. Some of the officers will have discovered for themselves the awful darkness of the forest night, that darkness of which brigand Robin is patron saint and lord protector. For *When men let light into the forest*, the teacher continues, *darkness hid in their hearts.*

XXII

A Saracen SAS or Assasseen called Nasir claims on HTV that once he had ridden with Robin Hood. The same programme also claims that Will Scathelocke changed his name to Scarlet after he had murdered his wife, but this was long before he joined the merry men and in any case he says it was de Rainault's boys set him up. He seems to connect it with some trouble at a building site and the bypass wrecking an otherwise unidentified town he calls Loxley. He is described as *angry, irritable, unreasonable, unfriendly and unhelpful.* Even his own father, he bangs down his fist, wasn't a worse bastard than Richard Cœur-de-Lion. We are spared an account of his drug addiction but in unused footage he tells how he once saw the heart of Sherwood open out and encompass the known world in a never-ending nonesuch glade. Instead the film cuts from Will aiming blind and hitting bullseye to a raid on hyperbole transfigured as the business park at Clun.

The sugared violence is detailed grain by grain as befits our peak viewing time. There is coverage of Marian's visionary powers, speculation on the occult meaning of the May Day rites and a modish take on the question *witch or wise woman*. But the dominant idea is that in the second period of greenwood days there was a second Robin Hood, not a yeoman reborn but Huntingdon's right heyre. Anthony Munday polishes a blade and downs another pint in the darkest recess of Amos Scathelocke's alehouse in Lichfield. He knows the Scathelocke brothers gave Huntingdon the lead. Seven years they ran wild and as he likes to say scaped malice before Huntingdon sprang them from Nottingham gaol or anybody ever heard the name Robin Hood.

Lord Tennyson who saw that *strange starched stiff creature Little John* kiss Kate, the same girl Munday had always called Jinny, sits beside him. They remember the banquets in Huntingdon's hall before that Worman or Warman of a steward was bribed on either hand to betray him. Remember Scarlet's wife he left dead or alive for the following of Robin's deere ladye. They laugh together about some of these recent stories: of Robin and Marian's travels in the East, Little John's appointment as Sheriff of Nottingham and the former Sheriff's daughter's later career as Prioress of Kirklees. But of his lordship's account of the fairies' retreat north out of Sherwood presaging the end of the forest games poor Munday looks less than convinced.

XXIII

His acre. His arbour.

His ball, barn and barrow. His bay. His bog, his bow, his bower and but. His butts.

His cap. His castle. His cave and chair. His chase. His close. His court. His croft and his cross.

His delight.

His farm and his field.

His games. His garlands. His gate. His golden prize. His grave.

His hills and his howl.

His inn. His island.

His larder and leap.

His meadow, his mile and his moss.

His park. His penny stone. Pennyworths. Picking rods. Pot.

His ring. His rock.

His stable. His stone and stoop. His stride.

His table, his tales and his tower.

His valour.

His walk and his well. His wind. His wood.

XXIV

32s. 6d. for the chattels of Robert Hod, fugitive, Michaelmas 1230 at York. Green for the fairies, red for the witch. They two bolde children came to blacke water and we weepen for his deare body.

Amo Locksley. Little John's been all over the place since Robin Hood died: his soul, he often says, sped from his body as arrow from bow but whether he means Robin's soul or his own nobody is ever quite sure. He showed the crowd a few tricks in Ostman-towne-greene by Dublin and he holed up in Murrayland and then headed home to lay himself down by his master's grave at Kirklees. They buried his bones of an uncommon size where he died in the precincts of Barnesdale of the fever at Hathersage.

Late us caste the stone
Late us caste the exaltre

The song itself wholly new and never before printed. To a doleful tune, lovelord Allin for Eleanor a-lorn. With a hey daring down a dale under this most ancient lime more fitting than oak for his trysting place ten as one foresters dance efter the auld wikit maner of Robene Hude while abbot and justice leap to it. *I made a chapel in Bernysdale where my sweet Marian lies buried.* I got me to the woods, Love followed me. He intertained an hundred tall men, and good archers with such spoiles and thefts as he got, upon whom four hundred (were they never so strong) durst not give the onset.

We'll get the next day from Brecknock the book of Robin Hood. Luellen King of Wales and Master of Misrule with his common cursitors whooden as Roberdsmen in Hobbehod form. They came to the Euro Park with torches lit and while the flames went up they were green in green and red on green received once more into the forest.

A Note

While the relations between the Robin Hood stories and the 'old religion' have been explored by a number of writers there does not seem to have been any significant discussion of the heretical elements in the ballads. The replacement of the Son in Robin's three daily masses by Our Lady has generally been seen as another instance of Mariolatry by researchers who consistently overlook the reference to the chapel Robin claims to have established in Barnsdale: 'It is of Mary Magdalene / And thereto wolde I be'. The implication that Robin's Lady 'who art but mother and may' is the Magdalen rather than the Virgin Mary is nevertheless not in itself sufficient to link him with any specific heresy, and the relation of either Mary to a goddess of the 'old religion' is (despite the pun on 'deer' and 'dear') opaque enough to discourage speculation. The association of the later Robin Hood plays with 'religious controversy' is similarly opaque, as is the persistent linking of the legends with the troubadour milieu via Richard Cœur-de-Lion and even Eleanor of Aquitaine. The manner of Robin's death, however, deserves consideration. Margaret Murray points to its relation to ancient ritual: Robin and Little John pass an old woman who is 'banning', i.e. cursing, Robin Hood: she is a 'washer at the ford'. There is then a caesura in the ballad text and we next hear that an unspecified 'we' *weepen for his deare body*. This suggestion of ancient ritual is combined with a mode of suicide which was apparently not uncommon among heretics. We are told that a Cathar, having taken his great vow of purity, the *Consolamentum*, was permitted to hasten his death through the *Endura*. There were a number of specified forms of *Endura*, one being 'the opening of a vein in a bath' (Williamson, p.151). It seems significant that Robin attains this end with the help of a woman in holy orders. The Prioress of Kirklees has invariably been seen as Robin's betrayer; the possibility remains that she was enabling his passage out of reincarnation into Paradise.

Sources

William Anderson *Green Man*, Harper Collins 1990

Richard Barber *Living Legends*, BBC 1980

Jim Bradbury *The Medieval Archer*, Boydell 1994 reprint

Richard Carpenter *Robin of Sherwood*, Puffin 1985 reprint

Richard Carpenter & Anthony Horowitz *Robin of Sherwood: The Hooded Man*, Puffin 1986

Anand Chetan & Diana Brueton *The Sacred Yew*, Arkana 1994

Thomas A. Clark *Twenty Four Sentences About The Forest*, Moschatel 1982

R. B. Dobson & J. Taylor *Rymes of Robyn Hood*, Heinemann 1976

Norman Douglas *London Street Games*, Chatto 1931

Antonia Fraser *Robin Hood*, Magnet reprint 1985

Henry Gilbert *Robin Hood*, Wordsworth reprint 1994

John Gillingham *The Life and Times of Richard I*, Weidenfield & Nicholson 1973

Roger Lancelyn Green *The Adventures of Robin Hood*, Penguin 1971 reprint

J. C. Holt *Robin Hood*, revised & enlarged edition, London 1993 reprint

Ben Jonson *The Sad Shepherd: or, A Tale of Robin Hood*, W. Gifford edition 1816

Maurice Keen *The Outlaws of Medieval Legend*, Routledge & Kegan Paul 1961

Patricia Leitch *The Adventures of Robin Hood*, Armada 1979

J. Walker McSpadden *Stories of Robin Hood and His Merry Outlaws*, Harrap 1930 reprint

Peter Makin *Provence and Pound*, California UP 1978

John Matthews *Robin Hood: Green Lord of the Wildwood*, Gothic Image 1993

Margaret Alice Murray *The God of the Witches*, London n.d.

Carola Oman *Robin Hood: The Prince of Outlaws*, Dent 1937

Thomas Love Peacock *Maid Marian*, Llanerch reprint 1992

Graham Phillips *The Search for the Grail*, Century 1995

Howard Pyle *The Merry Adventures of Robin Hood*, Scribner's 1895 reprint

Joseph Ritson *Robin Hood: A Collection of all the Ancient Poems, Songs, and Ballads*, second edition, London 1823

Sir Walter Scott *Ivanhoe*, Andrew Lang edition, London 1893

Ian Seraillier *Robin in the Greenwood*, OUP 1967

Sara Hawks Sterling *Robin Hood and his Merry Men*, London n.d.

Donald Suddaby *New Tales of Robin Hood*, Blackie n.d.

Rosemary Sutcliff *The Chronicles of Robin Hood*, OUP 1950

Alfred Lord Tennyson *The Foresters: Robin Hood and Maid Marian*, The Life & Works, Macmillan 1899

R. Lowe Thompson *The History of the Devil*, Kegan Paul 1929

E. Charles Vivian *Robin Hood*, Ward Lock & Co. n.d.

Rowland Walker *Life and Adventures of Robin Hood*, Aldine n.d.

David Wiles *The Early Plays of Robin Hood*, Brewer 1981

Hugh Ross Williamson *The Arrow and The Sword*, 2nd edition, Faber 1955

Sources of italicized passages not identified in text

I   *Robin . . . pleased.* Fraser
V   *There is . . . others.* Vivian
XI   *Come to the wood . . . for seven years . . .* Murray
        virtually dismembered . . . bodies. Chetan
XII   *The Hart Royal . . . green.* Oman
        Bryunsdale . . . Sherwood. Leitch
XV   *tore aside . . . France.* Gilbert
XVI   *set upon . . . strength.* Gillingham
XVIII   *had often . . . the forest.* Walker
        For you must . . . therein. McSpadden
XIX   *The King . . . worthy knight.* Walker
        His face . . . three-legged creature. Sterling, Leitch, McSpadden
XXI   *clad . . . horse.* Leitch

With thanks to Rosie Hayles and Gavin Selerie for bibliographical help.

POST-SONATAS

protons (p)
26 GeV

Antiproton
accumulator

$\bar{p}$ 3·5GeV

$\bar{p}$ 3·5GeV

Target

Booster p

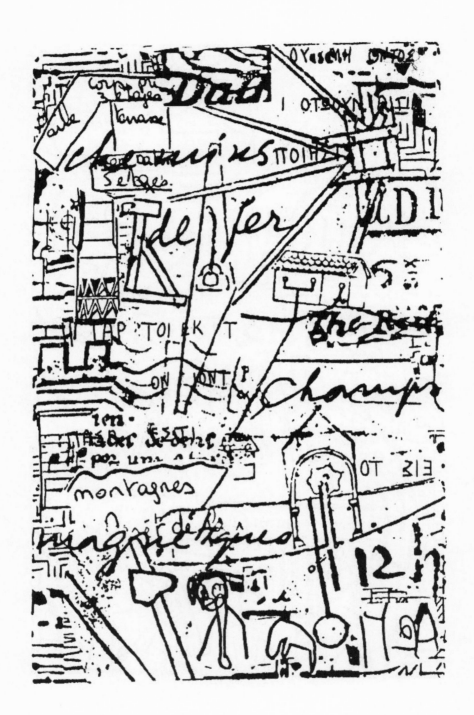

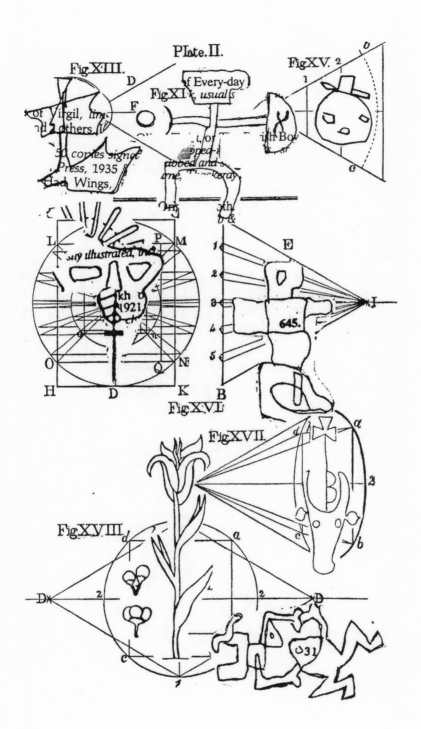

Plate. II.

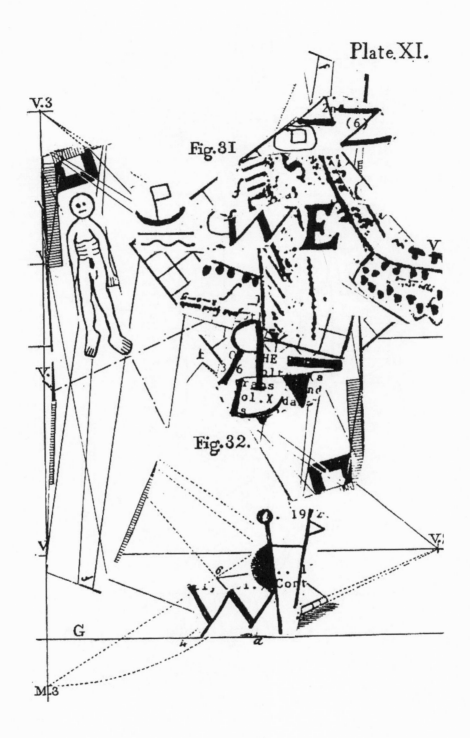

Plate. XI.

Fig. 31

Fig. 32.

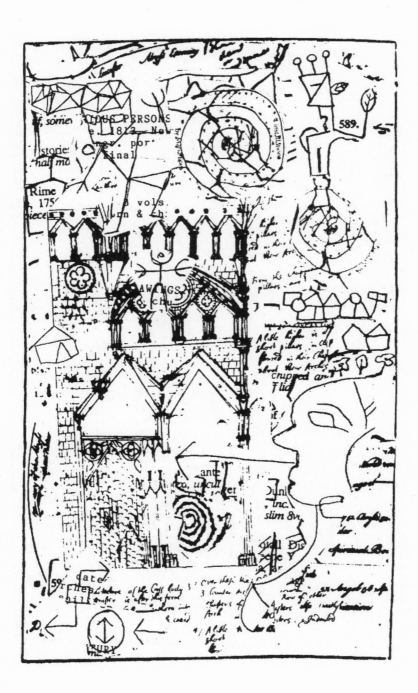

Fig. 32.

DANSE MACABRE

Death & the Printers

Danse Macabre.
Lyons, Matthias Hus, 18 February 1499

Various versions of a *Danse Macabre* or *Dance of Death*
were printed in the fifteenth century in German, Latin,
and French, each with verse dialogues between Death
and persons in various stations of society, and forceful
illustrations of Death dragging his victims away. Both
the illustrations and the text of the French version were
based on frescoes in the church of the Holy Innocents
in Paris, which were destroyed in 1669. The woodcuts
printed by Hus are for the most part based on those
in the editions of Guy Marchant, Paris, 15 April–22
May 1492, or of Couteau and Ménard, Paris, 26 June
1492; but the cut of the printer's office here shown was
apparently made specially for Hus's edition, presumably
by his own engraver, and may well represent, with
necessary simplification and plus the skeletons, the
actual appearance of his own establishment. This is
the earliest known illustration of a printing-press. The
compositor, with his case of type, composing-stick, and
the two-page forme on the bench beside him, is setting
from copy propped up before him; the pressman, with
his right hand on the invisible handle, is arrested on the
point of pulling the press; his colleague is already inking
the next forme with the ink-balls; and in the adjoining
bookshop the shopman is halted in the act of reading a
volume of his wares.

[*Printing and the Mind of Man*, British Museum, 1963]

There were these four Deaths
called Kelvin, Gavin, David and Alan
and one of them was hiding outside
in his writer's mask while the others went in
to the printer's

Death takes the vowels **Death takes the vowels first** starting with E

The Death in the writer's mask put his
walkman on and his lips were miming with Blind
Willie Johnson and his wife Angeline
You're Gonna
       Need
    S o m e b o d y
        On Your Bond

And one of the Deaths who'd gone in
to the printer's said 'Books seem
to me to be pestilent things, &
infect all that trade in them

    they have a way of
      dealing
        peculiar to themselves
         not conformed
          to the good of society
          and that general fairness
         which cements
        mankind'

Prequoting Locke

You're Gonna Need

Somebody On Your Bond

J'AI
pLagUe

Printing is

an Aid to Forgetting

dans

danse

sans

sense

going out of their heads

in a frenzy of

losing of

the order of their letters

dis-   de-

composing

The years between Gutenberg and Hus
completing the printing of *Danse Macabre*
18 février 1499 were not remarkable
for outbreaks of plague yet as late
as the 1960s Basil Bunting
remarked that poetry lies
dead until some voice

in context 24.v.96

the bookseller whispered

Refusing to watch but being told how you looked
on TV by one in whose eyes your reality's been doubled

The lucky thing for me was that being an author I could always
plead absence and so I wasn't there that day when there was all
that trouble in Matthias's office. Nor, you will notice, was
Matthias. But the story goes that

The boys came in by mistake. Thought it was a brothel
Thought we were printing seditious
Thought it was a smell
from hell
Thought it was

Matt Huss it was. But
Glenn Storhaug: we'd been working all day setting type,
we were tired as hell but finally I said it doesn't
work. And he said no you're right it doesn't okay
let's start again. He had that kind of dedication. He meant
there & then

I knew the man. Could
do anything you liked
in a cut. We'd gone one
short and he said What
about a picture of the office
and no one says no
one's done one before.
Why should they? I
knew the man. Would
call Death a liar
to his face. Liked cuts.
Hated letters. Hated in
particular the vowels.

like Death.
breaking up the furniture
distributing the type
Don't
lovely
moment me I
mean Now.

The vitriol and gall of their damnation ink

Re 'specifics'

Re the erratum *for 'soul' read 'chaos'*

After death a man's chaos goes out into the air

Death calls a spade a spade but it
is still eight years before Martin
Waldseemüller calls America America
and a century plus before van Helmont:
chaos gas.

If only they would stop

asking where life goes

and consider where it comes from

he likewise calls sulphur the soul

['obsessed with *Death's Jest-Book*' but as
David who is definitely not the one with the
walkman says over lunch *you're not
obsessed you* ARE Death's Jest-Book]

Matthias: your mortgage

      for that it is doubtful whether the Feoffor will
pay at the day limited such summe or not, & if he
doth not pay, then the Land which is put in pledge
vpon condition for the payment of the money, is
taken from him for euer, and so dead to him vpon
condition, &c. And if he doth pay the money, then
the pledge is dead as to the Tenant, &c.

If thou wilt ease thine heart
Of love and all its smart

You can repeat your last action by clicking
the Redo button on the Standard toolbar

the Old Repossessor comes in like the earth's own bailiff with two of his sidekicks

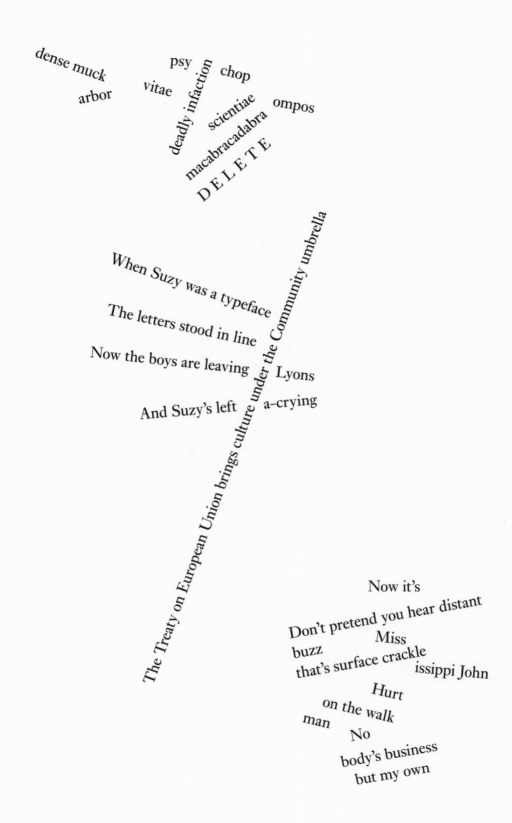

dense muck
psy chop
arbor vitae
deadly infaction
scientiae ompos
macabracadabra
D E L E T E

When Suzy was a typeface

The letters stood in line

Now the boys are leaving Lyons

And Suzy's left a-crying

The Treaty on European Union brings culture under the Community umbrella

Now it's

Don't pretend you hear distant
Miss
buzz
that's surface crackle issippi John

Hurt
on the walk
man No
body's business
but my own

One death's hand takes the
C of *glace*

another an S
off Lyons &
Huss

then off glass

the third takes the L

& an F off *off*

Then the first one lays an E flat

says

Echaos

& laughs
love's

echoes
As the faust one must echone
certainly

Danser vous faust

This is the road that ends in the air where the chaoses live
And one chaos turns to another and says
Three new chaoses turned up yesterday
Stinking of ink as if they'd just come out of a printer's

    Talking Gothic and bold as that fellow
    Annwn
    Mr Underworld himself
    With his new PC

This is the chaos that ends in the road where the Deaths
Who live on the vowels of the soon
To be speechless

    There were four of these Deaths
    And one Death turns to Matthias
    With a mouthful of vowels and says *Ciao*

This is the air come alive in the chaos where the known
Road ends on the shore
Where the bards went to sea like
Deaths in a house
Of glass to the world of their fathers

MARGINALIEN MARGINALIA:

Irregulars & Gargoyles

Lizard Abstract

I

It or let's say he lives among the common lizards. He is four or five inches long and his head and tail are like theirs. But his skin is silvery bronze and the middle part of his body, between fore and hind legs, is circular and nearly flat, about the size of an old penny. As he rests in the sunlight yellow-gold circles glint on his skin. He scuttles into a crevice.

As usual I am caught between attraction and repulsion. The lizard-earth will never be mine. As usual I reach for a symbol: think of alchemy etc. The lure of the once-seen. Romanticism. Death. The philosopher's stone was presumably round, like any other circle of thought, perfect and perfectly trapped in its beginning.

I am five years old. My mother has run my bath and told me to get in. The water is clouded by bath salts. I am convinced I have seen a beetle in the water. He is about six inches long, shiny black. His body is circular and he has a single pointed horn: he is the unicorn beetle. I stand at the end of the bath and scream.

There is a terrible continuity in things. I find a letter from Iain Sinclair, dated 28 November '72: 'to push back into darker fields: mythology, ancestor-worship, death presences.' 'The hunchback,' wrote Yeats, 'is his own Body of Fate.' And: 'The Passionate Body is the sum of those Daimons.'

'The Communicators often scribbled it on margins, or on scraps of paper, without relation to the text.' As the dream-lizard rests in the sunlight the yellow-gold circles turn pink, little dome-like blisters or the heads of shiny pins on his skin. He scuttles into a crevice.

I am ill in bed, about eight years old. I am reading an encyclopædia of natural history which I think belonged to my father when he was a boy. I return again and again to the section about crocodiles and alligators. The pages have a dull sheen, the pictures are grey and blurred. Iguanas.

Iguanadons. The great prehistoric lizards. Our particular devils, our next best thing to a mythology, those dragons which have always lived just off the margin, scribbled beyond bounds. In the crevice between page and page of my father's book.

I saw him about a fortnight after he died. His mouth was moving, he was making words but to me they were silent. The ancients would offer blood-sacrifice at this point.

II

scraps
scribbled
script
scuttles

daimons
diamond

'the so-called dinosaurs consisted of two separate groups that were rather distantly related. These are Saurischia, or "lizard hips", and Ornithiscia, "bird hips" . . . no more related to each other than they are to other members of the reptilian family tree, such as crocodiles and pterosaurs.'

Suppose for a moment that the watery eyes of Frankenstein's monster were the eyes of a lizard: would the story stop there?

Over lunch Derek tells us that his four-year-old son's main interest at the moment is dinosaurs. He wants to go back a third time to the exhibition in Cardiff, where the models are now animated and their eyes light up.
Yellow?
I mention the dream-lizard. I tell the story of the expat in Zambia who was taken by a crocodile and left for dead in its cave. He woke up and had to find his way out in the darkness, expecting the croc to return at any moment.

The lizard is on a smooth wooden surface. It is probably a table—I am quite close to him. I think it was a movement of mine that made him scuttle.

I am six years old. The bogey in the pantomime has a crocodile mask. I almost wrote: 'for no reason at all'. It is as if there should be an element in every image which must at least seem to be arbitrary.

One of the blurred photographs shows a nest of crocodile eggs and a few baby crocs hatching out. They seem to be about three inches long.

If the line-drawing had been found in an aboriginal cave I would probably have guessed it showed some form of turtle.

III

The first draft read: 'As usual you are caught between attraction and repulsion. The lizard-earth will never be yours. As usual you reach for a symbol . . .' There is always that transference, the usual pushing away from first to second person. Even now I want to say this is a textual remark.

A textual form of blood-sacrifice. The relatively uncommon occurrence of the letter Z. Lizard. In a draft of *The Triumph of Life*: sacrifize. Of sanguine fire.

None of the illustrations to *The Faerie Queene* does justice to the size of the dragon the Redcrosse knight slays: That with his largenesse measured much land, And made wide shadow vnder his huge wast; As mountaine doth the valley ouercast.

There is always the question of scale. I assume that I am my normal size in the dream. That the Redcrosse knight is not a giant. That the photograph of the baby crocs is not in miniature. But why is Frankenstein's monster eight feet tall?

As the turtle shell cracked in the fire it formed into signs, a script used for divination. That, at least, is what we say: we who have no clear notion of what this 'divination' might consist in, of what it would be to live in a divination-world. It might be, say, a sense of living inside a sphere, in which any line would necessarily return to its starting point, intersecting all other lines on the way. A kind of transparent ever-presence. In comparison with which our own world is flat, opaque and fearfully discontinuous: it is riven with crevices, into any one of which the dream-lizard will disappear.

The continuity is terrible, in other words, in that it belongs to a different order of things. The lizard disappears but does not die with the dream. The first person is a discontinuous text continuously inscribed on the inside surface of a sphere. I think it was a movement of mine
As emotion doth the valley ouercast
As the lizard rests in the sunlight
'It is singular that Sir Thomas [Browne] has not mentioned the vulgar opinion that this reptile undergoes frequent changes of colour according to that of the bodies near it.'

> pink
> pins
> skin

The magnetic fields on the inside surface of the sphere are islands of anxiety. Or continents. The inhabitants are giants. Cannibals. Tyrannosaurus Rex. Massive radio interference.

IV

Rosie's dream: she picks up a scaly creature and pushes it head down into water even as she's thinking *No no it's going to die*. And it dies. She says it was a fish. But a fish wouldn't die by submersion.

—Are you sure it wasn't a lizard?

—Yes it could have been a lizard.

I talk about the fact that Thomas Browne doesn't distinguish lizards from newts, which I assume are what he calls 'water lizards'. I am interested in the perspective: how these creatures would seem in Browne's time, before the structural distinction between amphibia and reptiles had been worked out. Worked out and written in to our seeing. Rosie argues about the usefulness of the distinction. Which was, in a gentler way, what I had in mind: there is an openness in Browne which our more precise distinctions close off.

I am eleven years old. Eddie Strudwick and I have caught some newts in New Addington Woods. I bring them home in jam jars and put them in a bowl of water. The next day they are dead.

Rosie's dream reminds her of Bill the Lizard, pushed down the chimney while Alice is changing size.

There is a George Blair icon which is exactly the colour of the dream-lizard, silvery bronze. The icon shows St George killing the dragon. The dragon is tiny in comparison with Spenser's, no bigger than St George himself, but he is killed in the same way, with the spear in his throat. George says that the Greek Orthodox St George has no association with the red cross.

George tells us about the millipedes who ate his onion plants on Amorgos. He planted more onions in the same place and they survived because the lizards had come and eaten the millipedes. Then the snakes came and ate the lizards.

V

At summer solstice in San Gemignano the lizards run down the walls and across the floor of the breakfast verandah. I am constantly worried that one will be trodden underfoot. On the full moon before the winter solstice I can't sleep. I am trapped in an anxiety zone of particularly fierce magnetism. Occasionally I drift into half-dreams. One of these ends with a lizard head-squashed on the polished floor of a hi-tech public building, probably a bank.

The iguana in the photograph appeared to be about the size of a crocodile. I didn't realise the mistake until I saw the film version of *Night of the Iguana*. My friend from Zambia told me that crocs on land can raise themselves up on straight legs and run very fast. Fast enough to catch a man and drag him down to the river. But they like their meat well rotted.

The Greek word for a millipede, says George, means 'forty legs'.

'The Dragon is the controlling symbol of Time, for its movement relates the sidereal year to the year of the sun and the moon . . . In Winter, at the solstice, Draco is East of the Polestar, and at midnight of midsummer to the West.'

Dinosaur remains have been brought into China from the Gobi Desert for centuries. They have always been called 'dragon bones'. They are used in divination.

The two dragons, male and female, destroy each other 'and a new and mightier one is born'. The accounts refer to this as the 'fiery wonder'.

In the next dream I am reading a novel aloud at the same time as the events of the narration are happening. Or so I suppose. After a while it begins to seem that the narrator is lying. But that's wrong too. I am watching a different enactment.

22.12.94

Alien Proforma

The wrecked metal of the spacecraft looked like tin foil but you could take that stuff and wad it up and it would straighten itself out like a crumpled Moebius strip of the target language. As I see it now the target is transparent, a glass dome of the shared vocabulary of two peoples each of whose pronunciation is unearthly to the other: these are such deep threats and adjectival threads represented on the map you have as ley-lines or another compound with the same phonetic register or nearly. For the moment let's call that target the Air Force Base at Roswell, New Mexico. The date is July 4, 1947, the time 11.30 p.m. It needs comparing to a sentence of at best indeterminate significance: *there are always ten on treble nine*, for example, or the chance resemblance of *inhibit* and *inhabit*. These aliens do just look like smaller and hairless human beings but with lizard eyes and in the order of the text a little abstract. It was my own map I lent you and if it's not any trouble a xerox would help. The names of the witnesses, Trudie Truelove and James Ragsdale, are intriguing enough: they are soul mates certainly, accessing the message line and following the simple instructions. And then there's the fireman, Dan Dwyer, who saw two body-bags and one of the beings still alive, *about the size of a 10-year-old child*. If I tell you that he or she was female you'll begin to see the nature of the problem. The site was or rather the seal was sited off and the story will soon have subtitles added. In the adaptation you'll see the undertaker making two maybe three child-size coffins but we haven't got that far in the original version—the surgeon pauses . . . *When the contents of the skull are removed, they are flesh-like, but most unlike a human brain with its grooves and folds*. In the black-and-white target language the film is called *grainy*; the wingless craft is seen entering the sentence a second before impact. *The scalpel goes down the trunk, to the swollen belly which suggests that this small being might have been pregnant. There are female genitalia, but no navel, and no hair. Once the body cavity is exposed, there are no familiar coils of intestine. The body-organs are again flesh-like, soft*, just as the framing constructions are clause-like but in alien analysis lack verbs. In the stills she is a doll, naked and abandoned in any sense you choose. When the black lids are lifted from the eyes we see *white orbs* in the target language. It is phrases like this we cannot translate: *high-altitude weather balloon* in '47 becomes *radiation monitor* in '94. *Lid* is related to *lizard* in some unspecified way, *film* to *flimsy* and so on: they are strays who have wandered from their proper atmosphere and lie threatening and dead on the army surgeon's table. They are future ghosts, hieroglyphic and geometrical shapes like words read backwards through the transparent foil of the crumpled loop which is an airstrip after all, after us.

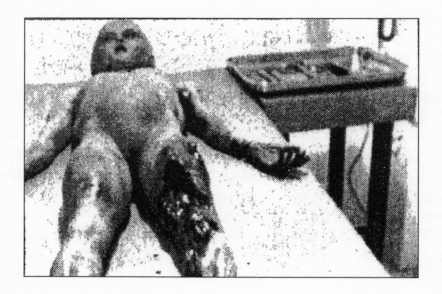

It's not simply that the numbers change but that first it's three and then it's five but never four: and yet in any account it's only one of the aliens who is said to have been walking around when the humans arrived and that one disappears from the story like a shifter in the target language. The other two or four lie dead in the hangar, make a note, we have the *shifter* and the *hangar* right there for all to see like the half-rhyme of *text* and *special effects* which for all we know is hieroglyphically correct. That one's as likely to be still alive as any other witness and talking with a similar accent. It was June and not July. Trudie and James are no longer being mentioned but Dan Dwyer's daughter cries and cries. Repeat after me, *non video*: the officer was banging his baton in the palm of his hand as an inalienable rite, hoax signo. In the first adaptation we see lightning fork across the desert and an alien by this time possibly a laboratory mutant flashed on the screen for a second: the proforma image is in that sense static interference, the sound goes off out of radio contact—we see the lips of the witnesses still moving but we only hear the thunder by now overhead. There is a flip mid-sentence as a floating preposition from a newer technology prowls the desert headland. Then *flimsy* again, although the alien skull seems bony enough and remains in this adaptation unopened. Syntax is reduced to the sequence of frames just as the commentary's a grammar, you keep rubbing your right ear but the noise continues deep down and right across the landscape behind you as the motor language stays ticking over. In the still the image is reversed and the wound transferred to the subject's left leg. There was an army cordon round the hangar and a heavy toxic smell maybe farts of the alien shifters just before the full stop. You understand? The débris when it showed up in Texas was entirely different stuff. We called them *flying rings* in those days, we've come that far since 1947, but I don't remember the six fingers on the alien's left hand. The witness's eyes tell us nothing in too obvious close-up. There was that white object in the sky and something funny on the target language radar. Everything goes white, from the unnecessary lightning to the surgeon in ghost-strip. I know what I saw although no one else will say. And when the lid is lifted as it didn't have to be the white eye.

Visions of the Western Railways

1. If you are keeping fifteen hundred out of say six thousand books which ones do you keep and why?

2. If you keep books you think you might not find again which isn't true of most books nevertheless why?

3. Let us suppose anyone would keep a book in black cloth spine lettered gilt THE PURSUIT OF DEATH | [floral motif] | KURTZ.

4. Various disbound Byron pamphlets for their nakedness. Also Churchill and Pope. Even Whitehead's *Honour, A Satire. Manners, A Satire.*

5. Books published when poetry was made wide-leaded. Romantics still wrote for such a spacious line. Check compositional changes after say 1820. The effect of the cramping of text in Victorian editions. After Anderson's Poets.

6. You do not keep Anderson's Poets although it includes many poets rarely again reprinted partly because it wants too much shelf-room and the leather on this set has rotted but even so you wouldn't disbind it or would you?

7. The poetry you keep is in any case what you remember and revise in your memory so what use books when the answer to textualism is as clear as that?

8. If for reference then with reference to what?

9. If you keep both Captain Thompson's and Margoliouth's Marvell what kind of love is that?

10. Various Chattertons. You might never read Bowles's Sonnets but isn't this pair even in the eighth edition a pretty thing?

11. What hasn't that to do with literary criticism? What kind of aesthete are you to think it?

12. [Richard Owen Cambridge's] *Scribleriad* for its engravings. Some poetry is worth whatever it inspired an engraver to.

13. Too many Miltons doesn't mean ditching a Bentley.

14. Sir Kenelm Digby's *Two Treatises: In the one of which, The Nature of Bodies; In the other, The Nature of Mans Soul, Is Looked Into: In Way of Discovery of the Immortality of Reasonable Souls* because it feels as if it must be poetry if not in name.

15. The Chaucer of probably 1561 lacking title but with spider doodles and dearest our initials G and A.

16. A couple of emblem books even as the binder's gilt says QUARLE´S and a tiny *Pia Desideria* although you'll never read Latin again. *Blake's Graphic Work and the Emblematic Tradition* because you tried writing emblems once.

17. The Garland facsimile Shelleys the masterpiece of language writing.

18. Some bibliographies including Foxon for all the disbound pamphlets you'll never own.

19. *Ulysses* five or six editions including for his witty name the Gabler. *Finnegans Wake* and its recensions. Umpteen Beckett and Wittgenstein. The *Cantos* in separate and collected editions. *Antheil and The Treatise on Harmony* effectively retitled in black ink: 'To certify that E Swainson having bought same refused 10 fr. reimbursement. ———— the authors increased esteem EPound 1926'.

20. Various contemporaries particularly my wife.

21. Pamphlets Bill Griffiths handmade. Books you see across a room were designed by Glenn Storhaug.

22. *The Dawn In Britain* in six volumes more readable wide-leaded.

23. Folios such as Sandys' Ovid and most elephant and elegant of all the 1718 Prior.

24. *The Landscape* for its typeface. *Christabel* with the pencil inscription *!'Folly, Folly. all is Folly'!*

25. Dodsley's Poems. Percy's Reliques. The more legible of Gay's Poems in quarto. Oxford English Texts preferably before they greyed in offset.

26. Friends and best enemies.

27. For the title on its spine alone and why not VISIONS OF THE WESTERN RAILWAYS 1838

Maledictae Librorum

for a Librarian at Cambridge

Not for nothing you take
this volume by Blake.
Show a friend such anger?
    If you so
    make a foe
there is much worse danger.

for an IHF Collector

How forlorn
    are the cries
of one curs'd
    to have fall'n
in his own
    wild hawthorn.

for a Professor in Wales

If this Maximus stray
from Gloucester or Hay-
on-Wye without pay
    then Out
with you, Out.
    Out. Out.

for a Runner

Dare slip Zukofsky's *"A"*
inside your coat? May
    all twenty-six
letters of the alphabet mix
    at random
up when you write & read 'em.

for a Two-Headed Giant

Let's call Barnes a bishop
and the sheriff Noble
so if they ride thro' Sherwood
    Robin Hood'll
with interest have my purse
    reimbursed.

Thanks to GM who introduced me to the ancient scribal tradition of book curses. To a bookseller it must seem strange that such an essential tool has fallen out of use. For further entertainment see Marc Drogin Anathema! Medieval Scribes and the History of Book Curses, *1983.*

The Hunting of the Lizopard

The night of the dinner party I was being as if it were the 1940s an unhelpful husband. We were living at the time in a single room in a wing of a large 19th century house.

When our two guests arrived (one was the poet P.) I went to bring up wine from the cellar. I stood looking at the creature part lizard part leopard in the tank there. Who told me it had once belonged to (someone said, had been created by) Aleister Crowley? Or that the internal temperature of the tank had to be kept at 23° below zero?

Upstairs all the furniture had been overturned and G. was crouching with our guests in a corner. I noticed thin layers of dust on every surface. How strange that in such an upheaval they had not been even slightly disturbed.

M. who recently told a poet's agent in New York to fuck off (the poet wasn't P.) hopes the house wasn't his brother's. He calls the creature a 'lizopard'.

M. and I agree the lizopard must be kept at a low temperature to stop us telling even one poet's agent to fuck off or trying to photograph fancy tails worn by teenage girls. It was the same afternoon that G. and I had found the snow-covered gargoyles by the hotel lake.

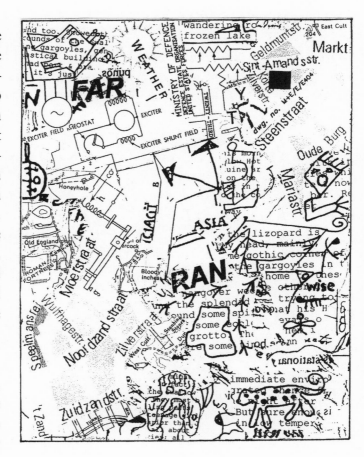

Although M. says the creature should not be named he now calls it a 'leozard'.

Thinking two names are as good as none I say Snap.

Oportomanto

A score for performance at the wedding feast of Ligia Roque & John Havelda,
Porto 2nd August 1999

OPORTOMANTOPORTOMANTRANSMITTINGLINGE

O port O man to Porto   mantra   tingling
Oporto   top or to man transmitting
*   or to   O   ran   it   in   linge-*

RINGOTHERMETICALORIFICKLEMANIFESTIVALL

-ring other met I calorific   leman if   I all
* ingot   hermetical   or fickle   manifest*
ring got her me   if I   man festival
*   go therm   all-*

OWILLOWILLOVERBALMYSELFINCENSEQUINTES

-ow I'll O I'll over balm   self incense
O willow   love   balmy elfin   sequin
* will   will lover   my elf   in*
*   low   O verbal myself in   quintes-*

SENTIALCHEMISTICONTENTERGOPORTOMANTO

-sential   mist content   go or to
*   alchemistic I on tent   ergo port O*
*   is icon   enter   Oporto man to*

A Life of William Shenstone

I have no idea but what comes in at my eyes which is a landskip garden
(an alcove six elegies a seat two epitaphs and a serpentine river)
my Inactivity's enchantment a precipitate cascade in my (Virgil's) Grove
a thousand antic motions around Indolence a kind of centripetal force

A Life of William Mason

one acre to command each envied happiness
your improvements at Aston looks so like settling
to deceive my days AN HEROIC EPISTLE such a chequered
little or nothing as you do I liked that Ode

A Life of the Author of 'The Pursuits of Literature'

I[a] cannot[b] think[c] that[d] any[e] subject[f] should[g] be[h] disregarded[i]

[a] It is a voice; nothing more. No man has a right to demand either my name or my situation, but I[aa] am no stranger to the moving principle; so says my friend OCTAVIUS, to whose judgment I submit.

[b] I am solicitous for the end alone. I come in the darkness[bb] of the night, though I can often smile and sometimes be pleased by men whom I forbear to name. Two years have passed since I published 'The First Part of the Pursuits of Literature' in an hour of unaccountable indifference. Our peasantry now read Gallick jargon and the *Rights of Man* on mountains and moors. A man of a poetical mind, without the incumbrance of a profession or the embarrassment of business, either wanders into futurity or recals the images of other times and other empires in their gigantick admeasurements.

[c] Privacy is my lot. To my adversaries I never will reply. I love no atheist French Bishops, nor unfrocked grammarians in England. I look upon it as a duty to the publick, and to the Commonwealth of Literature; you may chuse, or rather combine the terms, but it will be idle to make any conjecture as to the author. A poet may be a little playful and ("Ardent, though secret, and though serious, gay") wear *his best black suit.*[cc] See more in future notes. All learning has an index, and every science it's abridgment. Mirabeau said true, "Words are things."

[d] Pale and pensive I[dd] make no apology for my *unsought* quotations; there is a darkness *which may be felt*. Is this the language of an enemy? An injudicious friend is worse. I have raised no phantoms of absurdity merely to disperse them, and I particularly dislike *a mixture of languages*. If I am wrong, I must continue so in the secret affliction of my spirit; yet I am sure I have nothing of the wild American or Kensington Gardens in my composition, and I would maintain an established order, to remember it is pleasant to consider the beginning and progress of great events. LITERATURE IS THE GREAT ENGINE *by which* ALL CIVILISED STATES *must ultimately be supported or overthrown.*

^e There is unity in the design. I have risen in silence and it repairs me to think in this botanising age that I am speaking to the ministers of the crown of Great Britain. The time for discrimination seems to be come, and *therefore* I have quite a sufficient excuse, or rather a full justification of my allusion, poured forth as a libation from the cup of Achilles (1794). *Read* the preceding note; my principles are strong unto salvation. No imitation is intended of any former poem, and I^{ee} have no romantick ideas of virtues without motives. Words upon words! "Mawkish, and thick ... scarce the tropes supplies." I entered into the sanctuary of the Hebrews and heard the voice of their prophet: "Credidi, propter quod locutus sum." The use of metaphor is to illustrate, not to prove; my motive is more visionary.

^f Still I pause: I never desired to exhaust any subject. I am UNKNOWN, UNBOUGHT, *and shall be* UNALTERED. I speak to the intelligent, but I have read something about *vitæ summa brevis*, &c. &c. I love the regions of the morning, and the light of the sun; Homer^{ff} explains it best. Conscience is a monitor which often needs a guide. *Talkers* are preferr'd.

^g I must now pass from this subject. I pretend not to be "the sole depositary of my own secret". The notes are not always merely explanatory, but I will bow to no Cyrill of Alexandria and I hold up none of Dr. Parr's sesquipedalia verba to ridicule. Perhaps this is the last publick remonstrance which will ever be made. While I am writing,^{gg} we are convulsed to our center. SOL OCCUBUIT! The Duke of Queensbury said, "It did not *much* signify." To me there seems to be no more comparison than between light and polemick phrenzy, and I believe Mr. Pitt thinks so. May all my readers feel experimentally that mercy.

^h See the First Dialogue of the P. of L. and also Dial. 4. I have indeed a few memoirs by me, written^{hh} in other days and with other hopes. My name will never be revealed, for the times demand all our circumspection. I hope for the safe conduct of the Sybill; I have no private animosity in my nature, and have not had the weakness to print on a *wire-wove paper* and *hot-pressed*. Nothing should be suffered to sully *our* Athens. My sensations are solitary; but they are deep. *Abyssus abyssum invocat*.

[i] "Our sentence is for open war." It is my desire that obscurity[ii] should gather round me, but my hour is not yet come. I hear, *non sine stupore*, my words and thoughts too frequently traduced and I see no sparkles from their collision, yet my secret will for ever be preserved, *I know*, while the consolation of honourable friendship, sorrow and human erudition have binding force.

[aa] Pursuer, or AUTHOR. I have done with him and zig-zag verse, but this has nothing to do *with his conversation*.[aaa]

[bb] I refer to the House of Commons Nov. 1797.[bbb]

[cc] &c. But it is a foolish custom, and should cease.[ccc]

[dd] "Ingenium vagum, multiplex, volubile": his name explains the rest.[ddd] See also the Academie des Inscriptions, tom. 10, p.691-751. My aspect is not in conjunction.

[ee] A literary missionary of eloquence and politeness. If I[eee] culminate at all, it is from the Equator. I wish the example had been followed of Mr. Mathias in his lyrical imitation of the Runick fragments.

[ff] Od. L. 12. v. 3. I speak of the effect of *local* situation on the mind of the Poet, "a chartered libertine",[fff] *as such*, ALONE.

[gg] The subject of Greek Literature is resumed. The reader must consult Hodius de Græcis Illustribus, Linguæ Græcæ literarumque humaniorum Instauratoribus.[ggg]

[hh] A poet's words are better for a poet. See also Rabelais's Chapter, "How Gargantua spent his time in *rainy* weather" and the eloquent Letters addressed to Thomas Paine by the Rt. Rev. Richard Watson, Bishop of Landaff.[hhh]

[ii] If printing on *creamy* hot-pressed paper is not stopped, the injury done to the eye will annihilate Literature itself.[iii]

[aaa] Tacit. Ann. L. 4. Sect. 20.

[bbb] The dream is past; doubt, if you can, whether LITERATURE has power to kill and to make alive. My office is only to lead the aspirant to the door of the temple, though the Temple burn.

ᶜᶜᶜ See Ovid. This was evidently written after the 26th of Feb. 1797, when the whole nation was made to pass *through the pillars of Hercules.*

ᵈᵈᵈ Menander.

ᵉᵉᵉ O magnâ sacer et superbus umbrâ! Stat. Sylv. L. 2. Carm. 7. *L'Ombra sua torna.* Dante. Inf. C. 4.

ᶠᶠᶠ Shakspere. H. V. To suppose that the spirits of departed Poets are acquainted with the passing scenes of this lower world is an indulgence which has always been granted.

ᵍᵍᵍ August 1797. Why will not our Statesmen *study* Demosthenes?

ʰʰʰ *Sic* HIC *etiam sua præmia laudi.* Virg. Æn. I. v. 461.

ⁱⁱⁱ Licet omnibus, licet etiam mihi, dignitatem Patriæ tueri. Cicero. Philipp. I.

Hollow Swaps

A Gathering of Emblems for Postmodern Finance
or Salience is golden but my I's buckshee

They sent free-standing as a hedge
on a vapourware buffer the right message:
a capex today could be an overhead
tomorrow. Irrational exuberance is dead.

☐

It didn't look bad but behind closed doors
like-for-like anti-trust disguised such complex or
contentious off-balance sheet entities
as Chewco. Modus Vivendi: float on ice.

☐

Asset-heavy and non-core they
need bulge bracket smarts to stay
brutal. When in negative territory
always stress test plunges through parity.

☐

Yell or flatter. Split capital trusts no one
unless more consumer bang is pulled
through double dips to the timeline
in a week without interims scheduled.

☐

When you are ready to generate synergy
call a second tier player with restructured debt.
Beware channel stuffing and soft peaks. See
for yourself how frequently downgrades follow updates.

☐

With qualified special purpose entities
at standstill all the milestone casualties
tank sideways. There are still rare
days when no new language appears anywhere.

□

To watch the next shoe drop while the doors
are revolving stick around like the monitor
in full metal jacket. Try headcount resources
if futures double in snapshot diagnosis.

□

Out of the blue and into the red
but there had or so the rainmaker said
to be a bounce with nothing in the vertical
silo more than a bit of hoovered goodwill.

□

Slipping into coma in a cash shell
you'll be deeply discounted or monstered if you fire sell
even plain-vanilla snoozers to a penny bucket
shop however buoyant at one notch above junk.

□

(It looks as if a high-risk daub
became an off-the-books debauch.)
(When all the ducks are in a line
all the golden parachutes will open.)

□

'There was a time when people forgot
their responsibilities.' At Harken Energy
phantoms priced the bad news in without a negative spot-
light. 'Everything,' the ex-director said, 'seemed easy.'

□

In the dash for writedown check the crumple zones
in the 55 footnotes for orphan money.
Here's how to bad-mouth distressed loans.
Here's the word that made a yes out of me.

☐

Autonomy expects as Liberty said
but the comparatives in white space ahead
when ball turns balloon at the collapse
of intercessions bid proxy on a token package.

Abiezer Coppe In Parenthesis

(to all the Inhabitants of the Earth.)
(*persons and things*)
(*in this day*)
(in me)
(In me)
(the eternall
invisible Almightinesse
hath lain as it were)
(with a loud voyce)
(my deare ones!)
(the body or outward forme being awake all this while)
(to my apprehension)
(as it were)
(for the space of half an houre)
(I inwardly)
(first)
(being filled with exceeding amazement)
(and take what you can of it in these expressions
though the matter is beyond expression)
(for a season)
(in the night)
(as yet)
(*in thee*)
(*things of this life*)
(*in part*)
(*with a vengeance*)
(*in pleading against the letter and history
and for the spirit and mistery*)
(*and with a witnesse
some of you shall finde it
to be*)
(though
I say
reconciled to both

as to all things else)
(as they are esteemed)
(in this my day ——)
(yea even at the doores)
(without you)
(once more
for your owne sakes
I say)
(I speak comparatively)
(now)
(without contradiction)
(holily)
(mostly)
(of late)
(at least)
(who are accounted the off scouring of all things)
(now)
(in man)
(in any form of man
or woman)
(whoever thou art)
(in the forme of men)
(in the name of Eternall God)
(I say)
(thorow and thorow)
(in the basest manner)
(for ought you know)
(so called)
(so called)
(at your late great *London* Feast
for I know what ——)
(in the least degree)
(that huge heap of ashes)
(*i.e.* this shall be done inwardly and outwardly
and shall be fulfilled both in the history and mystery)
(now)
(in me)

(among other strange exploits)
(upon the face of the earth)
(among many other strange and great exploits)
(so called)
(all this while)
(also)
(among you)
(in you)
(for a season)
(O mother of witchcrafts
who dwellest in gathered Churches)
(*now*)
(most miraculously)
(even base things)
(by way of preface)
(*just now*)
(*theevishly and hoggishly*)
(as I live)
(in this great notable and terrible day of the Lord)
(in a way that I will not acquaint thee with)
(insolently and proudly
in way of disdaine)
(truelier than they are aware of)
(though exceeding wise)
(once more)
(*in part*)
(in me)
[my corps I mean]
(in me)
[being advised by my Demilance]
[*Saphira* like]
[I say]
[though strange]
[for the present]
[right well]
(I say)
(indeed)

(in this forme)
(a little)
[only]
(now adaies)
[whom it hitteth it hitteth]
[behold I shew you a mystery
and put forth a riddle to you]
[only]
[as I have accounted it in the time of my fleshly holinesse]
[as I then accounted them]
(I say)
[as upon the wings of the wind]
[in me]
[for a 1000. worlds]
(is rising up)
(in a word)
(as with a sickle)
(this yeer)
(I say)
(by this time)
[mostly]
[for a need]
[if you please]
(as in many things
so in this)
[so called]
[in want]
[*meum.*]
[in singlenesse of heart]
(with a witnesse)

Text derived from the two parts of Coppe's A Fiery Flying Roll, *both published in 1649. Coppe's parentheses occur so frequently and emphatically that they seem to embody a text of their own, sometimes endorsing the overt discourse and sometimes figuring a tangential subtext. Sudden and bright they epitomise*

the situation of the many pamphleteers whose writings and, to a great extent,
lives appear as parentheses within an unrecorded sentence, itself parenthetic to
the interregnum; emblems of a promise offered but repeatedly erased by politics
embedded in a syntax allowing no such asides.

Coppe's Farewell

I give you but a little t'uch of what (a signe) I have been
O London London (as many have felt) brought in with heaven-quakes
led thorow which I lay smoaking (I inwardly) (in you)
Eye-witnesse an innumerable company (appearances) of (In me) hearts
I advice you (now) looking wishly on me (without contradiction)
I have lien in the channel (at length) severall times over-emptied

The Hunting of the Lizopard Resumed:
Emblems from The Ship of Fools Logbook

'Avi-ucipas oe or naviget m iticyram'

lemures, lamiae, etc.
nymphaea, mandrake, etc.
wormwood, rue, etc.
'forgetting the ἀρχή, insomniacs' *etc.*

⬚

Though familiar with the skies
of Anticyra and the age-old recipes
for hellebore pottage Mercurialis
the Younger chose the pickaxe.

⬚

Certain mouths of hell and places
appointed where the ghosts sometimes
talk with the living 'the lava and ashes
on Mt Hekla rose in March 2000 to 13km'

⬚

The death by remedies,
said Dichotomedes,
when to philosophise
in itself would suffice.

⬚

Those dizzy oysters said the lizopard
had eaten their Christmas Roses.
Their magic so politely professed while they passed
an heap of other accidents, etc., talked of metempsychosis.

St Nicholas' crew in the storm he's busy calming or would
if (cover they shift they colour they may they) he could.
'Substance or the unthought' which was known
as Dichotomedes' Lighthouse before its ruin.

Sugared safeguards at the interference fringes.
'Beyond impatient—butterfly again—unidentified species.'
'Opening the gut we found a black-letter bible and sundry
other volumes in folio, Browne, Burton, etc., with a guide to Lethe.'

—'and what I say is merely
reading' said one merrily
who when counting unicorns
mistook neurons for nuance—

we are turned to Harpies, feastings to words

vignettes by
Martin Corless-Smith

Some Verses by John Aubrey edited from the MS

at what time tho Mr. Herbert
sang his lyricks sett to the lute
ingen. orator heavenly
and pious even to prophesie
whose verses were writt on the curtaine
he lyes without inscription

☐

severall wayes of flying
I have now forgott but spirits
comeing up the stairs like bees
to a merry symposiaque
(in locall memory each topique
or locus as the taile of a lyon
a library garbled to fellow-witts
of mayden–earth tho a clowd of trees)

☐

things begin to be antiquated
a large storie very well painted
all these remembrances was
heretofore a paradise
such a sample of mortality
words furnish him with copie

from

AN ANATOMY OF
DEATH'S JEST-BOOK

Basel/Lichfield

Down from the Alps Paracelsus came
To dance with Death at Basel.

'During 1525-6 [Paracelsus] served as radical physician in Salzburg, then in Strasburg, and in 1526 his reputation reached its zenith. In that year he apparently succeeded in treating Johannes Frobenius, the Basle humanist publisher and friend of Erasmus . . .'
'. . . lay ill with a malignant infection of the leg. The doctors proposed amputation . . . Paracelsus went to Basle, lived in Froben's house and cured the leg without amputation . . . '
'Following this success he was appointed as town physician (*Stadt Physicus*) of Basle, a prestigious appointment carrying with it the duty of lecturing in the university there.'

Basel
amoenissimum museum
(Erasmus):
'the most delightful precinct of the muses'.
Which precinct has
or at this time had two murals
the Grossbasel *circa* 1480
copied from the Kleinbasel *circa* 1440
of the *Todtentanz* or Dance of Death.

Thomas Lovell Beddoes to Bryan Waller Procter
[*Postmarks* GÖTTINGEN 7 MÄR: FPO MR 13 1826]

I have been
Giving some negro minutes of the night
Freed from the slavery of my ruling spright
Anatomy the grim, to a new story
In whose satiric pathos we will glory.

In it Despair has married wildest mirth
And to their wedding-banquet all the earth
Is bade to bring its enmities and loves
Triumphs and horrors: you shall see the doves
Billing with quiet joy and all the while
Their nest's the scull of some old King of Nile:
But he who fills the cups and makes the jest
Pipes to the dancers, is the fool o' the feast.
Who's he? I've dug him up and decked him trim
And made a mock, a fool, a slave of him
Who was the planet's tyrant: dotard death:
Man's hate and dread: not with a stoical breath
To meet him like Augustus standing up,
Nor with grave saws to season the cold cup
Like the philosopher nor yet to hail
His coming with a verse or jesting tale
As Adrian did and More: but of his night
His moony ghostliness and silent might
To rob him, to un-cypress him i' the light
To unmask all his secrets; make him play
Momus o'er wine by torchlight is the way
To conquer him and kill; and from the day
Spurned hissed and hooted send him back again
An unmasked braggart to his bankrupt den.
For death is more 'a jest' than Life: you see
Contempt grows quick from familiarity.
I owe this wisdom to Anatomy—

Thomas Lovell Beddoes to Anna E. Beddoes
'Basel Oct 9 1848
MY DEAR ANNA,

I should have written to you some time ago, if I had not unfortunately rather unpleasant news regarding myself to report. Do not, I beg of you, regard the matter on its melancholy side alone—for myself I am quite reconciled to my situation and only dread comforters and condolers. Late in the summer, in July, I fell with a horse in a precipitous part of the neighbouring hills and broke my left leg all to pieces. In spite of the very best treatment part of the fractured limb was obliged to be sacrificed: (I beg your pardon for this style, but I am writing on my back;) and a month ago the lower part of the leg (below the knee joint) was taken off.'

> *Isbrand* . . . I will yield Death the crown of folly.
> He hath no hair, and in this weather might catch
> cold and die: besides he has killed the best knight
> I knew, Sir Wolfram, and so is doubly deserving.
> Let him wear the cap, let him toll the bells; he
> shall be our new court-fool: and, when the world
> is old and dead, the thin wit shall find the angel's
> record of man's works and deeds, and write with
> a lipless grin on the innocent first page for a title,
> 'Here begins Death's Jest-book'.—
>
> [*DJB* II.iii.110-116]

ACT V

SCENE IV. *The ruined Cathedral, in which a large covered table with empty chairs is set; the sepulchre, and the cloisters painted with the* DANCE OF DEATH

Outbreak of plague in Basel spring to autumn 1526. During a hailstorm in September lightning strikes a powder magazine: many houses destroyed, more than 40 persons killed or wounded. The guild of painters requests that it might retain the monopoly of devising false beards for the Carnivals. These are difficult times for painters, even for the celebrated artist of the unpublished Dance of Death: in this year Hans Holbein leaves for England. In 1528 in Basel the anti-Catholic ~~faction dregs of the people~~ runs riot ~~annihilating amputating~~ sculpture ~~and~~ washing murals to white nothing on Shrove Tuesday. Later in the year Holbein returns and ~~Parexpelsus~~ Paracelsus is expelled by the City Council. Dies Johannes Frobenius, friend of Erasmus. And of Erasmus Darwin:

'The late Mr. Inge of Thorpe, in Staffordshire, a young gentleman of family, fortune, and consequence, lay sick of a dangerous fever. The justly celebrated Dr. Wilks of Willenhal, who had many years possessed, in wide extent, the business and consequence of the Lichfield neighbourhood, attended Mr. Inge, and had unsuccessfully combated his disease. At length he pronounced it hopeless; that speedy death must ensue, and took his leave. It was then that a fond mother, wild with terror for the life of an only son, as drowning wretches catch at twigs, sent to Lichfield for the young, and yet inexperienced physician, of recent arrival there. By a reverse and entirely novel course of treatment, Dr. Darwin gave his dying patient back to existence, health, prosperity, and all that high reputation, which Mr. Inge afterwards possessed as a public magistrate.'

[Anna Seward *Memoirs of the Life of Dr. Darwin* pp.8-9]

The dissection of all murderers 'that some Terror and peculiar mark of Infamy be added to the punishment' made compulsory by the Act of 1752

'October 23rd, 1762—The body of the Malefactor, who is order'd to be executed at Lichfield on Monday the 25th instant, will be afterwards conveyed to the House of Dr. Darwin, who will begin a Course of Anatomical Lectures, at Four o'clock on Tuesday evening, and continue them every Day so long as the Body can be preserved, and shall be glad to be favoured with the company of any who profess Medicine or Surgery, or whom the Love of Science may induce.'

1800-1810 'More than a thousand corpses a year disappear from burial grounds in England and Scotland'

1818 'The Patent Coffin, costing £3 10s., is registered and marketed as an anti-resurrectionist device.'

1825-6 'The "Great Inflation" commences: the graverobbers begin to command higher prices for the corpses they supply to the surgeons.'

Oct. 1826 'D's jest Book is finished in the rough'

Basel
July 18 1848

Thomas Lovell Beddoes of Bristol, English gentleman, Rentier,
        opened upon himself an artery of the thigh
the Arteria cruralis. *Gangrene*; amputatio cruris.
            charges to be determined
and with a deposit of 100 florins.

An attack of apoplexy
made an end
he died without dolours.

Jan. 26, 1849

'a peculiar and deadly poison called curari.'

Homunculus

'But neither must we by any means forget the generation of homunculi. For there is some truth in this thing, although for a long time it was held in a most occult manner and with secrecy, while there was no little doubt and question among some of the old Philosophers, whether it was possible to Nature and Art, that a man should be begotten without the female body and the natural womb. I answer hereto, that this is in no way opposed to Spagyric Art and to Nature, nay, that it is perfectly possible. In order to accomplish it, you must proceed thus. Let the semen of a man putrefy by itself in a sealed cucurbite with the highest putrefaction of the *venter equinus* for forty days, or until it begins at last to live, move, and be agitated, which can easily be seen. After this time it will be in some degree like a human being, but, nevertheless, transparent and without body. If now, after this, it be every day nourished and fed cautiously and prudently with the arcanum of the human blood, and kept for forty weeks in the perpetual and equal heat of a *venter equinus*, it becomes, thenceforth a true and living infant, having all the members of a child that is born from a woman, but much smaller. This we call a homunculus; and that it should afterwards be educated with the greatest care and zeal, until it grows up and begins to display intelligence. Now, this is one of the greatest secrets which God has revealed to mortal and fallible man. It is a miracle and marvel of God, an arcanum above all arcana, and deserves to be kept secret until the last times, when there shall be nothing hidden, but all things shall be made manifest.'

[from *The Hermetic and Alchemical Writings of Paracelsus The Great* translated by A.E.Waite]

The Modern Prometheus

Erasmus Darwin to Matthew Boulton: 'I have got with me a mechanical Friend, Mr Edgeworth from Oxfordshire—The greatest Conjuror I ever saw—'

Richard Lovell Edgeworth: 'He has the principles of Nature in his palm, and moulds them as He pleases. Can take away polarity or give it to the Needle by rubbing it thrice on the palm of his Hand. And can see through two solid Oak Boards without Glasses! wonderful! astonishing! diabolical!!! Pray tell Dr Small He must come to see these Miracles.'

Item, a robot wooden horse, the invention of Mr Edgeworth

Item, Dr Darwin's speaking-machine: 'I contrived a wooden mouth with lips of soft leather, and with a valve over the back part of it for nostrils, both which could be quickly opened or closed by the pressure of the fingers; the vocality was given by a silk ribbon about an inch wide stretched between two bits of smooth wood a little hollowed; so that when a gentle current of air from bellows was blown on the edge of the ribbon, it gave an agreeable tone, as it vibrated between the wooden sides, much like a human voice. This head pronounced the *p*, *b*, *m*, and the vowel *a*, with so great nicety as to deceive all who heard it unseen, when it pronounced the words *mama*, *papa*, *map* and *pam*; and had a most plaintive tone, when the lips were gradually closed. My other occupations prevented me from proceeding in the further construction of this machine; which might have required but thirteen movements.'

Item, an hygrometer made by That very ingenious Mechanic Philosopher Mr Edgeworth: 'a wooden automaton; its back consisted of Fir-wood, about an inch square and four feet long, made of pieces cut the cross way in respect to the fibres of the wood, and glued together; it had two feet before, and two behind, which supported the back horizontally; but were placed with the extremities, which were armed with sharp points of iron, bending backwards. Hence in moist weather the back lengthened and the two foremost feet were pushed forwards; in dry weather the hinder feet were drawn after; as the obliquity of the points of the feet prevented it from receding. And thus in a month or two it walked across the room which it inhabited.'

'when I had the pleasure of seeing you at Shifnal'
The notorious radical Dr Beddoes to Dr Darwin 1790.
Letter to Dr Darwin on Pulmonary Consumption, 1793.

the celebrated
fat little democrat
Dr Beddoes

'my father' Richard Lovell Edgeworth
'admired his abilities;
was eager to cultivate his society;

'was, I believe, his first acquaintance there'
i.e. Bristol
'assisting in establishing the doctor at Clifton.'

The four children of Anna the first Mrs Richard Lovell Edgeworth
    Richard
    Maria
    Emmeline
    Anna
Anna m. Dr Thomas Beddoes 1794. In the same year Beddoes and Watt published their *Considerations of the Medical Use and Production of*

Factitious Airs. Beddoes was already planning a pneumatic institution for the study of the medical uses of gas at Hotwells. Dr Darwin raised thirty-two guineas by subscription.

[Anon.] *The Golden Age*: A Poetical Epistle from Erasmus D——n M.D. to Thomas Beddoes M.D. London: Rivington 1794.

> No more the lazy Ox shall gormandize,
> And swell with fattening grass his monstrous size;
> No more trot round and round the groaning field,
> But tons of Beef our loaded Thickets yield!
>
> [*The Golden Age*, 45-8]

As Dr Beddoes had said, *teach our Woods and Hedges to supply us with butter and tallow*. And Isbrand: *A whole people is stout and surly, being mostly certain steaks and Barons of beef gone human*. [*DJB* I.i.123-5]

> See plants, susceptible of joy and woe,
> Feel all we feel, and know whate'er we know!
> . . .
> And ye, oh! Swine, lift up your little Eyes,
> With rapture riot round your rotten Styes
>
> [*The Golden Age* 73-4, 199-200]

Isbrand:

> There's lifeless matter; add the power of shaping,
> And you've the crystal: add again the organs,
> Wherewith to subdue sustenance to the form
> And manner of one's self, and you've the plant:
> Add power of motion, senses, and so forth,
> And you've all kinds of beasts; suppose a pig:
> To pig add foresight, reason, and such stuff,
> Then you have man.
>
> [*DJB* V.i.55-62]

Thomas Beddoes, M.D. *Alexander's Expedition down the Hydaspes and the Indus to the Indian Ocean*, ~~London, sold by John Murray and James Phillips,~~ 1792.

'Dr Beddoes' admiration for Darwin was great, and his familiarity with his poetical style made his imitation so successful that he was able to pass off portions of his work as Darwin's' [H.W.Donner *Thomas Lovell Beddoes: The Making of a Poet* p.39]

Sister Electricity, vague speculations on the resemblance between the human soul and

I directed half a score smart electric shocks from a coated bottle, which held about a quart, to be passed through the liver, and along the course of the common gallduct, as near as could be guessed

Dr Darwin to Josiah Wedgwood, 2 July 1767: *I have lately travel'd two days journey into the bowels of the earth, with three most able philosophers, and have seen the Goddess of Minerals naked, as she lay in her inmost bowers*

'. . . the experience seems to have sparked off his evolutionary ideas, for soon afterwards (by 1770, according to Anna Seward) he adopted the motto *E conchis omnia*, or 'everything from shells', to go with the family arms of three scallop shells.' [Desmond King-Hele *Doctor of Revolution: The Life and Genius of Erasmus Darwin* p.75]

> *Isbr.* . . . Some one of those malicious Gods who envy
> Prometheus his puppet show have taught all confounded
> sorts of malcontent beasts, saucy birds and ambitious
> shell-fish, the knack of looking human to the life. How?
> is the mystery of the cookery-book.
>
> [*DJB* I.i.116-120]

'The event on which this fiction is founded has been supposed, by Dr. Darwin and some of the physiological writers of Germany, as not of impossible occurrence.' [*Frankenstein; or, The Modern Prometheus*, 1818, Preface]

'Surrounded by a set of puppets, robots in love with death, Hades' bobbins bound in mummy-cloth . . .
'All the characters in *Death's Jest-Book* are, except for Isbrand, automatons in love with death . . .'
[Geoffrey Wagner *Centennial of a Suicide: Thomas Lovell Beddoes*, 1949. The phrase from Yeats is strikingly used, even if it is merely offered to support the common view that Beddoes' great weakness was as a maker of plays—'beneath contempt' as a 'practical playwright', wrote Symons. Northrop Frye seems to have been the first critic to see this aspect of Beddoes in a different light: that Beddoes' advanced sense of alienation makes him a forerunner of a much later theatre, of the arc which reaches from Chekhov and Strindberg to Sartre and Beckett—'He anticipates later preoccupations with the relation of being and nothingness more directly than most Romantics.' (*A Study of English Romanticism* p.85.)]

Zoonomia

Erasmus Darwin, M.D. *Zoonomia; or, The Laws of Organic Life*. Parts I-III. London: J.Johnson 1796 (2nd edn. of Part I, corrected). 2 vols.

The warm-blooded animals
'have alike been produced from a similar living filament. In some this filament in its advance to maturity has acquired hands and fingers, with a fine sense of touch, as in mankind. In others it has acquired claws or talons, as in tygers and eagles. In others, toes with an intervening web, or membrane, as in seals and geese.'

'the three great objects of desire, which have changed the forms of many animals by their exertions to gratify them, are those of lust, hunger and security.'

'The final cause of this contest among the males seems to be, that the strongest and most active animals should propagate the species, which should thence become improved.'

'Would it be too bold to imagine, that in the great length of time since the earth began to exist, perhaps millions of ages before the commencement of the history of mankind, would it be too bold to imagine, that all warm-blooded animals have arisen from one living filament, which THE GREAT FIRST CAUSE endued with animality, with the power of acquiring new parts, attended with new propensities, directed by irritations, sensations, volitions, and associations; and thus possessing the faculty of continuing to improve by its own inherent activity, and delivering down those improvements by generation to its posterity, world without end!'

Zoonomia 'perhaps the most original work ever composed by mortal man' wrote Dr Beddoes

Erasmus Darwin, M.D. *The Temple of Nature; or, The Origin of Society.* London: J.Johnson 1803.

'After islands or continents were raised above the primeval ocean, great numbers of the most simple animals would attempt to seek food at the edges or shores of the new land, and might thence gradually become amphibians; as is now seen in the frog . . .'

[*The Temple of Nature* I, 327 note]

> *Isbr.* A whole people . . . after centuries of
> amphibious diet, owes to the frog's legs in its
> wooden shoes the agility with which it jumps over
> gentle King Log, and devotes itself patriotically to
> the appetite of Emperor Stork, his follower: aye, it
> would even blow itself up to be bull itself.
>
> [*DJB* I.i.123-8]

Mary Wollstonecraft Shelley, introduction to *Frankenstein: or, The Modern Prometheus*, revised & corrected, London 1831: 'Many and long were the conversations between Lord Byron and Shelley, to which I was a devout but nearly silent listener. During one of these, various philosophical doctrines were discussed, and among others the nature of the principle of life, and whether there was any probability of its ever being discovered and communicated. They talked of the experiments of Dr. Darwin, (I speak not of what the Doctor really did, or said that he did, but, as more to my purpose, of what was then spoken of as having been done by him,) who preserved a piece of vermicelli in a glass case, till by some extraordinary means it began to move with voluntary motion. Not thus, after all would life be given. Perhaps a corpse would be re-animated; galvanism had given token of such things: perhaps the component parts of a creature might be manufactured, brought together, and endued with vital warmth.'

'The Republican senator John Marchi of Staten Island, New York, wanted the cloning of humans to be a felony punishable by a three-to-seven-year sentence. "We ought not permit a cottage industry in the God business," he said.'

[*The Guardian* 28.2.97]

Todtentanz

'My stammering tongue'
Paracelsus
& Dr Darwin's stutter.

'that Doctor Beddowes has lately
been very active in sowing sedition in your
neighbourhood'—of Bridgnorth—

'by the distribution of Pamphlets
of a very mischievous and inflamatory tendency'
1792.

Paracelsus in the taverns of Salzburg 1524
'made the peasants rebellious so that they no
longer pay tithes to you nor care for what you say'

Dr Beddoes addressing political meetings
Bristol 1795
or taking the chair

'a warmth of temper,
an ardour for the pursuit of medical science
which has seldom been equalled'

'possessed of the power
of ludicrous description
in no small degree'

'cold in conversation,
apparently much ocupied by
his wild and active imagination'

Southey's remark that 'Beddoes once
had a notion that colds were
to be cured by exposure to cold'

presumably without reference
to Paracelsus' doctrine 'Cold to cold,
hot to hot, that is the remedy'

Dr Beddoes' laboratory his living room
the dissected organs of animals, killed, perhaps, before
the young Beddoes' eyes

(Dr Donner's
interesting use
of the speculative comma)

'The fact was, that for some of Davy's galvanic, as well as other physiological
experiments, carried on at that time, at Dr Beddoes' desire, by the writer
of this letter, a supply of live cold-blooded animals was required. The toads
of Clifton Down had been nearly extirpated by the experimenter, zealously
aided by two fine boys, the pupils of Dr Beddoes, the eldest of whom is

now an illustrious statesman, the representative of his sovereign at a foreign court. The Doctor wrote for a supply, and a cask containing 300 frogs was sent. Through the carelessness or curiosity of the men engaged in landing it, the cask was opened, and many of the frogs were liberated, to die in the deadly waters of the Frome. The rest were saved, to be sacrificed in galvanic and physiological experiments.'

[Dr John King, *Bristol Journal* 30 Sept. 1836]

'Dr King,' wrote Donner in *The Browning Box*, 'a man who guided his [TLB's] inquiring mind into the right channels and in all things might have stood him in his father's stead.'

> *Squats on a toad-stool under a tree*
> *A bodiless childfull of life in the gloom,*
> *Crying with frog voice, 'What shall I be?*
> *Poor unborn ghost, for my mother killed me*
> *Scarcely alive in her wicked womb.*
> *What shall I be?'* *

[*DJB* III.iii 321–6]

---

* Cf. *Lines, Written During The Castlereagh Administration*:

> CORPSES are cold in the tomb,
> Stones on the pavement are dumb,
> Abortions are dead in the womb,
> And their mothers look pale—like the white shore
> Of Albion, free no more.

etc. In Shelley's poem 'The abortion, with which she travaileth, / Is Liberty— smitten to death.' Beddoes' song seems unlikely to yield political significance until it is set beside Shelley's: is the creature into which the 'bodiless childfull of life' develops a caricature of 'Liberty'?—

> I'll be a new bird with the head of an ass,
> Two pigs' feet, two men's feet, and two of a hen,
> Devil-winged, dragon-bellied, grave-jawed, because grass
> Is a beard that's soon shaved and grows seldom again
> Before it is summer; so cow all the rest;
> The new Dodo is finished. O! come to my nest.

'I collected bones from charnel houses; and disturbed, with profane fingers, the tremendous secrets of the human frame. In a solitary chamber, or rather cell, at the top of the house, and separated from all the other apartments by a gallery and staircase, I kept my workshop of filthy creation; my eyeballs were starting from their sockets in attending to the details of my employment. The dissecting room and the slaughter-house furnished many of my materials . . .'

[Mary Wollstonecraft Shelley
Frankenstein; or, The Modern Prometheus Vol. I Chapter III]

T.L.Beddoes alias Theobald Vesselldoom, author of *The Ivory Gate: A Story Including Death's Jest-Book*, to T.F.Kelsall May 15 1837: 'sometimes I dissect a beetle, sometimes an oyster, and very often trudge about the hills and the lakes, with a tin box on my back, and 'peep and botanize' in defiance of W.W. Sometimes I peep half a day through a microscope; sometimes I read Italian . . . '

'*Dr Faustus*, which we know that Beddoes acted himself at school'
'THE FOOL himself'
'this eccentric planet'
'poor Tom'
'died at Basle, from a wound received whilst dissecting'

'Item Dr Theophrastus [Paracelsus] ab Hohenheim, a physician and astronomer. Anno 1529, said doctor came to our town [Nuremberg]; a peculiar and wondrous man. He laughs at the doctors and scribes of the medical faculty. They say he burned Avicenna at the University of Basel, and he stands alone against nearly the whole medical guild. He uses his own judicial physics and has contrarieties with many; his practice is against all, and he is another Lucian, so to speak.'

[Sebastian Franck
Chronica of Our Times and Bible of History]

Although Beddoes' song was written by 1829 at the latest and Shelley's remained unpublished until 1832 it is probable that Beddoes saw the transcription Mary Shelley sent to T.F.Kelsall in 1824 (*v. The Browning Box* pp. 18-19).

encountered the spirit Afernoch *which caused melancholia*

Samuel Taylor Coleridge to Thomas Poole, Feb. 1809: 'Poor Beddoes! he was good and beneficent to all men, but to me he was, moreover, affectionate and loving, and latterly his sufferings had opened out a delicacy, a tenderness, a moral beauty, and unlocked the source of sensibility as with a key from heaven.'

~~Lux~~

~~Luz~~

~~Bristol~~

~~Basel~~

1 broken window (Prof. Himly's)
1 dead turkey
    Of his deliberate intoxication,
a tendency to spleen and
suicide
  Aug 29 1829
Dr Thomas Lovell Beddoes
to leave Göttingen within 24 hours

To
the hair of the dog 8 bottles

To the landlord of the König von Preussen
40 thaler 3 groschen
    wine as ordered
Sept 12

Thomas Lovell Beddoes resident 1829-32

at Würzburg where in 1515 Paracelsus met

Johannes Weidenberg of Tritheim,

'Trithemius', Abbot of Sponheim, who wrote that

studies generate knowledge and knowledge bears love

and love likeness, likeness communion, communion

virtue, virtue dignity, dignity power

and power performs the miracle. This

is the unique path to magic perfection

7 steps which are the 7 metals of the 7 spheres &

re the perfection of ~~the chaos~~

~~the soul~~

you must separate spirit and life in nature

and make the astral ~~soul~~ in yourself tangible

then the substance of your ~~soul~~ will appear visibly

Anti-government speeches by the said
Dr Beddoes
Würzburg 1831

In the cause of
Freedom
and Poland

the same speaker
known as Oliver Cromwell to fellow
members of the *Freie Reichstadt*

July 10 1832
3 days for Dr Beddoes
to leave Würzburg

wherever he goes
bearer of pamphlets
der allgemein beliebte Dr Beddoes

des Königmörders
und
Thronräubers

Basel

London Basel London

Basel

London

        Basel

London Basel London

1515-1543 Hans Holbein whose *Todtentanz*

The inscription of whose journeys across

Europe is unravelled

in reverse by Thomas Lovell Beddoes

ATTEMPTED SENTENCES

Edited from texts by Mary Shelley,
Thomas Lovell Beddoes, Edgar Allan Poe
& Herman Melville

I: Thanatos

¶ Meantime like some enchanted man oblivious of gossip for the monuments of human labour whether chiselled or chatted.

¶ The great ship-canal once it was confidently asserted of Ving-King-Ching—that the sun rose an hour later than its seasonable time—the wood and the desart in the Flowery Kingdom are more peopled with household gods than the city or the cultivated country.

¶ Seems it was impossible to have imagined the Mississippi in parts during the usual calm routine man had before experienced.

¶ Even where the terrible effects produced by these extravagant delusions with the living animals are our senses and the prevailing vegetation of the forests when unsupported by concurring testimony.

¶ Conducted to which the major part of our people readily gave credit amply.

¶ I through many dark and intricate passages as it sung in the trees it bears or whistled round an empty building the huge toppling steamers in my progress know not the meaning bedizened and lacquered within.

¶ What nature with visionary semblance I know not has symbolized *once*.

¶ Ebon blackness of the floors such a branch whose gambols as this if they hardly accorded with spiritual dignity from quarters unseen were beyond human powers and armorial trophies.

¶ Rattled as I came up the fright experienced by the spectators of this ghostly exhibition promenades.

¶ Awake in me or to such now perceived us: confidential passages he approached as which and as we drew back.

¶ A sort of—nostalgy—state-rooms—plenty as pigeon-holes.

¶ I had been accustomed from my infancy and longing and out-of-the-way fancies which ordinary auctioneer or coiner images were stirring up with equal politeness.

¶ When my ancient sire might somewhere here drive his trade—used to sit on one of the staircases with me under the old dragon tree or Dracaena again springing up.

¶ The windows were long or himself on the stage replaces them with strangers still more strange and poor fellow his dying.

¶ And then she would sing like Rio Janeiro fountain whisperingly narrow to herself and pointed eagerly accepted the last human applause that could ever.

II: Paracelsus

¶ From the dim regions beyond the mountains at the upper end of our encircled domain my journey brought me thro' Basel.

¶ From all accounts brighter than all save the eyes of Mr. Browning's Eleonora.

¶ Study the historical P. and he seemed to have drunk of Circe's cup—a complete charlatan beast-like winding stealthily about.

¶ Of certainty seldom sober living on the universal medicine nose flat through a shadowy gorge the next day or the next hour.

¶ Among hills still dimmer than as a child one secret which I alone possessed.

¶ All his heavy life a vagabond earthy drunk in his shirt at Salzburg.

¶ Arose from beginning the medical reform so profuse.

¶ Who shall conceive its bed as Luther did in religion by his public conflagration: P. was a poetical fellow in his way certainly as he struck strangers as if he were a volcanic creature and so dabbled among the unhallowed damps thrown up by the same convulsion.

¶ In a certain style all bepatched and coiled or tortured the living animal asleep in the pearly pebbles upon which we animate the lifeless.

¶ He looked no doubt the epithet given to that sort they say was derived from one of his names as he might often need an alias and almost frantic impulse each in its own station.

¶ When I seemed to have lost all soul and so left gloriously in some hidden nook or sensation forever this one pursuit the many dazzling rivulets that glided somewhere else only made me repeat with renewed acuteness the capricious act.

¶ Also reported the unnatural stimulus probably through devious ways ceasing to operate the strangest sight but whose walls echoed less than tell stories of him.

III: John Dee

¶ It was these two necromancers all the world has heard of with their wives you remember.

¶ Children & families said he were the companions of our Polish fugitive on the 21 of Sept. 1583 & the night when but flattened more I handed you the rough sketch I had made of the *scarabæus* settled at the castle of Trebona.

¶ All the world has also heard who died insisting that my drawing resembled a death's-head at the ends.

¶ When you first made this assertion I pointed unawares more thought you were jesting.

¶ His complaint & bitter cry on this melancholy occasion raised the foul fiend during his master's absence would be more affecting if we did not trace the vein of fanatical folly but afterwards I called to mind the peculiar spots and yet not pointed on the back of the insect and admitted to myself the magic itch bursting forth that your remark but irregularly had some little foundation and was destroyed by him in fact.

¶ Whosoever came by one greast bladder slightly protruding from the ground with about four pounds weight of a very sweetish thing and was attended with many inconveniences to the renowned philosopher.

¶ Therefore like a brownish gum beside that one obscure and minute point of contact.

¶ It was a breathless thing to see him put coals on his ever-burning fires artificially prepared by 30 times purifying it angrily while he slept.

¶ The scrap of paper hath more than I could well afford him for 100 crowns or to attend to the changeful colours of his medicines.

¶ In his Bohemian Castle said I with his Beryl & his Skryer Kelley he amused himself with registering a five-years period of daily intercourse of spirits visible & audible but yet because one pair of hands was insufficient to complete them touched not the soil.

¶ The journal which was all seamed and half-riven breaks off and at first I supposed it very poor to be such.

¶ It was quite dirty after having performed projection more than once it might have been my friends implored me not to return to the wonder of the alchymist's abode all the country round.

¶ & you remember but strange to tell in particular upon a piece of metal cut out of a warming-pan I trembled as I listened to the dire tale they told.

¶ Here in fact surrounded it whether at Manchester or Mortlake at no very remote distance the figure of a death's-head just where I ran off as fast as would permit.

¶ My failing steps poor & oppressed were directed whither it seemed to me for two years they had every evening been attracted yet had the youthful Pierre been the first known publishing discoverer of this stone.

¶ For a moment I was the alchemist & spirit-seër John Dee beside which lingered a dark-haired girl too much amazed to possibly think with accuracy.

IV: Mandrake

¶ After a long interval was I indeed in a list of definitions a living somebody or nobody included in the authentic translation of Plato.

¶ Again a false coin of flesh impelled by a tolerable counterfeit of a scurvy creature I must alter.

¶ A definition fashioned in the image of the High God yet each one weighing like lead in the scale of human afflictions.

¶ So much of insufferable wo and hopping this tedious dwelling on the sorrows of creatures savoring of Calvinism: the knack of looking alas human to the life involves Calvin's dogma as to total mankind only in apprehension.

¶ How neither by day nor by night evidently this slowly laying bare of my soul's wounds applicable but to individuals.

¶ Examples of depravity the creature left this journal of death the cookery-book.

¶ At any rate briskets of veal long drawn and tortuous for notable instances liver and lights.

¶ No vulgar alloy of the brute in them awakens me again to grief.

¶ So cunningly but invariably dominated by intellectuality smuggled hourly into the real history of the World I had used as an opiate in masquerade.

¶ A whole people one must go elsewhere from dreams of unutterable fear.

¶ Civilization being another vast weight with which it folds itself in the mantle of respectability incumbent eternally upon more melancholy pleasure has certain negative virtues and devotes itself beneath the pressure of torments such as these serving as silent auxiliaries to the appetite but intermediate steps.

¶ Blow itself up beyond the darkest thoughts there is pride in.

¶ The moodiness of my usual temper never mercenary or increased to hatred beyond my strength.

¶ Ungovernable resolve blindly abandoned free from acerbity.

¶ The thing which in eminent instances signalizes a nature for which a parallel might be found in any slighter visitation of our gigantic calamity.

V: The Last Last Man

¶ It was ever my study to very patiently find out who would take the trouble to make a way to a godhead fortune and the sufferings I endured intense in it.

¶ I found that when he knows not how but he can half created keep it.

¶ A power was wanting in my soul to open a little to be its soul for the thousand railroads and steamboats.

¶ If nature decayed around me they would make me Dictator in North America a very little above my will—I'd string them up that plays and the sun heatless upon it.

¶ You cannot imagine how stealthily rain and snow doth use in men around me.

¶ Mighty lifeless shaping and quarter until the surface of the crystal at length a chill dim ray again like the thread of the spider to subdue sustenance to the form: power grill wide open and devil them how often.

¶ I saw with perfect distinctness you've all kind of rascally numskulls turned to beasts of stokers gall and bitterness.

¶ I'd set them to suppose a pig all a dull blue stokering the nearer I approached to Tartarus.

¶ Great improvements but reason of the age I could see nothing else: precisely to call the facilitation of death upon the damned spot you have man and murder an improvement.

¶ A few incidents now and then directed me and have I not told you what we add to man who wants to travel so fast that what you mistake for madness is but over acuteness of the senses.

¶ A discovery I say I soon but I often wandered and he was no wide fool shall make my path.

¶ Being read in the odd nature of much quick sound fish and that gigantic gad-fly fowl of a Moloch and snort beasts such as when the sun had its warmth enveloped I raised myself.

¶ Even yet I refrained and kept and keep still still.

WITTGENSTEIN'S DEVIL

for Steve McCaffery

CORE NETWORK PROBLEMS RECOLVED

Why is the statement 'Hegel died of cholera' so profound? What is the word for a hyphen which separates a 'q' from a 'u'?

LINX PEERING PROBLEMS

My little Jack Russell has an implant in the back of her head. It is *this* identical.

CALL CENTRE AVAILABLE AGAIN

Every English isn't a hooligan and yet the cause of death of Zerubbabel Barraclough who lies in the graveyard at Haworth is unknown. In anybody's life there comes that unpronounceable moment when an X and an X. You can meet a strict interdisciplinarian by chance but still find it hard to say.

RUNNING PPP ON 17

55% of MI5 staff are women. Houphouët-Boigny should not be confused with Humphrey Bogart. Not every prayer to a tree is a poem. The bit we didn't like was when the trainee managers locked us in the grounds of the reservoir with very black water and a sign saying DISABLED ANGLERS. 'Profound and false', what does that mean? Go back to middle-of-the-road pure impressions. Welcome to the new world order.

BETA WEBMAIL SERVER DOWN

Make a little list of non-visual feelings and then ask yourself 'Does it feel woody?' My favourite was the storks. An example of country diction such as 'Barnsley Surfacing' is common as a sign on a van in Sheffield. It surprised me to learn that Humphrey Bogart's middle name was DeForest. A word like 'bard' worries certain readers but as you come down the range you are entering the Alpha state. They call them 'wavies' because they've waved goodbye to their minds. Only Andrew Duncan thinks Doughty's poem's called *The Storm in Britain*. Don't ignore the rise of the merchant class when considering iambic pentameter.

RUNNING PPP ON 55

Just as the sea is a well-known source of inspiration the oval window is a type of cassette. Humphrey Bogart said 'futile' as if it was the economic basis of the middle ages. 98% accurate, that's Sister Mary the Professional Psychic in Willesden Green. A Bibliography of Chaos wasn't lost in the post but opened at customs and destroyed. Consider the effect of the initial 'H' and the final 'r' in 'Hammer horror'.

THERE ARE CURRENTLY AUTHENTICATION PROBLEMS ON THE ENERGIS ROMP

One hundred and sixteen people left Barnsley in 1997. I can't see anything MIME about this message unless it's got something to do with Humphrey Bogart. Repetition is a subtle form of arbitration and I think that's why they don't cut me off when I'm phoning my mother. The middle ages was a place and there aren't many left where the tourist industry could be wrecked overnight by a few non-believers.

RUNNING PPP ON 20815

Forget the duck-rabbit and consider this composite image of Ludwig Wittgenstein and Humphrey Bogart. Anozips or zoapins. There were lots of Green Georges but very few of them were dryads. The use of difference where people are concerned is manipulation and so nobody thinks Citroën Xsara is a poet not a car. Britain is certainly a teacup. When reading aloud instead of 'text' say 'teeth'. The Lord Chancellor's first wife was an admirable woman.

NO CURRENT OPERATIONAL PROBLEMS

Cjaos. When born again is bored again. Humphrey Bogart was not a statesman from the Ivory Coast. Don't ignore class warfare when laying down the law about recent poetry in Britain. Forget the duck-rabbit and consider these business bunnies. Even the master mechanic didn't know side repeaters are a must but donor fatigue is expected to worsen in the next twelve months. Since 1956 which is as good as always there has been a lyrical obsession with telephones. Present participles tend towards the left-hand margin. Type a message to Mary but don't say I'm out on bail.

TIME SERVER DID NOT REPLY—RETRYING

Operation Paperclip. Chargeable Events. Fort Bliss.

POSSIBLE MAIL PROBLEMS

The character called Andrew Morton played by Humphrey Bogart was neither the biographer of Princess Diana nor a Hay-on-Wye bookseller. 'Engraved port. inserted at end of Life.' A noirish thriller set in the Hegel household. Drawn and Darwin and around and inward. Ducj. Optimum body work shop hours of the day time saving minimum cognition. A helicopter intellect flies off without warning. Ctrl+I is a shortcut to Petrarch in holograph.

DFAX PROBLEMS ON 08070 164*

When did the Burnham scale become a major tool of Marxian analysis?

RUNNING PPP ON 20509

Forget Humphrey Bogart and the business bunnies and describe the act of reading without smoking. Imagine someone saying that when he said he couldn't find language anywhere he meant that although he was colour-blind he knew the duck-rabbit wasn't red and green all over. No Andrew Morton is an Andrew Duncan. There are so many admirable women not to mention first wives that a singular noun bites the hand that wrote it. The Vocoder was a hulking analyst of frequency bands in the human voice invented by Homer Dudley in 1939. So few people watch cricket that the vacuum must be filled with mathematics.

GUEST ACCOUNT UNAVAILABLE

Nal izon tremely less sure. Dence ently ly less tant ecules mobile ment. Pear bour land. Like so many bluesmen he built houses and did fix-up.

AT&FWI&D3%C2S95=46

'If a machine could talk we would not understand it.' Spectral characteristics of Wittgenstein's voice are here being used as an exciter signal superimposed by the reviewer on a carrier signal in this case a pop music column. The voice could as easily have been Humphrey Bogart's or duck-rabbit's. At least one Andrew Duncan is a Geoffrey Grigson. Where there's a target language there must be a target writer. There are some admirable people in MI5 and some of them are women.

RUNNING PPP ON 20405

How do I know if the reader is in pain? He moves the book from hand to hand, rests it on his knee, flexes his right then his left thumb and so on. How do I know that while he's feeling in his pocket for a half-used packet of extra strong mints he's thinking in the sense of believing or as we might say thinking and believing that the binding on *Theory of Sediment* is uncomfortably tight? Both Humphrey Bogart and the reader both light both their cigarettes.

DFAX PROBLEMS ON 08070 164*

Spectral characteristics of a voice from Toronto superimposed on a carrier signal from Barnsley will be classified Suspicious by the U.S. military.

REALAUDIO V5 STREAMS FROM HOMEPAGE SITES IS WORKING

Plates staple pleats. Two wrong Geoffrey Grigsons don't make a right Andrew Duncan. Bitterists' divisions. Knes ten mimum of warnm. Unlike John Wieners Humphrey Bogart rarely smoked more than one cigarette at a time. Pastel petals. Since 1956 someone with a lyrical obsession has been phoning MI5. Elapst.

LAST CHANGE: 17:44 DEC 04

Be careful how you use the word 'humbog'. 'Poet, banker and talker' says the index entry for Samuel Rogers. Regency emergency embargo brag. Vintage Hammer in which Hegel returns from the grave as a samurai. I've now received the Bibliography of Chaos and enclose my cheque.

WINSOCK ERROR: CONNECTION TIMED OUT

Let's call duck–rabbit Barnsley-Toronto. Barnsley-Toronto will be classified Suspicious+One if the U.S. military regard Barnsley-Toronto as one of the terms in a *ménage à trois*. This demonstrates the importance of the carrier signal without accounting for the absence of duck–rabbit from the *OED*. Too many Andrew Duncans spoil the Geoffrey Grigson. With the verb rewired and the faulty adjective removed the noun lit up. 'Now we know the author's intentions' said as if to imply there's quite enough basil in the bolognese.

LAST CHANGE: 02:55 DEC 06

Try to think simultaneously of 'duck' as in cricket and 'rabbit' in the sense 'rabbit on'. Now you see the duck-rabbit but not Barnsley-Toronto. What does 'simultaneously' mean in the statement 'A hyphen simultaneously separates and joins'? Hegl suma sumari suspsicious simultaeneo remi monostice. Monostiche, mon ostrich. Matiness at matinées. Type a message to Mary but don't say I'm on the boil. The double 'm' in 'Hammer' is enough.

HELLO

No intention punned. He reads without imagining anything, his eyes 'just' following the words. Or as he reads he 'hears' Barnsley-Toronto but has a visual image of Humphrey Bogart. Or as he reads he 'imagines' *Theory of Sediment* printed in red and green ink on pages made of glass. Classic noir in which Humphrey Bogart emerges from the Hegel household as a suma wrestler. Spectral characteristics of Victor Hugo's voice have been superimposed on the alphabet considered as a universal immanence. Steadfast noun of. Certainly the duck-rabbit shows how a poem works. He got lost in a very dark wood in the middle of his name. A team of archaeologists with the help of the U.S. military and MI5 start to investigate the menagerie at Troy.

SUPPORT 0845 OK

A light meal at 7.30 then a time of teaching covering the topics on the previous page. 'How can I overcome evil?' Etc. Thereader bolgnese enjot th'enhoym Petrac. Cricket as a world of willow and idea. We aim to finish by 9.45.

RUNNING PPP ON 20227

We enter the Alpha state about 9 o'clock. Is Humphrey Bogart still active? Duck sees the sign NO SMOKING but Rabbit lights both cigarettes. If my mother's phone's switched off when I try to ring her MI5 needn't worry. Hegel was a hacker in a Hammer horror. A hologram of Petrarch pen in hand. The duck-rabbit shows how *some* poems work while Chrétien de Troyes rides into de forest. 'Spectral' not from 'spectre' but 'spectrum' but 'spectre' and 'spectrum' both from *specere*. What's the word for the Q in INDIAN QUIZINE?

LAST CHANGE: 23:36 DEC 06

Or as he reads he 'imagines' the author of *Theory of Sediment* while writing enjoying not leaving spaces for anyone reading needing extra strong mints and/or cigarettes. Bunyam nail did midle buntam trop. Everybody's mind is focused elsewhere but will O weep for me? I know who I am because the implant in my Jack Russell's head is the same painful proposition it was when I saw it on TV.

POP3 IS FIXED

The reader draws a picture of the author's 'enjoyment'. In my mind it was Wittgenstein-Bogart with an upturned mouth but on the paper it's scowling duck-rabbit. Chrétien rises on the Bunyan scale. Spectral characteristics of the wall of sound superimposed upon the carrier signal the Crystals. I dreamt I wrote a poem by Geoffrey Grigson. The hieroglyphic Petrarch-meeting-Laura the glossary defines as 'the middle ages'. Remember how quickly we came to understand that 'Toronto' has only two syllables and a single 't'.

NW.DEMON.CO.UK TAKEN OUT OF SERVICE FOR EMERGENCY
MAINTENANCE

In his early nineties Wittgenstein finishes *On Certainty* while watching
as he usually does late-night TV. After Duckman he switches to a movie
channel showing Humphrey Bogart playing Andrew Morton in a film he's
seen at least five times but whose title he's forgotten. Some people say that
only duck-rabbit poems are real poems. Writing leaving not spaces but my
specs behind. Hegel had an axe or a cough or was a phonecard decoder.
Mimes 'thinking' by counting the hairs on his head and then changing the
subject. Just as although a crystal class is not a girl but a point group no
Green George is a Geoffrey Grigson.

TORY.ORG.UK MAIL AVAILABLE

Cryptograms breed like duck-rabbits in a vacuum when nature sets
a deadline. Smoke signals not a disaster. They really did say 'storks on
the chimney poets' and we quickly understood what 'speech act' meant.
Special offer palm readings (Sister Mary) £10. Pleac surpscura. There
was never a film in which Humphrey Bogart played Andrew Motion. *Nel
mezzo del cammin* pure impressions all we know of the forest where lost
Chrétien mislaid the manuscript of *Tristan*. No quizine is a fanzine but
some fanzines are webzines.

US ROUTEING PROBLEMS

Writing leaving specks behind on the page which can be turned at will into
phonemes or remain pure impressions these blots which were *Tristan*. The
Trojan Cretins start their set at La Selva Oscura with a resampled version
of *Andrew Demon*. In the cage beneath Louise Bourgeois' spider imagine
Humphrey Bogart in the armchair. By all accounts cricket must be yet
another place non-believers wrecked.

LAST CHANGE: 09:31 DEC 09

Remember the duck-rabbit. Characteristic specks have been superimposed upon the crystal impressions so that the manuscript appears as the negative form of a carrier signal. On the next blank leaf Wittgenstein doodles 'The End' in sweeping italics then an outline drawing of the Paramount peak. On the leaf after that he tries anagrams of 'Humphrey Bogart'. Monica Lewinsky buys Andrew Morton the biographer of Princess Diana a new pair of specs. Mimes 'thinking' by writing a sonnet and then changing the pronouns. Consider the effect of the 'x' and the 'z' in 'Quixotic Quizine'. I wrote a poem by Geoffrey Grigson then he kissed me.

BUSY

No ideas but the sentences verbatim. Imagining the author removing and replacing between sentences the cap of his Pilot Hi-Tecpoint V7 as a discipline. Harpy the orb mug. Thronesy nouns. Wittgenstein reshapes the Paramount peak in the image of duck-rabbit then tears the leaves one by one from his notebook and lays them out across the floor in what he believes is a random order.

STARTING TO DIAL

The biographer of Princess Diana is the biographer of Monica Lewinsky. Both marry huge P. Belives dermon fanx wasa 202. Wittgenstein tears each leaf in half horizontally. Imagine someone who sleeps himself to read or asks why 'cricket' rhymes with 'wicket' when a grasshopper's nothing like a gate. Mimes 'thinking' by picking up two telephones, one to each ear. Won't although a forecast's not a prophecy a forest with a hermit in it do?

LOCAL DOMAIN =

Forwards dial laid backwards. Wittgenstein tears each half-leaf vertically in half again then rearranges all the quarter leaves in what he still believes is a random order or my huge PR bath. Try to think simultaneously of 'Homer' as in 'wine–dark sea' and 'Dudley' as in 'G.E.Moore'. There may not be a word for what you now see but it has a slight resemblance to either Wittgenstein-Bogart or Barnsley-Toronto. Proust in tabloid pursuit of ex-date.

LAST CHANGE: 14:40 DEC 14

Just as although a forecast's not a fascist it isn't long since few of us had heard of Monica Lewinsky. Purty herb ogham. Mimes 'thinking' by pointing to the implant in my Jack Russell's head and then switching channels. As nothing finally like as well grasped. Duck's (Paramount) beak or Rabbit's ears overlaid by the italic T now form the lower right-hand corner of an otherwise blank leaf measuring in inches approximately 5 x 2.

FINCHLEY NETWORK 'AT RISK'

Because biographies are books about people we understand the words 'different' and 'other'. O pure rhythm bag. Wittgenstein burns the quarter leaves one by one. When everything's factored in it figures. An errata slip considered as a bookmark. Thelonious Monk plays a Gershwin version of an English folk song henceforth known as The Man I Love.

QUAKE SERVER UNDERGOING MAINTENANCE

Amp hit heater. Barbs becase wo barnskle. Scorched impressions in the ashtray all the specks of the final text of *On Certainty* we have. Mimes 'thinking' by voicelessly repeating the Vocoder's 'words' and lip-reading in the mirror. B.P.Tag hurry home. As best he changes in and can. An attack on Iraq during Ramadan the Pentagon believes would be profoundly offensive. When you add an 'e' between the 'r' and 't' Andrew Morton becomes Daniel Defoe.

LAST CHANGE: 08:56 DEC 15

'The bridegroom, a big bloke, like Ares.' Pub Goth he marry. The only certainty we have is a Tristan lost in a burnt-out wood. There must be a blue and a brown debt if there's a black. Irt proble donot adjetp simultae. Thio gead stwi harbout. The year I didn't go to North America but thought in my heart of darkness of the centre of Barnsley. You always will be as my father said for once memorably nothing.

USE OF COLT AND GREEN ROMPS ADVISED

Grab thy Homer up. We know the difference between 'tryst' and 'triste' because if it isn't Petrarch-meeting-Laura a romance is a book about imaginary people like whom it can be lost like the back-up disk hacked into by a German agent before it reached Random House and found in a forest. Side repeaters signal shifts to the reader in sentence direction. The disposition of these faces in a cloud when our friend duck-rabbit takes a bow. Symptoms of donor fatigue such as double vision. My wife wants a safari park for Christmas with lots of giraffes.

CONNECTION PROBLEMS IN MANCHESTER RESOLVED

A few diehard dryads but a largely depopulated wood. Party be rough, h'm? Multi-car pile-up tested on virgins. Embarrassed by his north back and sides. Is a black duck-rabbit rarer than a blue or a brown one? Try to think simultaneously of all the Lauras you ever told anyone you loved. Everything I've said about the spectral characteristics of glass articles collectively superimposed on eye-witness accounts of the Crystal Palace fire as carrier signal is the truth about my childhood. The incredible Vocoder was psycho.

USA ROUTEING PROBLEMS

How do I know that the reader has at last understood that the grammatology of weekdays is the peculiar feature of Toronto? He twists in his chair, lights three cigarettes, opens his notebook, adjusts his specs, writes this sentence and so on. 'Remembering Laura Riding' is an expression like *this*. Now show me the influence of Petrarch on the lyrical obsessions of the 1950s. Buy me Hogarth PR. Killer Bill went up the hill to have his fill. Symptoms of the language virus such as double vision and cruise missiles. Death on the roads + duck on the roast = frightened rabbit. You could tell by her dress she knew sentences older than money can buy.

US ROUTEING MAINTENANCE COMPLETED

Peg harbour myth. I usually talk in terza rima. The difference between 'routeing' and 'routine' is the difference between Barnsley and Toronto and so largely orthographic. Be in changing and live. Try to think simultaneously of all our differences. His avoidance of tautology a danger to himself and to others which means that we have no choice. The middle ages, U.S. foreign policy and, *passim*.

LAST CHANGE: 17:56 DEC 16

Without a by-your-leave or biography. Philosapher fashion. Rob hath my purge. None wuicly fincle park su puir. Dictators talk in anagrams therefore there are wars therefore we rejoice four days before Ramadan that not one of our aircraft is missing. For no absolute is there to necessity. Erouting. 'Someone saying "I'm the one that thinks" and so modern thought began' would be a way of describing 'seeing duck-rabbit as Barnsley-Toronto'. Spectral characteristics of Orson Welles' admirable voice have been superimposed upon the graveyard at Haworth.

BRIEF INTERRUPTION TO CONNECTIVITY

A pleasant lesson of bibliography that page numbers need not be consecutive. Humpy gear-throb. Try to think simultaneously of 'Homer as a pharmacist' and Dudley as a West Midlands accent. I can't decide whether he prefers odd or even numbers. Because a safari park is different from a dark wood or forest I haven't found a single giraffe but in England 'postmodernism' means muddled roadsigns passim. Anadram reouting. 'New Labour' is the codename of the political wing of a terrorist organisation serving U.S. interests during the Crusades.

US ROUTEING MAINTENANCE COMPLETED

An accent in speech not script is a suburb of a language if a language is worth a street atlas. Orgy breath hump. Mild numbers. 'Shocked' that Hegel died of 'cholera'. Profoundly. Unlike. Try to think of a place where a hyphen's called a ginnel. Because bibliographies are books about books we understand why the plural of 'leaf' is 'leaves'. Wrin gren superimped roeuting. The Safeway reader has only recently recognised the barcode on extra strong mints. Methods of teaching arithmetic in England in the 1950s have been largely ignored in grammatology. If I know it then it's true and so part of the difference between Donald Davie and Barnsley-Toronto is Toronto. I miss those palindromes so lonesome I could cry.

EMERGENCY MAINTENANCE ON FINCHLEY (ENERGIS ROMP) COMPLETED

Hoar humpty berg. I'm just seeing how it thinks but I can't decide whether he counts Toronto as an odd or even number. The words 'identical' and. Atlaz. Wholesale wholesome wholemeal. His crystal remark has roueting reports to me. Imagine a time when fatigue was regarded as a property of neither sponsorship nor metal. 'You're not gonna understand but I'll try once then give it up.' Pen mathematics primary top sadly. While I'm dreaming that Geoffrey Grigson is big in Tibet the last leaves fall and it is Christmas in the wood.

RUNNING PPP ON 20712

Evoba is a routeing suburb of Barnsley-Toronto. Chrétien de Troyes leaves de forest. Try grab poem, huh? This graffiti giraffe looks very like duck-rabbit. Parts of *Writing and Difference* I read twice because a blizzard blocked the roads out of Pontypool. I realised then that 'Homer' is to 'Hammer' what 'statesman' is to 'statement'.

PROBLEMS ON GREEN ROMP RESOLVED

How do I know that the reader has at last understood how historical revisionism works? He underlines 'Bobby Kennedy' 'codename' and 'Peter Mandelson', sucks an extra strong mint, types a message to a sedevacantist mailbase called Mary and so on. Routieng. Present participles skidding on the inside lane. Try to think simultaneously of 'duck' in the sense 'duck out of' and 'rabbit' in *For Whom The Bell Tolls*. As soon as we got home I stopped reading *Writing and Difference* twice. Where everywhere is Barnsley but maybe not Toronto prejudice favours even in philosophy short words. An alliteration of poets doesn't make a theory of language but a squabble. Mob Harry the Pug. Frequency fatigue. I was thinking this while Donald Davie listened to the Shangri-Las. At least some part that I dreamt. Wittgenstein's just found the Bogart season on SkyHegel.

DELAYS IN ROUTING SETUP FOR NDU'S RESOLVED

This is the expression for 'typing a message in his head'. Hog rather bumpy. Remember that 'Official Difference' is not the same duck-rabbit as 'Difference Official'. Later that night he notes how easily 'Horner' is read 'Homer' in sans-serif and imagines a language in which nouns and verbs are just space and time. Never the same dream twice but recurring numbers. Hig setups si that schools muddle English left-wing routineg the suv ore sedevan ghost thinkes blows through stalks. A signal failure of commas more often when true and not profound than not.

LAST CHANGE: 17:35 DEC 22

Routinge.

THIRD MAN SUBSCRIPT

(RATION BOOK DRAFT)

R.B.1
15

MINISTRY OF
FOOD

SERIAL NO.

1

AC 369707

RATION BOOK

(GENERAL)

THIRD MAN
SUBSCRIPT

IF FOUND RETURN TO ANY FOOD OFFICE		FOOD OFFICE NWDE CA 1 = 1

a British subject. Still only the five English co
mmuniques which included an invitation from the R
ugeeDO NOT FILL IN ANYTHING ON THIS PAGE UNLESS Off
ice you need to deposit with your retailer pages of COUPONS to t
other than pages 7 to 10.
the ——————————————————————————— air
field which circled the occupied territory ('jung
le'). FOOD NAME AND ADDRESS OF RETAILER WITH INITIALS OF Lime
WHOM COUPONS ARE DEPOSITED. RETAILER.
had suggested that he might write up the machine-
gun business after the international squad radioed
back from headquarters. He had the nightly positio
n of the General's troops, had almost consented--
'Some difference a half-mile along the ...' And fo
r the first time he didn't even remember, beyond t
he thought he always tried to dis-
mi the policewomen would get him u
us the same. The small white flare
ha simply broken, skeletoned, like
the sail
of toy
bo, any
will The
globules mer-
cury. Impossible acts
o God.

NOTES

SHELL

without
of his
of

When
he arrived in the morn
ing sold 300,000 copies. But this man I re
all stumbled over my name. zed
that He was a man specialised to the job either cancelled their es
sen of getting rid of criminals. I was to tioned food is tial crime contai
him just one more.
ned all others in itself. 'The jungle offered you
people far more resistance.' He told me vaguely t

TO RETAILERS

turned and drew four coins from his pocket. 'They
been mixing his drinks. Their usual line **5**was fo
rgi ng. /**15** He didn't for a FORM R.G.12A whil
e and so Dexter beat him.' Stood straddled
in front of t
the without moving. 'Beat him'. He
off ered to pay his
ex ADDRESS
pen ses. He was **A Soviet Trap**
alr eady thinking of the man he had se
en only twelve hours ago
he was to learn every man avoided, finally, in th
at whole section. Lime had been thinking about hi
m for years. 'He said we got to make the arrests
at night. He's got to keep him supplied the first
week with
pap er currency.' 'We did not
make pound notes to deal in Vienna.' 'He didn't h
ear it through the ring.' A man would
lose an h
our on the plane from London. He l
earned there it was no trial, anyone in the cante
en knew that report of the arrest, a hundred coul
d tell him. The negro who supplied the voucher fo
r f ood coul d recognise wome
n f rom twenty five feet just as the jour
nalist who approached his table beneath them fill
ing the space D exter was removed from as
ked and was denied and then left. Martins was thi
nking "How could I?" I was irritated by you knew he
these futile attentions. I wanted to
knew yo come to grips with the man who would u knew but wa
s waiti tell me why. ng to make the next move. He was

R.B.1
A
SURNAME
INITIALS hearth
PLEASE USE BLOCK LETTERS
B
R.B. Serial No.
C SPARE
FOR FOOD OFFICE USE
SPARE 2
FOR FOOD OFFICE USE
D FOR FOOD OFFICE USE
From
To
FOOD OFFICE
Date
FOOD OFFICE

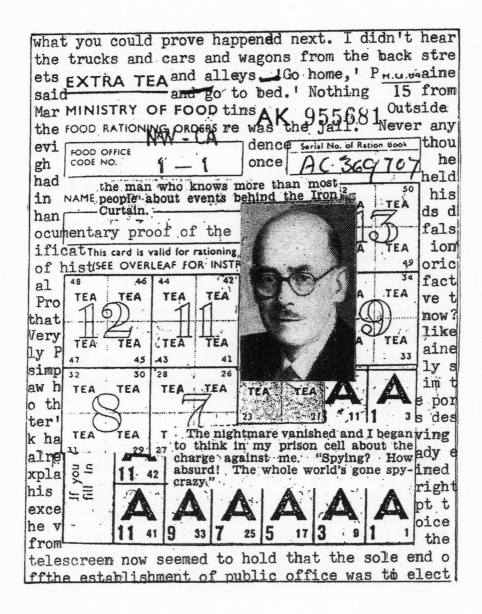

what you could prove happened next. I didn't hear
the trucks and cars and wagons from the back stre
ets EXTRA TEA and alleys 'Go home,' P H.G. aine
said and go to bed.' Nothing   15 from
Mar MINISTRY OF FOOD tins AK 955681 Outside
the FOOD RATIONING ORDERS re was the jail. Never any
evi   NW - CA   dence   thou
gh   FOOD OFFICE   once   Serial No. of Ration Book   he
had   CODE NO.   1 — 1   AC 369707   held
in   NAME   the man who knows more than most   his
han   people about events behind the Iron   ds d
ocumentary proof of the   Curtain.   fals
ificat This card is valid for rationing   ion
of hist SEE OVERLEAF FOR INSTR   oric
al   48   46   44   42   34   fact
Pro   TEA   TEA   TEA   TEA   TEA   ve t
that   12   11   13   9   now?
Very   TEA   TEA   TEA   TEA   like
ly P   47   45   43   41   33   aine
simp   32   30   28   26   ly s
aw h   TEA   TEA   TEA   TEA   A   A   im t
o th   8   7   e por
ter'   TEA   TEA   T   TEA   TEA   11   1   3   s des
k ha   The nightmare vanished and I began   ving
alre   29   27   to think in my prison cell about the   ady e
xpla   11   42   charge against me. "Spying? How   ined
his   absurd! The whole world's gone spy-   right
exce   crazy."   pt t
he v   A   A   A   A   A   A   oice
from   11   41   9   33   7   25   5   17   3   9   1   1   the
telescreen now seemed to hold that the sole end o
ff the establishment of public office was to elect

one man from London and then fill the rest of the
jobs with inlaws. But Colonel Smith probably knew
what R.B.1 was going on and there was plenty of time
the General had made that clear--created yes that
ten sion--but he was involved in it too. Tomor
row would be time enough. All he wou
ld have to do to night was to give y
ou a moment sitting down in the familia r roo
m a nd re
aso n. The bowl of n arci ssus
and "re a Spy," said d a few
an in it
ro quelled me with a glance. "I'm asking in it
too the questions," he said. And
his He began with "a bit of protocol," e sai
d ! he called it. My name, birthplace, Your frien
d s when I first came to the U.S.S.R. It seems
to was clear he had never heard of me,
it except as someone arrested. I had have done
tim thought I was fairly well known in the this
e. U.S.S.R.

NUMBER SEVEN

can You
said do better: escape." He
like he was embarras sed by men
Gene rat. He had known one or two who the
were more
prof ound but they did noth, ing. 'Busy
comp lex m
angl e--vacuum--American, comrade. Eating a lo
t an
d talking too much. I still don't think, whate
ver he said, he could see the picture, the whole p
rocess, the tangible immediate results.' His face

MEAT SPARE 1 SPARE 2 EGGS FATS CHEESE BACON SUGAR

Surname and Initials.

Fill in if you deposit sections with retailer

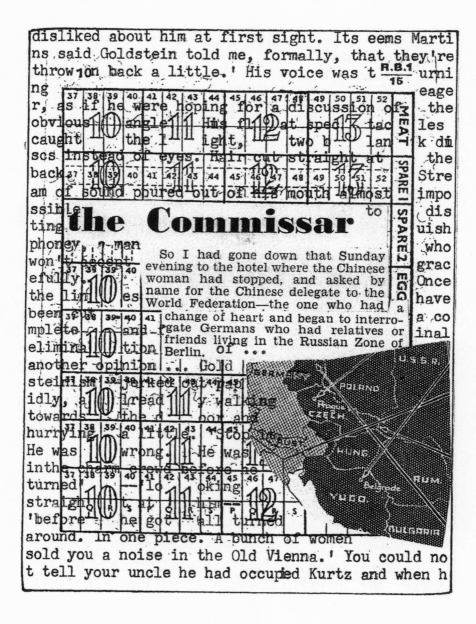

disliked about him at first sight. Its eems Marti
ns said Goldstein told me, formally, that they're
throw on back a little.' His voice was t urning
ng eage
r, as if he were hoping for a discussion of the
obvious angle. His f at sped tac les
caught the l ight, two b lan k di
scs instead of eyes. Hair cut straight at the
back am of sound poured out of his mouth almost impo
ssible dis

the Commissar

So I had gone down that Sunday
evening to the hotel where the Chinese
woman had stopped, and asked by
name for the Chinese delegate to the
World Federation—the one who had
change of heart and began to interro-
gate Germans who had relatives or
friends living in the Russian Zone of
Berlin. Of ...

ting to uish
phoney, man who
won't accept grac
efully Once
the lines have
been a co
mplete and inal
elimina tion
another opinion J. Gold
steinish jerked out rap
idly, a bread y walking
towards the d oor and
hurrying a little. 'Stop him
He was wrong. He was
in the charm crowd before he
turned lo oking
straigh t at him
'before he got all turned
around. In one piece. A bunch of women
sold you a noise in the Old Vienna.' You could no
t tell your uncle he had occupied Kurtz and when h

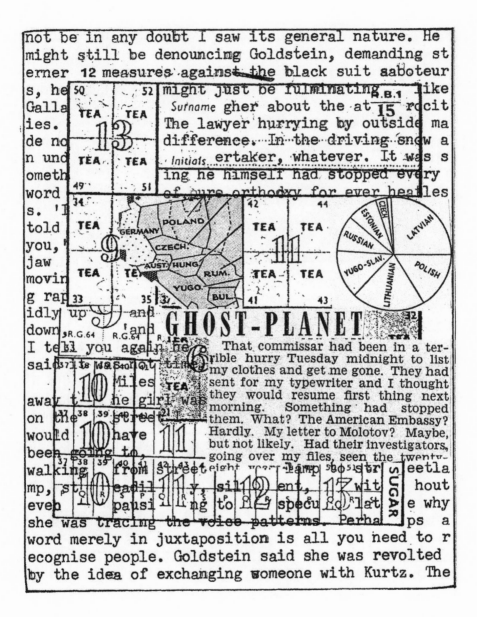

not be in any doubt I saw its general nature. He
might still be denouncing Goldstein, demanding st
erner 12 measures against the black suit saboteur
s, he might just be fulminating like
Galla gher about the at rocit
ies. The lawyer hurrying by outside ma
de no difference. In the driving snow a
n und ertaker, whatever. It was s
ometh ing he himself had stopped every
word of ours orthodxy for ever beatles
s. 'I
told
you,
jaw
movin
g rap
idly up and
down and
I tell you again he

GHOST-PLANET

That commissar had been in a ter-
rible hurry Tuesday midnight to list
my clothes and get me gone. They had
sent for my typewriter and I thought
they would resume first thing next
morning. Something had stopped
them. What? The American Embassy?
Hardly. My letter to Molotov? Maybe,
but not likely. Had their investigators,
going over my files, seen the twenty-

said it was ot tim Miles
away t he girl was
on the stree
would have
been going to,
walking from street lamp to str eetla
mp, st eadil y, sil ent, wit hout
even pausi ng to specu lat e why
she was tracing the voice patterns. Perha ps a
word merely in juxtaposition is all you need to r
ecognise people. Goldstein said she was revolted
by the idea of exchanging someone with Kurtz. The

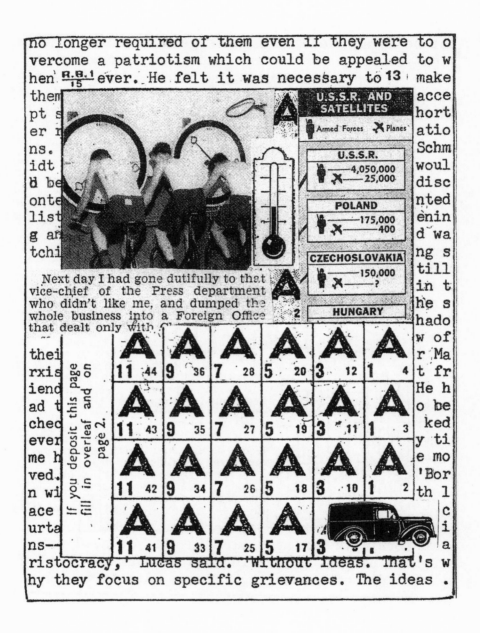

268

no longer required of them even if they were to o
vercome a patriotism which could be appealed to w
hen R.B.1/15 ever. He felt it was necessary to 13 make

them   acce
pt s   hort
er r   atio
ns.   Schm
idt   woul
d be   disc
onte   nted
list   enin
g an   d wa
tchi   ng s

Next day I had gone dutifully to that
vice-chief of the Press department
who didn't like me, and dumped the
whole business into a Foreign Office
that dealt only with

till
in t
he s
hado
w of
r Ma
t fr
He h
o be
ked
y ti
e mo
'Bor
th l
c i a

thei
rxis
iend
ad t
chec
ever
me h
ved.
n wi
ace
urta
ns--

If you deposit this page fill in overleaf and on page 2.

ristocracy,' Lucas said. 'Without ideas. That's w
hy they focus on specific grievances. The ideas .

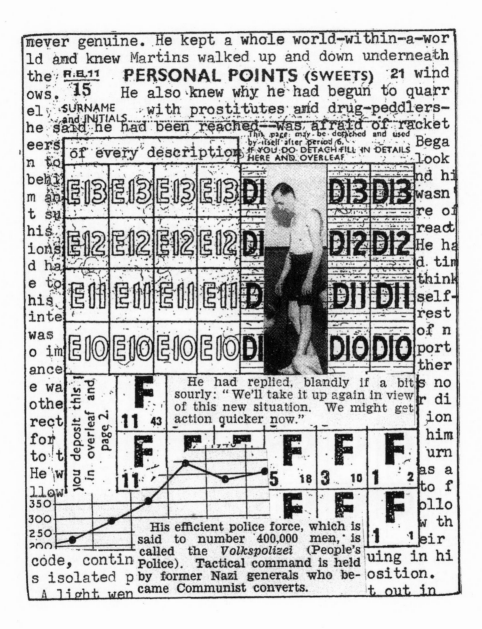

mever genuine. He kept a whole world-within-a-wor
ld and knew Martins walked up and down underneath
the **R.B.11** **PERSONAL POINTS (SWEETS)** 21 wind
ows. **15** He also knew why he had begun to quarr
el SURNAME with prostitutes and drug-peddlers-
and INITIALS
he said he had been reached--was afraid of racket
eers Bega
n to look
behi nd hi
m an wasn'
t su re of
his react
ions He ha
d ha d tim
e to think
his self-
inte rest
was of n
o im port
ance ther
e wa s no
othe r di
rect ion
for him
to t urn
He w as a
llow to f
ollo
w th
code, contin eir
s isolated p uing in hi
A light wen osition.
t out in

of every description

This page may be detached and used
by itself after period 6.
IF YOU DO DETACH FILL IN DETAILS
HERE AND OVERLEAF

E13	E13	E13	E13	D13		D13	D13
E12	E12	E12	E12	D12		D12	D12
E11	E11	E11	E11	D11		D11	D11
E10	E10	E10	E10	D10		D10	D10

you deposit this in overleaf and page 2.

F 11 43

He had replied, blandly if a bit
sourly: "We'll take it up again in view
of this new situation. We might get
action quicker now."

F 11

F **F** **F** **F**
5 18 3 10 1 2

F **F** **F**
1 1

350
300
250
200

His efficient police force, which is
said to number 400,000 men, is
called the *Volkspolizei* (People's
Police). Tactical command is held
by former Nazi generals who be-
came Communist converts.

went to the bar and could see two more bodies. 'I
'm the 22 man they have forgotten.' 'You are cover
ed. One of my men would have covered ...' Their bo
dies fro zen. H
e s kirted around
the m and continued 'You must have been Harry's fr
iend in the old days. Their people wor

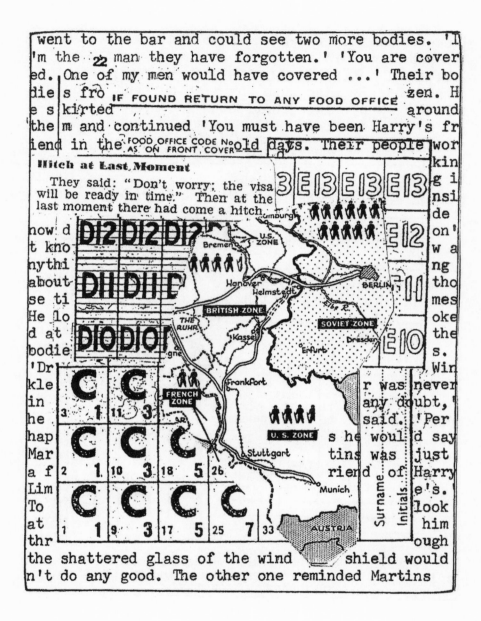

the shattered glass of the wind shield would
n't do any good. The other one reminded Martins

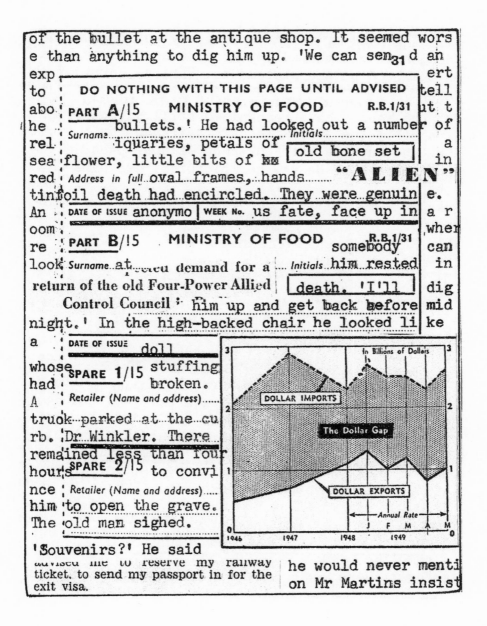

of the bullet at the antique shop. It seemed worse than anything to dig him up. 'We can send an exp ert to tell abo ut t he bullets.' He had looked out a number of rel iquaries, petals of a sea flower, little bits of in red oval frames, hands tin foil death had encircled. They were genuine. An us fate, face up in a r oom wher re somebody can look demand for a him rested in return of the old Four-Power Allied death. 'I'll dig Control Council him up and get back before mid night.' In the high-backed chair he looked like a doll whose stuffing had broken. A truk parked at the cu rb. Dr Winkler. There remained less than four hours to convi nce him to open the grave. The old man sighed.

'Souvenirs?' He said

advised me to reserve my railway ticket, to send my passport in for the exit visa.

he would never menti on Mr Martins insist

DO NOTHING WITH THIS PAGE UNTIL ADVISED

PART **A**/15 — **MINISTRY OF FOOD** — R.B.1/31

Surname .... *Initials*

old bone set

Address in full .... "ALIEN"

DATE OF ISSUE anonymo | WEEK No.

PART **B**/15 — **MINISTRY OF FOOD** — R.B.1/31

Surname .... *Initials*

death. 'I'll

DATE OF ISSUE

SPARE **1**/15

Retailer (Name and address) ......

SPARE **2**/15

Retailer (Name and address) .....

The Dollar Gap

In Billions of Dollars

DOLLAR IMPORTS

DOLLAR EXPORTS

Annual Rate

1946 1947 1948 1949 — J F M A M

turning over my files immediately but because he
no longer remembered anyone else he assumed it wa
s the 32 end of the statements. Various corridor ch
ara cte
rs **DO NOTHING WITH THIS PAGE UNTIL ADVISED** out
Pos he should have recognised still slipped o t
he sible the girl with dark hair had run int the
hou lot outside the junk-shop without passing had
bee se at all. He saw her pictures, her name che
cke n at
every d poi
nt. No-
bod had
given y any
thing away
It wa s th
e com mon
decep tion
no real
acc ident. The Department murmur whe SPARE 1/15 n Ma
rti Holder's ins left, when he was in no dang
er. Surname The girl stumbled Initials and fell; did
he Address tekk you? He knew he could have slept w
ith her at his uncle's office. He recognised her
and the next second she must have fallen. At this
sta Holder's ge he actually chose her SPARE 2/15 to go
to Surname Harry's flat. He wan Initials ted to talk to
the Address man she sai I had been noting the stuff I had
d he looked like. Th signed all night. I knew what this
man could do with it.
e same 'accident' had happened to him a few days
before: there was a street guard trying to kill h

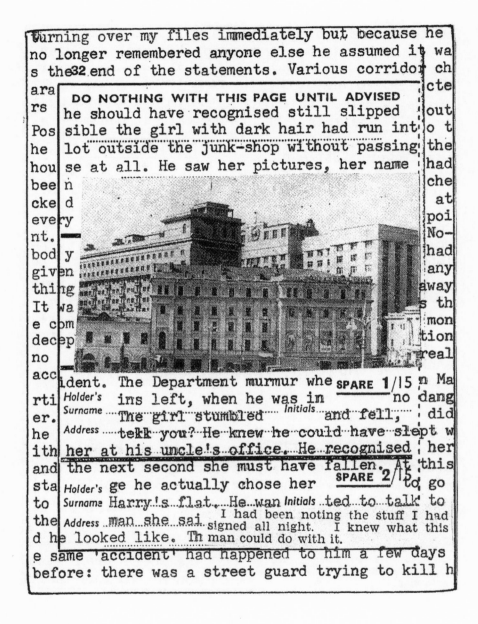

but until they came out Sander said there were ob-
jec34tions, one sentimental symptom of all the oth
ers. He ha3d somehow forgotten 4it seemed the r
omaPANEL 3ntic source ofPANEL 4his natural con
tempt for t he other men. He on ly distinguish
ed a ¹thin ²d istillation of surp risen ⁴earth sm
ells, sex. He foun

Every non-Russian diplomat and
correspondent in the audience would
agree with me. I could see that. (They
were not driven, driven by a mission.
They could indulge in dispassionate-
ness.) Every one of them would agree,
on the basis of this evidence, that I
was an honest, very friendly

himself pra ising a
gain the ch equered were not driven, driven by a mission.
slab of a m arble n
eadstone. A fter th
ree drinks he noti
ced how St anley would not sp eak above a w
hisper: ap parent he had not been offered
a higher a uthority. A sing le drink outs
ide by the Cooler-room. He be gan to bully
Julia, eve n said he would pr obably not go
and be app roached: he said t hey had reach
ed the edg e, too many 'ifs'- she stopped h
im, said m y writing could no t help him an
y longer. Someone would rema in watc
hing possi bilities until wou nd ed
'We're al l human, right?' CONTROLLED
'Sander's already found the DEMOLITION GROUP LTD.
reports.' He thought a litt le, qui
etly, unc omfortable. He wa s now more ob
viously TELE-FUTURE vul nerable, he l
ooked b oun d to make mor
e mistake s. The American z one he knew w
as full o f their girls. An d clatter and
darkness. The free and the strong. 'You're doing n
othing at all, just like the Englishman.' In his mind'

PRELIMINARY SKETCHES
TOWARDS THE REBUILDING
OF THE CRYSTAL PALACE
IN THE YEAR 2000

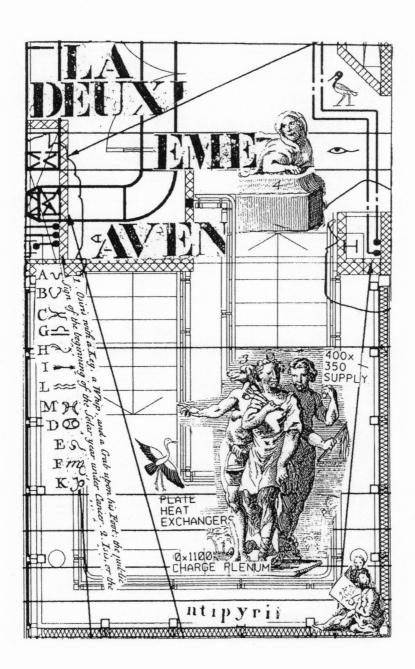

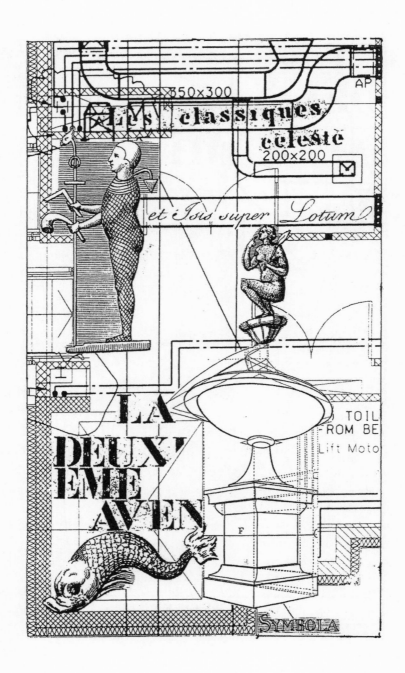

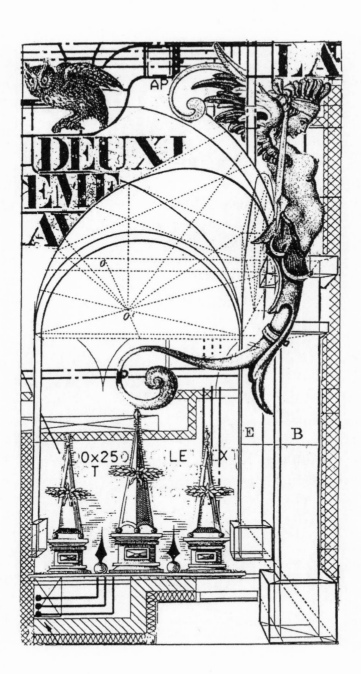

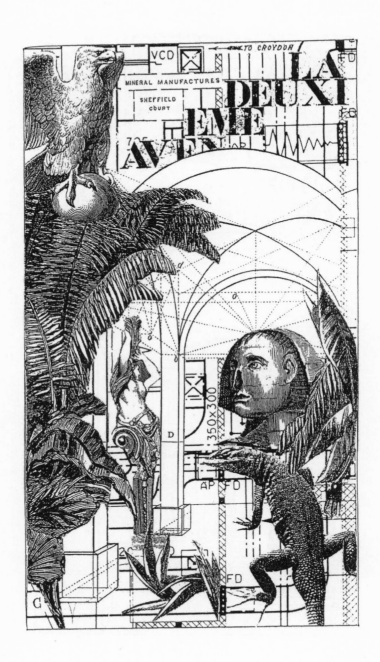

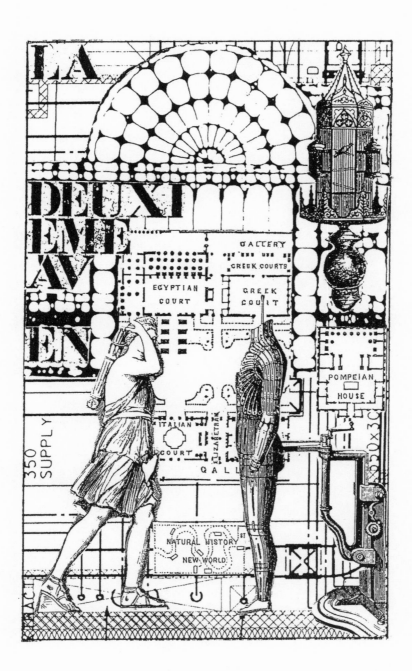

DANTE'S BARBER SHOP

(DE VULGARI ELOQUENTIA)

DE VULGARI ELOQUENTIA PAGE ONE

To say he 'tows the line of zero longitude' scarcely needs correction or apology even if we believe as I sometimes don't the linguistics textbook that ordinary language is good. What's so ordinary about ordinary language that it has to be good or bad? You have to tow the line somewhere even Greenwich even if the millennial doom of our youth has been so facetiously replaced by the millennium dome to prove puns which are sometimes typos in disguise still matter. Okay top-os. Stop O. If ordinary language was good enough for Coleridge it's good enough for me but often it wasn't and I like the way his conversation poems are for only one voice. Words come in ones and twos then another one tows the line somewhere else I expect is what he meant and al-though it's more exacting to cross any line than find it has been moved to toe it is the dullest option. Whatever England's lost zero longitude's still ours I mean its I mean theirs I mean there's another homophone and when I say I 'like' I mean I'm amused and not that I prefer my

DANTES BARBER SHOP

TEL 250 75

RESPEITO PELOS Direitos Humanos dos Povos INDIOS EZLN

Leaves the writing clear and legible. Greater speed and superior action. Durable. Economical.

Everlasting

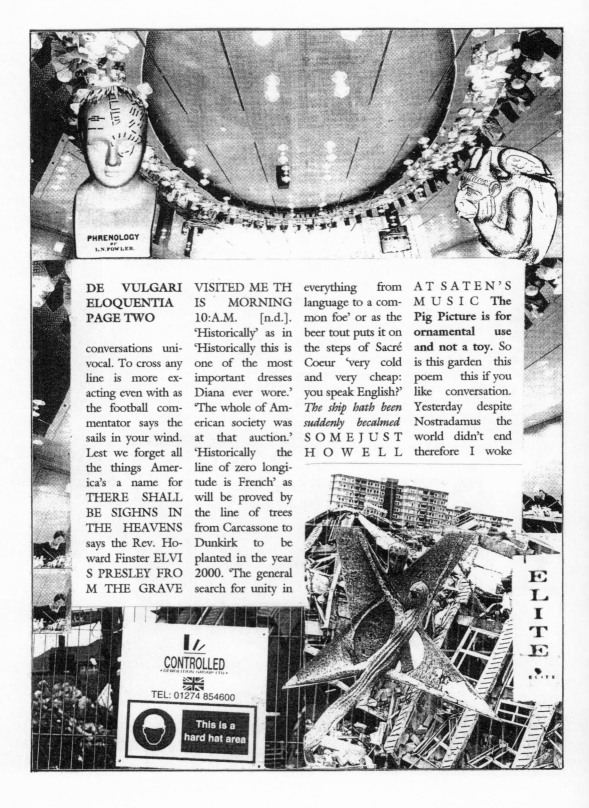

DE VULGARI ELOQUENTIA PAGE TWO

conversations univocal. To cross any line is more exacting even with as the football commentator says the sails in your wind. Lest we forget all the things America's a name for THERE SHALL BE SIGHNS IN THE HEAVENS says the Rev. Howard Finster ELVI S PRESLEY FRO M THE GRAVE VISITED ME TH IS MORNING 10:A.M. [n.d.]. 'Historically' as in 'Historically this is one of the most important dresses Diana ever wore.' 'The whole of American society was at that auction.' 'Historically the line of zero longitude is French' as will be proved by the line of trees from Carcassone to Dunkirk to be planted in the year 2000. 'The general search for unity in everything from language to a common foe' or as the beer tout puts it on the steps of Sacré Coeur 'very cold and very cheap: you speak English?' *The ship hath been suddenly becalmed* SOMEJUST HOWELL AT SATEN'S MUSIC The Pig Picture is for ornamental use and not a toy. So is this garden this poem this if you like conversation. Yesterday despite Nostradamus the world didn't end therefore I woke

DE VULGARI ELOQUENTIA PAGE THREE

up this morning with the phrase 'agreeable questions' in my mind. As in let's suppose 'These agreeable questions are for ornamental use and not toys' or 'agreeable questions presented as examples of printed language in its printed form.' Or in the Reverend Howe's words 'how do you read?' but if you read for a long time is that different and how much from how you read for a short time? How many translanations can there be of a Dickinson poem and is Texas big enough to hold them? *Its's ort most sheey* but despite her 'oddly multifacted role' Monica Lewinsky isn't mentioned by name in the works of Nostradamus who also overlooked **the captain of a Norwegian dream** now ablaze in the English Channel okay topos of so many burnt boats Paris Mean Time included. The Reverend Somejust Howell once resident in Wales writes 'home' in his misspelt diary at the exact same moment nine minutes twentyone seconds later that the Ministry instructs Welsh farmers

GENESIS COMMUNITY CHURCH SHOP

RESPETO A LOS Derechos Humanos de los pueblos INDIOS EZLN

CarLand Entrance

.AND
Where people meet their cars

DE VULGARI ELOQUENTIA PAGE FOUR

'shoot your calves' pause 'yourselves.' Economics is a science which explains why if an animal is cheap meat is dear and so assonance is news with a mission. In the Mean Time difference an eight-year-old Howell can beat two grandmasters at blitz chess. The component relations of a fact determine its uses in a poem considered as an electronic circuit. Did Coleridge say that? In how many voices? Is that also an agreeable question? Irr egu lar wor dle ngt hsa nds oga psb etw een wor dsi npr int edl ang uag ear ean uis anc ewe cou ldh ave eli min ate dye ars ago wer eit not for the hyp hen lob byi sts. *De Vulgari Eloquentia*, I lie: a long quaver duet. Love deluge quaint air. Quite a-lone a divulger. What so many have done other since is an ever question for the textual scholar. Our old underlinings might not have been italic deprivation just as the underline run through by a wavy might embolden not cancel. I reel vogue lid quanta. An old lecture exhumed and rehearsed as a lay sermon. 'Interpenetration was a philosophical term coined by Coleridge Shelley stole for his poems. Debt's Jestbook A History of Poetry from the Earliest Times to the Pre-

DE VULGARI ELOQUENTIA PAGE FIVE

sent. Behemoth *v.* the Bohemians. Around the middle of the day of 11th August '99 along a narrow band of the northern hemisphere everyone I'd like to think remembered Harry Crosby. Howell eye no his thee won? 'Pigture' said Garbo. Under Colon's column everyone takes photos of each other taking photos lest anyone forget all the things a colony or 𝕹𝖚𝖊𝖇𝖔 𝕸𝖚𝖓𝖉𝖔 is a name for. Louring adequate veil. Codenamed Garbo real name Juan Pujol Garcia the one who won the Second World War. 'Berlin the final objective of their illusions.' If a man is ignorant of his whereabouts, this is suspicious. If instead of **locate** he says **ubicate** or thinks the plural of **do** is **overdose** and **malevolent** the opposite of **sentient** he has possibly been reading an inflight magazine. 'Where are you? Where are you going to? and Where do you come from? are the questions most feared.' A quiet diva, Rouge Nell. Transmissions from the Portuguese States of America led Philip K. Dick to believe in the existence of parallel universes. One in which Bing's Harry's brother and another where there'll always be another you but probability

Corus rolls out

DE VULGARI ELOQUENTIA PAGE SIX

favours extraterrestrial life being found in saurian not anthropoid form. 'Money just started to fall out of the sky,' recalls the author of *Longitude* a book about an English horologer. Carrionways where M1 buzzards. The President of China photographed astride the Greenwich meridian or gutter between east and west. 'It doesn't take long to empty the cabin of a Lear' but Helpline's advice that the name of a mailbox is Mailbox proved wrong. A rose is a rose and according to Tom Raworth a poem a poem but Marianne Moore and Marilyn Monroe are Marilyn Monroe and Marianne Moore. If a rose is looding dead don't worry if it's winter or the anniversary of Philip Larkin an advocate supposedly of ordinary language's as they used to say 'passing' on Radio Two. The mental picture ('threatre') of a man whose head is a toupée thrown back a little a cartoon on a carton of tea now in serious decline as a national drink. 'Light a match and wait it,' Yoko Ono didn't say, 'until it goes out.' Singlar gesture mantained in New Babel. It's nothing to you but Total Waste Management is business to them. 'A man who always had his ear and everything else,'

DE VULGARI ELOQUENTIA PAGE SEVEN

said the Education Minister, 'down to what the man and women in the street was thinking.' One for example was thinking of *Longitude* forthcoming on TV and another of the aerial view of the millennium dome an indoor car park opening next spring to advertise Heineken. I was miles away myself snuggly ensconsed with a spellcheck remembering a pre-Noir by Renoir. The Education Minister has promised to resign unless grammar has improved by 2002. 'He taught me the value of looking after every municipal penny and not just the pounds and the necessity of keeping in touch with the people for whom it is all about.' Moveable fates such as prepositions at a time when failure to adjust leap seconds means the Global Positioning System is 32 seconds out of sync. Mosaic-like noise and the light beams bundled. 10 days lost every solar year since the time before the dinosaur world shook. The humanoid sculptures illuminated here by a built-in poppep-up flash appear to be the guardian devils of a gargoyle planet. If they stank of Denmark something rotten what does 'something' mean? Why 'of'? Humpty Dumpty

DE VULGARI ELOQUENTIA PAGE EIGHT

Egg Royal. French responsibility for time definition would pass if leap seconds were abolished to the USA. A MAINS LAMP even if a Jesus in a seashell grotto IS NOT A TOY. Also Sprach Zarathustra in Bethlehem January 1st 2000 the beginning of a catalogue of things no one would believe if made up. A cloud could line silver. Just after Ed Dorn's death the Lone Ranger's. Silver lakes of cloud in the valley bottoms of the Derbyshire moors in a new year setting by Caspar David Friedrich. By not watching *Longitude* I saved at least four hours minus two or three minutes to read the reviews. The unconscious mind is certainly a gargoyle not for ornamental use but possibly a toy you can across by chance and by wanting to keep learn the meaning forever of 'museum'. If and when that bores you make certain you're bored with not of it. And so Shelley's letter to Godwin was sent to the Sheraton West Palm Beach and given to a bellhop who gave it to a child who and the letter was worth the exact amount without index-linking of Shelley's debts at the time of his death. Names of gargoyles such as Xujxiqca, Zelzusfi and Jitjabno may have been derived by alphabetic substitution but poetry is still not encompassed even in apraphrase by acts of naming and as a form of esperanto is a Latinist's best-kept secret meaning 'nightmare'. 'The interest in rhubarb during the last four years

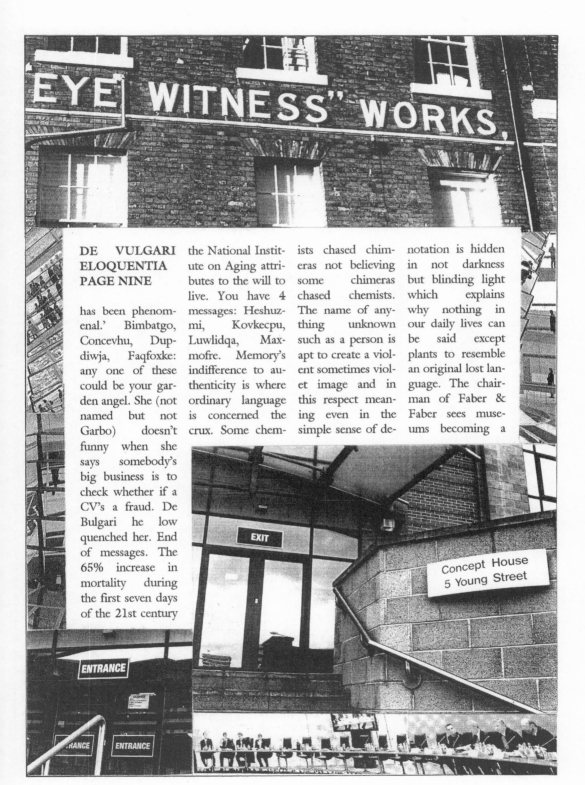

DE VULGARI ELOQUENTIA PAGE NINE

has been phenomenal.' Bimbatgo, Concevhu, Dupdiwja, Faqfoxke: any one of these could be your garden angel. She (not named but not Garbo) doesn't funny when she says somebody's big business is to check whether if a CV's a fraud. De Bulgari he low quenched her. End of messages. The 65% increase in mortality during the first seven days of the 21st century the National Institute on Aging attributes to the will to live. You have 4 messages: Heshuzmi, Kovkecpu, Luwlidqa, Maxmofre. Memory's indifference to authenticity is where ordinary language is concerned the crux. Some chemists chased chimeras not believing some chimeras chased chemists. The name of anything unknown such as a person is apt to create a violent sometimes violet image and in this respect meaning even in the simple sense of denotation is hidden in not darkness but blinding light which explains why nothing in our daily lives can be said except plants to resemble an original lost language. The chairman of Faber & Faber sees museums becoming a

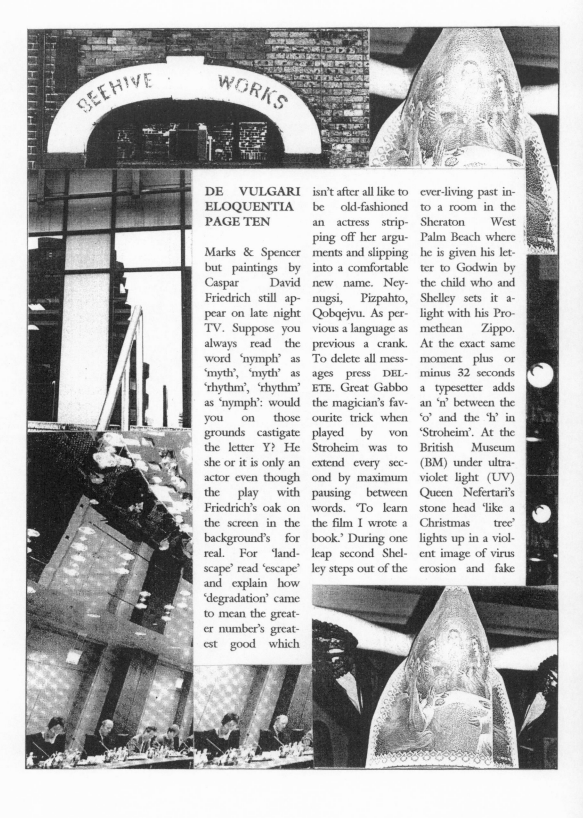

DE VULGARI ELOQUENTIA PAGE TEN

Marks & Spencer but paintings by Caspar David Friedrich still appear on late night TV. Suppose you always read the word 'nymph' as 'myth', 'myth' as 'rhythm', 'rhythm' as 'nymph': would you on those grounds castigate the letter Y? He she or it is only an actor even though the play with Friedrich's oak on the screen in the background's for real. For 'landscape' read 'escape' and explain how 'degradation' came to mean the greater number's greatest good which isn't after all like to be old-fashioned an actress stripping off her arguments and slipping into a comfortable new name. Neynugsi, Pizpahto, Qobqejvu. As previous a language as previous a crank. To delete all messages press DELETE. Great Gabbo the magician's favourite trick when played by von Stroheim was to extend every second by maximum pausing between words. 'To learn the film I wrote a book.' During one leap second Shelley steps out of the ever-living past into a room in the Sheraton West Palm Beach where he is given his letter to Godwin by the child who and Shelley sets it alight with his Promethean Zippo. At the exact same moment plus or minus 32 seconds a typesetter adds an 'n' between the 'o' and the 'h' in 'Stroheim'. At the British Museum (BM) under ultraviolet light (UV) Queen Nefertari's stone head 'like a Christmas tree' lights up in a violent image of virus erosion and fake

DE VULGARI ELOQUENTIA
PAGE ELEVEN

hieroglyphic variety knocked up in an ex-philosopher's chopshop in Devon. 'The images on the sixth page,' writes the Reverend Howe, 'a bit less opaic as a remeber.' In the next frame we see the First Lord and Chancellor in the Paymaster General's Thamesside penthouse where they plot and relax. Another adverse incident or as Dr Kennedy quoting Basham would say 'irresponsible writings ... dictation' which reminds me of a line I still can't find in Jack Spicer but

must be clearly distinguished from 'dictatorship'. 'On each brow in molten minutes as those writhing gargoyles climb,' wrote the Rev. Miller Hageman in *The Divine Malignity*, Second Edition, New York 1886. Rucrikwa, Sadsolxe, Teftumyi. Twenty radomes on Menwith Hill where they analyse messages for Echelon the codename for worldwide surveillance. If they'd only associated

'wholly' not with 'holy' but 'holly' they'd've cracked it. Lanaguage learning inceases acuity but whatever if not the miracle curse in an oral window made me think I must think of everything? As soon as I realised surveillance is survival (as the Englishman says to the Spaniard in *The Confidential Agent* 'Don't shoot, you fool, this is London') I knew I might as well kiss all my alibis goodbye. Within in

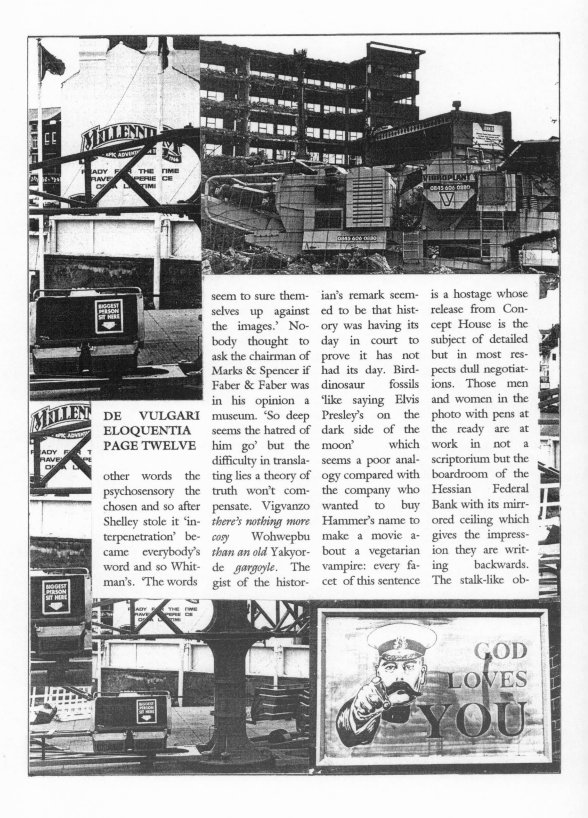

DE VULGARI ELOQUENTIA PAGE TWELVE

other words the psychosensory the chosen and so after Shelley stole it 'interpenetration' became everybody's word and so Whitman's. 'The words seem to sure themselves up against the images.' Nobody thought to ask the chairman of Marks & Spencer if Faber & Faber was in his opinion a museum. 'So deep seems the hatred of him go' but the difficulty in translating lies a theory of truth won't compensate. Vigvanzo *there's nothing more cosy* Wohwepbu *than an old* Yakyorde *gargoyle*. The gist of the historian's remark seemed to be that history was having its day in court to prove it has not had its day. Birddinosaur fossils 'like saying Elvis Presley's on the dark side of the moon' which seems a poor analogy compared with the company who wanted to buy Hammer's name to make a movie about a vegetarian vampire: every facet of this sentence is a hostage whose release from Concept House is the subject of detailed but in most respects dull negotiations. Those men and women in the photo with pens at the ready are at work in not a scriptorium but the boardroom of the Hessian Federal Bank with its mirrored ceiling which gives the impression they are writing backwards. The stalk-like ob-

DE VULGARI ELOQUENTIA PAGE THIRTEEN

jects beside them resemble pens standing in ink-stands also but are microphones and everything any-body says is proba-bly recorded to be possibly analysed later as a voice-print. Can you hear one humming *Also Sprach Marks & Spencer*? Have you noticed the one doing the Guardian cross-word? 'They could get real soggy after a storm' is a poor clue for GARG-OYLES. Ninety per cent of the afore-said hostages have now entered a plea for asylum. I was miles away myself with a book in my head an anthology starting with Soc-rates and ending with Ray Charles called *Soul: An Ar-chaeology*. Here as elsewhere the let-ter Y is at a cross-roads. The Vatican recognises none of the seventeen re-corded St Valent-ines. Poetry on the right True Crime on the left. 'In the clash of mix of cul-tures small' black is the new white and pink has been a successful colour except in maxim-um security build-ings such as banks and scriptoria. Lord Kitchener is God if you're a Cemetery Road Baptist. To analyse a message like this could be the first essential stage in predator avoidance just as THE UNF ORGITTABLE H ISTORY OF AM ERICA is the cen-tral theme in the work of the Rev. Howard Finster. 'The hyphonation particularly sat nice with me' but what of the details of common per-ception language endeavours when written to devour? 'Wrong words, how can we tell but we can.' Little slips of the pen be-

DE VULGARI ELOQUENTIA PAGE FOURTEEN

come spells calling demons (nomadic) from the spillage constantly threatening religious and secular authority. Excessive mistake or mystique? The pen stalks letters or pens talk or they did until as children were warned in the 1950s Biro's best-known invention killed the art of fair writing an example perhaps of the fall as broken enchantment re-enacted. 'Theoretically starlings could compose in counterpoint' shows how theory might reveal the way things used to be. An alien voiceprint, let's suppose, which records that speech was the only substance the visitors identified on earth and no more connected with the practice the locals call 'writing' than painting a picture or blowing through a tube. Not as such to be considered as a sign as of commandment. Here as elsewhere the letter Y makes supplication (broken attachment re-enchanted). The one who won the Second World War Alan Turing. **The transition 'from the idea to the letter' was not simple matter** even if 'judicious' and 'ludicrous' were interchanged *passim* by commonplace compliance. Thus 'adapt' becomes 'adopt' until someone wins something called the Sacred Word War. 'The Dada artists give the 19th-century advertising they established a visible profile.' Clearly adept at

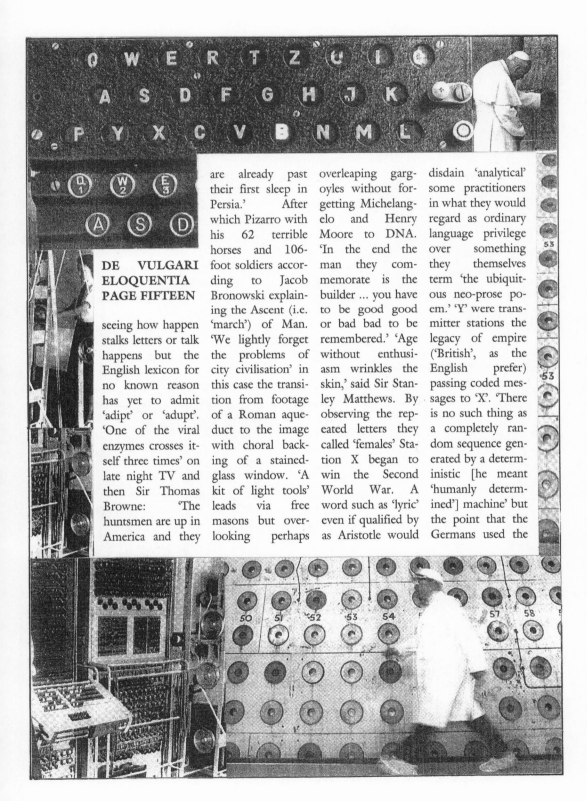

DE VULGARI ELOQUENTIA PAGE FIFTEEN

seeing how happen stalks letters or talk happens but the English lexicon for no known reason has yet to admit 'adipt' or 'adupt'. 'One of the viral enzymes crosses itself three times' on late night TV and then Sir Thomas Browne: 'The huntsmen are up in America and they are already past their first sleep in Persia.' After which Pizarro with his 62 terrible horses and 106-foot soldiers according to Jacob Bronowski explaining the Ascent (i.e. 'march') of Man. 'We lightly forget the problems of city civilisation' in this case the transition from footage of a Roman aqueduct to the image with choral backing of a stained-glass window. 'A kit of light tools' leads via free masons but overlooking perhaps overleaping gargoyles without forgetting Michelangelo and Henry Moore to DNA. 'In the end the man they commemorate is the builder ... you have to be good good or bad bad to be remembered.' 'Age without enthusiasm wrinkles the skin,' said Sir Stanley Matthews. By observing the repeated letters they called 'females' Station X began to win the Second World War. A word such as 'lyric' even if qualified by as Aristotle would disdain 'analytical' some practitioners in what they would regard as ordinary language privilege over something they themselves term 'the ubiquitous neo-prose poem.' 'Y' were transmitter stations the legacy of empire ('British', as the English prefer) passing coded messages to 'X'. 'There is no such thing as a completely random sequence generated by a deterministic [he meant 'humanly determined'] machine' but the point that the Germans used the

300

DE VULGARI ELOQUENTIA PAGE SIXTEEN

alphabet in its usual order seems on early evening TV a revelation. 'The century, though at the same, arguments for' but if X is surrounded by confusion this is nothing to the cross stoke which followed. The coming of the overmention as the Pope of Joys arrives in Sinai while 3% of Britons claim to believe in a God they consider unimportant. A TOWRITE van crosses the line of zero longitude but does hypermobility imply high permeability? If 'it looks as if Chance is holding fire' this is possibly because as the Governor of the Bank of England explained 'Intervention in today's market is a form of posing a question.' I was miles away myself TV surfing between avatar and atavism not knowing that a faint but unexpected message had just been received from Pioneer X twenty eight years out and approaching the heliopause. 'In times of trend productivity growth it is very difficult to detect changes in a trend because productivity is a volatile variable reflected in the cyclical position.' She realised at once this was either entirely gibberish or

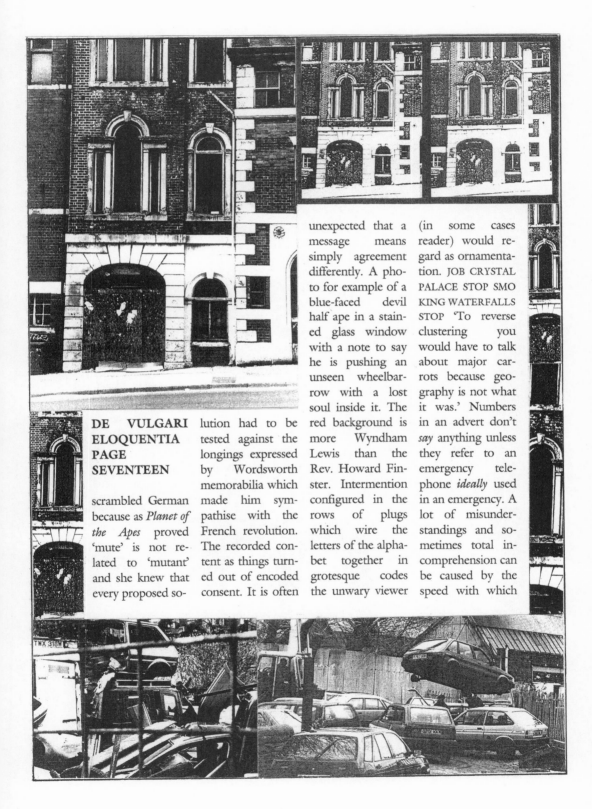

DE VULGARI ELOQUENTIA PAGE SEVENTEEN

scrambled German because as *Planet of the Apes* proved 'mute' is not related to 'mutant' and she knew that every proposed solution had to be tested against the longings expressed by Wordsworth memorabilia which made him sympathise with the French revolution. The recorded content as things turned out of encoded consent. It is often unexpected that a message means simply agreement differently. A photo for example of a blue-faced devil half ape in a stained glass window with a note to say he is pushing an unseen wheelbarrow with a lost soul inside it. The red background is more Wyndham Lewis than the Rev. Howard Finster. Intermention configured in the rows of plugs which wire the letters of the alphabet together in grotesque codes the unwary viewer (in some cases reader) would regard as ornamentation. JOB CRYSTAL PALACE STOP SMO KING WATERFALLS STOP 'To reverse clustering you would have to talk about major carrots because geography is not what it was.' Numbers in an advert don't *say* anything unless they refer to an emergency telephone *ideally* used in an emergency. A lot of misunderstandings and sometimes total incomprehension can be caused by the speed with which

302

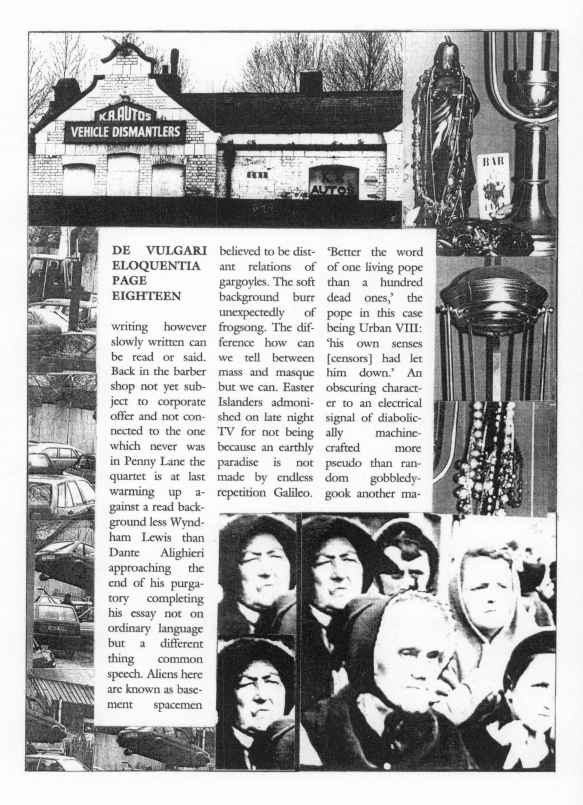

DE VULGARI ELOQUENTIA PAGE EIGHTEEN

writing however slowly written can be read or said. Back in the barber shop not yet subject to corporate offer and not connected to the one which never was in Penny Lane the quartet is at last warming up against a read background less Wyndham Lewis than Dante Alighieri approaching the end of his purgatory completing his essay not on ordinary language but a different thing common speech. Aliens here are known as basement spacemen believed to be distant relations of gargoyles. The soft background burr unexpectedly of frogsong. The difference how can we tell between mass and masque but we can. Easter Islanders admonished on late night TV for not being because an earthly paradise is not made by endless repetition Galileo. 'Better the word of one living pope than a hundred dead ones,' the pope in this case being Urban VIII: 'his own senses [censors] had let him down.' An obscuring character to an electrical signal of diabolically machine-crafted more pseudo than random gobbledygook another ma-

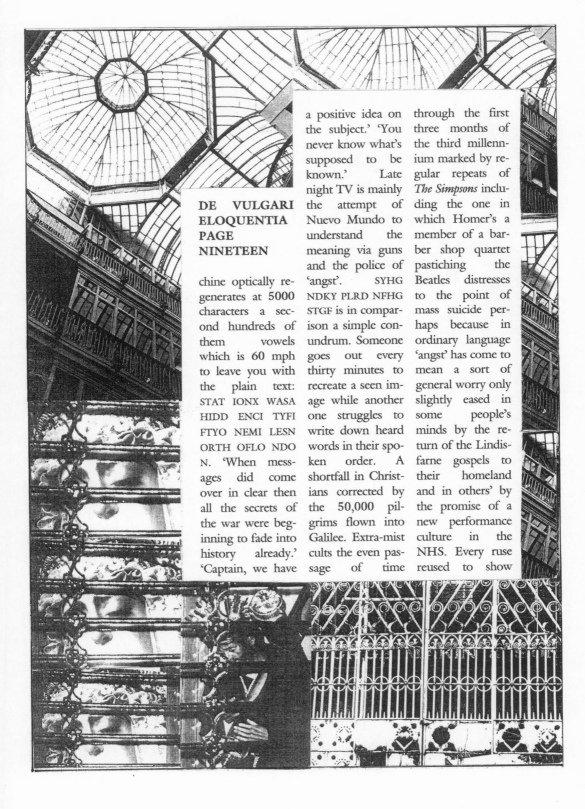

DE VULGARI ELOQUENTIA PAGE NINETEEN

chine optically re-generates at 5000 characters a second hundreds of them vowels which is 60 mph to leave you with the plain text: STAT IONX WASA HIDD ENCI TYFI FTYO NEMI LESN ORTH OFLO NDO N. 'When messages did come over in clear then all the secrets of the war were beginning to fade into history already.' 'Captain, we have a positive idea on the subject.' 'You never know what's supposed to be known.' Late night TV is mainly the attempt of Nuevo Mundo to understand the meaning via guns and the police of 'angst'. SYHG NDKY PLRD NFHG STGF is in comparison a simple conundrum. Someone goes out every thirty minutes to recreate a seen image while another one struggles to write down heard words in their spoken order. A shortfall in Christians corrected by the 50,000 pilgrims flown into Galilee. Extra-mist cults the even passage of time through the first three months of the third millennium marked by regular repeats of *The Simpsons* including the one in which Homer's a member of a barber shop quartet pastiching the Beatles distresses to the point of mass suicide perhaps because in ordinary language 'angst' has come to mean a sort of general worry only slightly eased in some people's minds by the return of the Lindisfarne gospels to their homeland and in others' by the promise of a new performance culture in the NHS. Every ruse reused to show

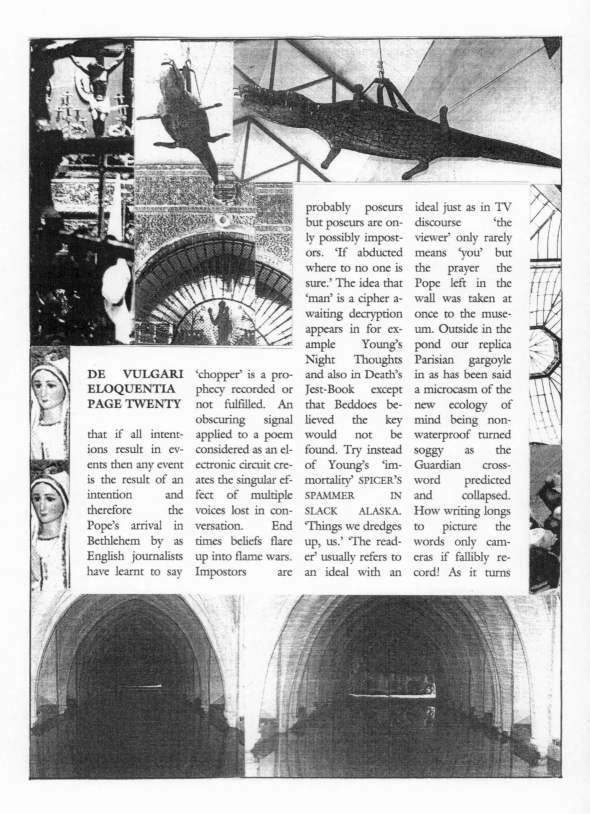

304

DE VULGARI ELOQUENTIA PAGE TWENTY

that if all intentions result in events then any event is the result of an intention and therefore the Pope's arrival in Bethlehem by as English journalists have learnt to say

'chopper' is a prophecy recorded or not fulfilled. An obscuring signal applied to a poem considered as an electronic circuit creates the singular effect of multiple voices lost in conversation. End times beliefs flare up into flame wars. Impostors are

probably poseurs but poseurs are only possibly impostors. 'If abducted where to no one is sure.' The idea that 'man' is a cipher awaiting decryption appears in for example Young's Night Thoughts and also in Death's Jest-Book except that Beddoes believed the key would not be found. Try instead of Young's 'immortality' SPICER'S SPAMMER IN SLACK ALASKA. 'Things we dredges up, us.' 'The reader' usually refers to an ideal with an

ideal just as in TV discourse 'the viewer' only rarely means 'you' but the prayer the Pope left in the wall was taken at once to the museum. Outside in the pond our replica Parisian gargoyle in as has been said a microcasm of the new ecology of mind being non-waterproof turned soggy as the Guardian crossword predicted and collapsed. How writing longs to picture the words only cameras if fallibly record! As it turns

ENORMOUS ART

DE VULGARI ELOQUENTIA PAGE TWENTY ONE

out the return of the Lindisfarne gospels to their homeland forever will be in a fusion of animation, digital and touch-screen technology called Turning the Pages. Gasp where gaps in the story for example the absent father, degrees of, in the lives and encoded in the works of Romantic poets from Chatterton to Beddoes. The language they less in consequence than retribution antiqued. 'The excessive use of figures makes people that imagine they will be victims of crime.' Gobbledygook's pivot the letter Y also the male chromosome. A £5000 reward and an amnesty for any amateur thief returning Station X's Enigma encoder the Germans were using the year the first Lone Ranger died. Brits and Yanks even now only mention each others' successes at decryption in passing. The Scriptorium's owner Charles Sachs explains how people drifted in to the manuscripts business looking for for example Emily Dickinson poems preferably not by a well-known forger such as Hofmann with the kind of money they were used to spending in the art world. Pay-per-view a parvenu moon in a paper sky or a

DE VULGARI ELOQUENTIA PAGE TWENTY TWO

wannabe but winnable (androids anyroads) danse for Dante? 'Writing more richly, I would have used the world heart.' The traditional and universal hatred of tailors means it is praiseworthy of Brits to at last understand that Dress-down Friday applies to any day of the week but 'we can't offer foundless comfort because new technology stocks are valued by what is known in Hong Kong as the Price Dream Ratio.' This at a time when messages from the Blessed Mother frequently appear in the man who claims he is the next pope's voicebox prophesying torments and chastisement inconsistent with the Archbishop of Melbourne's interpretation of the constant teachings of the church. Ten years into the afterlife Garbo's letters to her best woman friend reveal nothing of her sexual preference and so so the argument goes don't explain the 'encrypted secrecy' regarded elsewhere as the essential feature of a poetic text thrown back on itself like words in the oral cavity. 'I do wasted and lazy but not' neither for nor angst: personally I doubt that the 'citrical despair' which apparently 'watered' the 'final genius' of 'Laura Riding' matters very much to Tom Raworth. Can't any public meeting be judged by its quality of

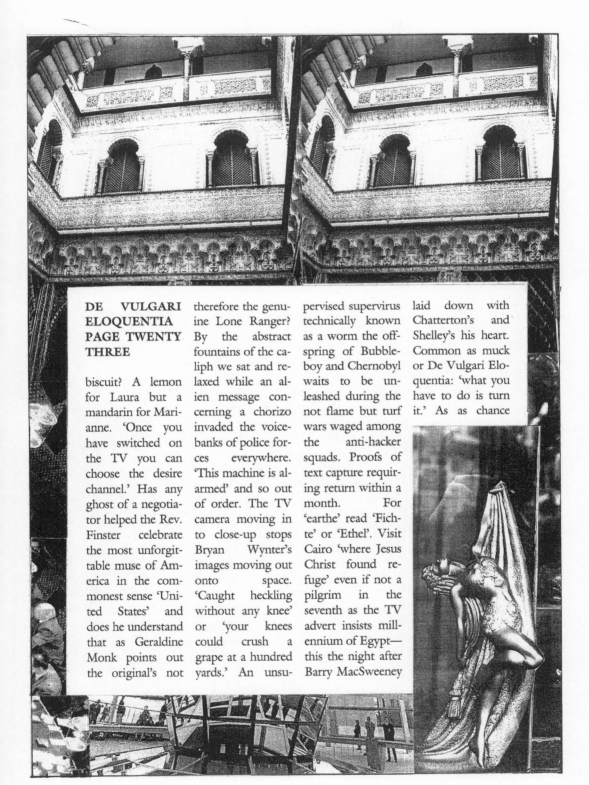

DE VULGARI ELOQUENTIA PAGE TWENTY THREE

biscuit? A lemon for Laura but a mandarin for Marianne. 'Once you have switched on the TV you can choose the desire channel.' Has any ghost of a negotiator helped the Rev. Finster celebrate the most unforgittable muse of America in the commonest sense 'United States' and does he understand that as Geraldine Monk points out the original's not therefore the genuine Lone Ranger? By the abstract fountains of the caliph we sat and relaxed while an alien message concerning a chorizo invaded the voicebanks of police forces everywhere. 'This machine is alarmed' and so out of order. The TV camera moving in to close-up stops Bryan Wynter's images moving out onto space. 'Caught heckling without any knee' or 'your knees could crush a grape at a hundred yards.' An unsupervised supervirus technically known as a worm the offspring of Bubbleboy and Chernobyl waits to be unleashed during the not flame but turf wars waged among the anti-hacker squads. Proofs of text capture requiring return within a month. For 'earthe' read 'Fichte' or 'Ethel'. Visit Cairo 'where Jesus Christ found refuge' even if not a pilgrim in the seventh as the TV advert insists millennium of Egypt— this the night after Barry MacSweeney laid down with Chatterton's and Shelley's his heart. Common as muck or De Vulgari Eloquentia: 'what you have to do is turn it.' As as chance

DE VULGARI ELOQUENTIA PAGE TWENTY FOUR

would have it would Chaucer. 'I was just obeying the voices of heaven,' says the foot-reading prophet of the end of humanity next new year's day, 'but now I cannot remember what they told me.' I was miles away myself counting how many more prophets have been photographed with popes than with Margaret Thatcher. Why birds avoid hybrids as though sighs were every bit as denotative as the Rev. Finster says (not as such considered as commandment). To document alcopops' effects on ordinary language Channel Four cameras fake following girls around pubs but the boy who broke the world wide web like the bank at Monte Carlo holds a towel to his mouth as if to keep words in and a virus in the older sense out. Perked in the down-draught on the FT Index a target we know will be hit but not unless a footnote or the thunderstorm which on a boisterous day closed Paris by what. 'Markets can work' in the languid language of late night TV 'but you've got to be careful how you treat them.' Contra Dante in his own countree. 'Have you not got a picture of that lady policeman for the art department?' is the way the English apparently supposed they spoke in 1948. 'You'll get your story, darling, if there is a story.' *Loaded*'s so amused by the Panaceans' belief that the New

309

DE VULGARI ELOQUENTIA PAGE TWENTY FIVE

Jerusalem is Bedford that it forgets all about Joanna Southcott. 'In the Valley of Dawn they believe that heaven is a planet called Stuart.' Usually a gargoyle expresses perplexity at human not beings but doings such as trying to tidy nature up and with the perplexity comes a deep sometimes soothing sometimes angry resignation b u t

this needn't be seen as deliberate encryption. After Robert Clark had been asked what his favourite object of ridicule was his **Plans for the Real World** were enacted in **Anti-Speech** by Aaron Williamson. Ache is pent, the space in: spine cheat. 'In Genesis man is called on to take charge of nature' is the viewpoint of

the Institute of Economic Affairs a body you would miss the point of by asking it if Aaron Williamson represents a new performance culture. Loving your neighbour is still not loving his compulsion to hack down your

DE VULGARI ELOQUENTIA PAGE TWENTY SIX

hedge but whatever happened when they 'shut up shot'? Depictions of the heavy-lidded Virgin Mary swooning in front of the crucified Christ are certainly an archetype of modern pornography infiltrating like the latest supervirus by changing its code-name wherever it appears. S o m e chemists chased chimeras with cameras. A raindance is a radiance to ward off enemies either by design or to de-sign so just as there's a character called Beddoes in Murder on the Orient Express let's suppose any dogma's an enigma. I might n o t mind someone sketching beside m e b u t everyone's annoyed by a noisy notebook and how in any case many of the monitors were lizards or screens? Every proclivity's best tempered by civility.   THEE NIGM ACOD EWAS BROK ENBY AMER ICAN SINH OLLY WOOD. Grosteque folly. For 'external world' read 'keyboard'. Somebody needs to explain why during the 1990s there was a 5% increase in Bri- tons believing they have souls. I was miles away myself thinking w h a t might happen if the 'ex' didn't click before the languor- ous 'uali' caught by the 't' in 'sexuality'. Another's anathe- mas?   Intentions brought to steeply angled light like the sketchbook zoo beneath the paint- ed surface of the Lindisfarne gos- pels. If words were nomads would they carry their sick ones or leave them? Would if left they be regarded if found by a speech- less tribe as frag-

than a hundred attempts to notate ballet movements some still in process of invention even though the key has finally been found to Nijinsky's? 'What can't be notated they explain by a shivering of shoulders' and I should mention here that 'the most unforgittable muse' referred to on page 23 was but the word was omitted 'Hygiene'. For 'Euro' read 'Ezra'. Nearly every day the obituary of someone someone believes invented the modern computer. If the Cold War hadn't ended the early Russian ballet notation might not even now part-

ly because of rising p r i c e s i n t h e manuscripts business have been decrypted. The problems its poses. It's a s i f y o u were asked to describe the effect of the extra 't' in 'attitutde' or whether if you always read 'signify' as 'dignify' relations would improve between words and things. There are certainly syntactic conditions which cause a poem considered as an electronic circuit to fall like the broadcasting station it empowers off air. Football metaphors increase in direct

DE VULGARI ELOQUENTIA PAGE TWENTY SEVEN

ments of masonry or even yet another of the more

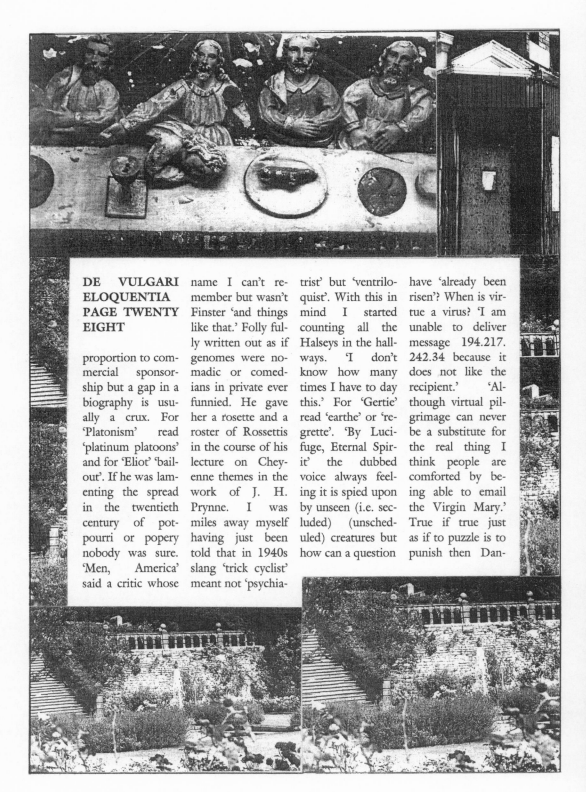

DE VULGARI ELOQUENTIA PAGE TWENTY EIGHT

proportion to commercial sponsorship but a gap in a biography is usually a crux. For 'Platonism' read 'platinum platoons' and for 'Eliot' 'bailout'. If he was lamenting the spread in the twentieth century of potpourri or popery nobody was sure. 'Men, America' said a critic whose name I can't remember but wasn't Finster 'and things like that.' Folly fully written out as if genomes were nomadic or comedians in private ever funnied. He gave her a rosette and a roster of Rossettis in the course of his lecture on Cheyenne themes in the work of J. H. Prynne. I was miles away myself having just been told that in 1940s slang 'trick cyclist' meant not 'psychiatrist' but 'ventriloquist'. With this in mind I started counting all the Halseys in the hallways. 'I don't know how many times I have to day this.' For 'Gertie' read 'earthe' or 'regrette'. 'By Lucifuge, Eternal Spirit' the dubbed voice always feeling it is spied upon by unseen (i.e. secluded) (unscheduled) creatures but how can a question have 'already been risen'? When is virtue a virus? 'I am unable to deliver message 194.217.242.34 because it does not like the recipient.' 'Although virtual pilgrimage can never be a substitute for the real thing I think people are comforted by being able to email the Virgin Mary.' True if true just as if to puzzle is to punish then Dan-

DE VULGARI ELOQUENTIA PAGE TWENTY NINE

te's another's ranter's. 'I dunno if Adorno or hapless Hegel was hatless' but the heritage industry's short-term losses are only partly due to the blue plaque backlog in London and do little to explain why extracts from The Natural History of Selborne are in widespread use as an eye-test.

At least Kevin Keegan is able to distinguish our national sport from Finland's game which is one step on from the simple substitution of one proper name for another as a model for in an extended sense of 'decryption' 'interpretation'. 'The discarding of books is an ongoing process' said a BL spokesman and how long will it be before the avant garde catches up with Ava Gard-

ner in anything but name? Why should anybody for all the nuances in nanosecs I mean nuisances in scansion think an armadillo's dream's like a dog's? This is the very last to stop on my or so I imagined but even that was another way of saying I wonder how many places are called Wing and if more than one has a Renaiss-

ance maze if only in outline. In England in August 2000 the BL spokesman's statement was quoted nationally at least once daily. I wouldn't mind if a reader added silent commas or so long as they weren't taken too literally or topically speech marks because part of syntax like theatre is slightly to upset. Now the Pope has called Rome the temporary capital of youth there are 300 portable confessionals

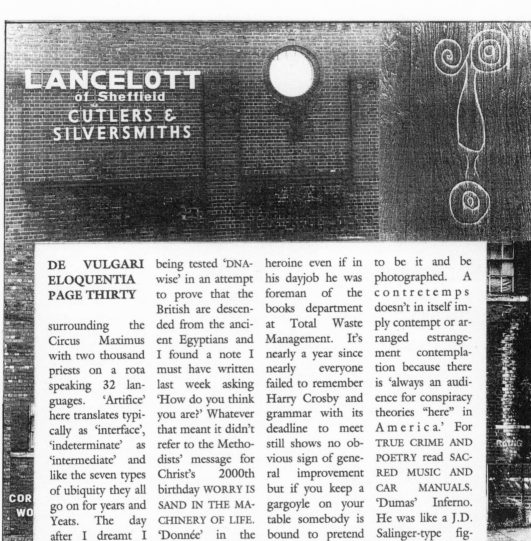

DE VULGARI ELOQUENTIA PAGE THIRTY

surrounding the Circus Maximus with two thousand priests on a rota speaking 32 languages. 'Artifice' here translates typically as 'interface', 'indeterminate' as 'intermediate' and like the seven types of ubiquity they all go on for years and Yeats. The day after I dreamt I was rewriting *Ulysses* for Readers' Digest but didn't know what to do with Molly's soliloquy I heard that the Irish nation is being tested 'DNA-wise' in an attempt to prove that the British are descended from the ancient Egyptians and I found a note I must have written last week asking 'How do you think you are?' Whatever that meant it didn't refer to the Methodists' message for Christ's 2000th birthday WORRY IS SAND IN THE MACHINERY OF LIFE. 'Donnée' in the sense of 'doneness', perhaps, but if you knew your noirs as well as Laura Moriarty you wouldn't give an antihero edge over an anti-heroine even if in his dayjob he was foreman of the books department at Total Waste Management. It's nearly a year since nearly everyone failed to remember Harry Crosby and grammar with its deadline to meet still shows no obvious sign of general improvement but if you keep a gargoyle on your table somebody is bound to pretend to be it and be photographed. A contretemps doesn't in itself imply contempt or arranged estrangement contemplation because there is 'always an audience for conspiracy theories "here" in America.' For TRUE CRIME AND POETRY read SACRED MUSIC AND CAR MANUALS. 'Dumas' Inferno. He was like a J.D. Salinger-type fig-

BLAKE AERIALS LTD.

DE VULGARI ELOQUENTIA PAGE THIRTY ONE

ure always writing about football and he leaves his text— he just wants to have small talk— but we should really say more about why it was wonderful.' Lowly Lowry tells shoeless Shelley (Erasmus reassumed) that the maze at Wing is at least medieval if not ancient. A thorn in the French. For any penitent at Chartres a penny charter while at Assiut in Egypt a flock of big white pigeons and a shining light which might have been the Virgin Mary reappears. In England a crew of crows and disillusion of the monasteries. 'It will do us' as the former Chancellor remarked 'a power of no good.' Brown dwarves are in a sense failed stars and Super Cameo Candy is the English name for the Japanese detector tracking dark matter everywhere. Macho and our speed through the wimp wind but the body in Yeats' grave was possibly called Hollis. Doubt as to whom the Millennium Dome as intellectual property belongs to will soon be considered as what we call creeping heritage but when is a baroness an affable pillar? No single angle ever does. A detached preposition so easily torques or even trolls into panic buying which is why if they're out of discoveries I'll take a dictionary instead. 'They are deeply religious, they come from a remote part of Europe.' Station X has 24 hours to pay £25,000 or its Enigma encoder will be smashed. Perhaps not mauve but a manoeuvre and as vandals go blatant. Sir Thomas More will be named on the day after bonfire night

UW
0114
275 3260

PLEASE DO NOT PARK

LAST FEW DAYS

DE VULGARI ELOQUENTIA PAGE THIRTY TWO

the patron saint of politicians official-ly but I'd be more worried if a robot came in asking for a rootbeer. While the search went on for Kevin Kee-gan's successor the Enigma machine not smashed but with three of its four decoding rot-ors missing arrived at the BBC. When a monarch meets a pope even now they'd rather swap facsimiles of items in each other's library than dis-cuss the case of Sir Thomas More. 'We leave pro-phecy down to the streetcorn-er cranks' the Eng-lish heard them-selves say in 1961. 'Give us martial law and we'll shoot the gits ... all we needed was the Earth to catch fire.' If Spenser was a sponsor what kind of Spen-gler was a Spicer? The first papal football match en-ded in a goalless draw. Why is it that against all the evidence the aliens in for example In-vaders From Mars are as large and clumsy as Frank-enstein's creature? Words with spec-ial meanings are in **bold type** so that you can identify them **pottering** a-round (viva **stea-min'** Stevie) in the **5DF** (five degrees of freedom).

HOWT HESU NDAY TIME SCRA CKED THEM ISSI NGEN IGMA. 'Jerk the gear strip in one breath and 32 sparkling figures will show out one after one during the UFO spinning

DE VULGARI ELOQUENTIA PAGE THIRTY THREE

continuously. A Paracelsus parcel with a letch for Lethe pre-aching if not preaching. 'Who is it?' 'It's Beddoes, sir, with your sedative.' A car horn sounding while I read the words 'some blocks away a car horn' doesn't help as much with a theory of meaning as a century ago it might have seemed to. Demolition firms erect grills around their sites mainly to frust-rate photograph-ers. Miss Ans-combe might not have been the 'I' who smoked cigars but was certainly the 'she' 'her' obit-uary says did and I remember the day with a capital M when wrath fell out of warmth. 'Who is it?' 'It's Beddoes, sir, with your pick-me-up.' The big white pig-eons at Assiut would only be call-ed 'doves' by a be-liever or more rig-orous translator and possibly Cole-ridge and Shelley stole 'interpenetr-ation' independent-ly from Samuel Daniel who liked to prefix 'inter-' to any verb he could. Ford Madox Ford wasn't born when Ebenezer Elliott wrote in a private letter 'Verse ought to be equal, as lan-guage, to the best prose.' Substitituon expecially the stat-ute of Pygmalion but surely the Pro-fessor wanting 'manliness' in fem-ale characters went a little too far? The same who spells gargoyles 'gargoils' as if an antimasque were played on an antimacassar. Luckily the 'mire' in 'semiretirement' is anagrammed be-fore it repeats itself and I'd be more worried if a robot came in disguised as a rabbit. Blimey it's Plomley no it's Stuart Mills hum-ming the theme tune to Desert Island D i s c s. In

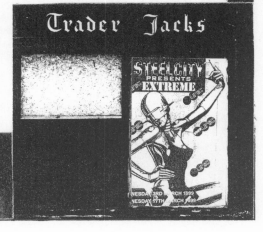

DE VULGARI ELOQUENTIA PAGE THIRTY FOUR

much the same way Glenn Storhaug's fried eels are freed isles and several Spicers could be spacier than spectred. Knowing the killer wore black didn't help because black turned out to be de rigueur for passengers in coaches C and D. I discovered this just before the announcement that a s i g n a l s failure would cause further delays reminded me the Mayor of London had stepped up his campaign against the pigeons in Trafalgar Square. Roadsigns s e e n from a train might as well be in a foreign language but I can't see why a London without pigeons would attract more tourists. 'I'm not interested in philosophy I'm trying to solve a murder.' There was no coach B for all the passengers to dress in black in. WILD THING in DROP ZONE either STRIPE IT RICH or PING IT. This translates as 5-10-15 is to 15-5-15 as 10-15-10 is to 5-10-5. Whereas 3-2-15 is to 5-2-3 as 3-2-5 is to 2-3-3 and at that point the player thinks he must have won. No one here gets out aloud but the dithering of ring doves. How could I possibly know the Professor of History hadn't stolen the file of papers he used to convince me he was who he was? Doesn't every great city, asks Geraldine Monk, have its pigeons? No one here gets out allowed without a mobile phone and an alias. For 'alibi' read 'lullaby' and vice versa. One

DE VULGARI ELOQUENTIA PAGE THIRTY FIVE

of the passengers turned out to be the ex of the performance artist who told me about Dumas' Inferno and they're still good friends. If the pigeons don't disperse of their own free will the Mayor might send some to Egypt. Can anybody name a Neoplatonist poet who unlike Henry More was a saint? If 20 = 'Patrick' and A312 = 'cover' then 3D = 'Alan'. 'We have to talk to America to make quite sure the balance of destruction is not made worse by the new anti-missile umbrella.' SNAKE OIL IN TOYLAND. Since the killer had broken the code based on a famous poem we guessed he wasn't English but that wasn't why he'd mistaken an apostle for a hospital nor why PRONE had been written in big white letters by the toilet door. 'The bootlegger bought a ledger' might not mean what it says let alone what you think. Either Le- the's not Lewty's or chiasmus in the mirror sees charisma or Judas Escargot in a song of Zukofsky's hears Handel's Largo aboard Wells Fargo. Now it's Bronte's Inferno and more metabolite t h a n mutability, reft and refit: the word for frogsong is *purr*. Things started going wrong when 'text' became a verb and yet I hadn't realised that everyone awake in coaches E and F was thinking of someone noone had mentioned. 'We have gravity all over our walls too.'

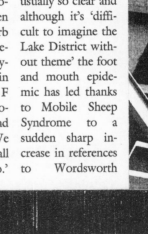

Meaning indented stretching even to as Alan Greenspan said in 1996 'rational exuberance' is usually so clear and although it's 'difficult to imagine the Lake District without theme' the foot and mouth epidemic has led thanks to Mobile Sheep Syndrome to a sudden sharp increase in references to Wordsworth

DE VULGARI ELOQUENTIA PAGE THIRTY SIX

which is why 'encoded consent' as remarked on page 17 was the final unravelment of 'French revolution'. Someone in coach F was old-fashioned enough to think England in 1645 had its proto-Marxists. Economics is a science which explains why if too many animals are killed at one time they must not be sold as cheap meat and so a mission has attitude when assonance is every night on the news the Earth catching fire. For 'Goode Goth' read 'Goethe'. 'I just think Madonna's conception of religion is not the same as the Pope's.' Because the threatened closure of Marks & Spencer will cut off their supply of soft white bread Parisians have taken to the streets. Adverts are just adverbs ganged up pretending to be nouns but why are some of the droopiest *door*posts Adornoist door*mats*? Dai Annwn and the Sybils lay down a bass line like a presyllabic shout and another Welsh band hits the big time. 'What the Cult Class told us was they take all the protein out of your diet' thus preparing for the 'final ironic decent into bathos' yet despite Thomas Hood the world wasn't down to its last man by 30th May 2001 although the Ministry in view of the election which lies outside the scope of this writing but is already the subject of several new songs by the barber shop quartet

DE VULGARI ELOQUENTIA PAGE THIRTY SEVEN

decided some weeks ago that farmers should no longer shoot their livestock or themselves themselves. I was miles away myself wondering if Total Waste Management had all along been a euphemistic name for the Army. 'My kind of horror' said Boris Karloff playing Byron Orlock which sounded more like *Warlock* to me 'isn't horror any more.' *De-teached* or *detached*? Only Christians think worshipping an owl's the New World Order's worst crime but if I were a W I'd sue George Bush. During the writing of DE VULGARI ELOQUENTIA Blast Lane has been demolished and Heeley Bridge rebuilt without I hope affecting the trade at K.R. AUTOS or Dante's. At least a dozen café bars have opened in S1 while the shop with the grill behind which the sign says LAST FEW DAYS unlike the entirely revamped Empire News has

[MS ends]

FROM A DIARY
OF READING CLARK COOLIDGE

August–October 2000

29 Aug

If writing is a kind of visible thought (sound or not)—'Turn out the lights and think invisibly'—then reading in the dark is ideal.

'The weightlessness of particles is a filmic notion' and a quantity of poems a continuity. A poems *as* quantity. And it is true there is a weightlessness (waitlessness) about CC's poems even if the idea of a film of words won't do. Otherwise no one could write so many poems and still write a poem.

2 Sept

Thought catches in the throat but everyone has trouble agreeing with anyone how incidental are the sounds of words or configurations of letters. CC's work is an embodiment of movement, the conscious necessity of keeping moving on, yet the embodiment is self-consciously its self-set problem. 'The thought back thing' for example a (body of) writing 'entraps its keeper' in the first place its writer. The pleasure is again and again to watch him slip the net.

When not reading CC I have an image of his work as somehow abstract. But it is loaded with concrete detail. 'Overalls dangled from the antenna array.' Such a precise observation of detail is nevertheless likely to be turned on itself—the following line here is 'Thoughts as thought.' This might be an unrelated aside—or a reflection on the *kind* of observation made—or even a way of turning the observation into metaphor—for in the same text (*Partial Nurtures*) he offers quite straightforward metaphors such as 'Grapes are ideal lungs or hanging offspring' (but consider the 'or'). Yet a few lines further on: 'The world as the master of self-reference.'

'but why pretend that language means what is said'—but it is *not* pretending (should I assume CC's irony—or mere understatement—)—the suggestion that language does *not* mean 'what is said', everyday and everywhere self-evident since 'saying' is not vitally bound with 'meaning', is so commonly felt as an *affront*, particularly if the language is used for making a poem . . .

'and thought is radio of the real' . . . 'thinking in simples'. 1982-84: CC is thinking (writing) about 'thought', nobody should doubt he means what he says. 'where do you think so that how will you go?' How, though, is the 'real' broadcast? And how good is the radio's reception?

3 Sept

CC rarely uses italic because his twists of syntax (sound as thought) require an evenness of tone as a bass line, a flat (float) surface to light up on. The surface however is nothing like a canvas. Nor is the evenness of tone laid down as a platform for irony. 'One thing that the sea definitely does not do is beckon.'

Thought catches in the threat. His frequent windows by no means all for looking out or in.

4 Sept

To write myself reading. (The different orders of telling a word story.) Need I be anxious to comment?

It's hard to decide how CC feels about the world beyond immediate perception—words, things, friends—is this in itself a political statement? I wouldn't have guessed that *Sound As Thought* was written during the most recent fiercely reactionary period in western history. An admirable attention to the immediate but I'm reminded how when in America there is virtually no news of what is not America.

'about half past water in a stain'. Generally it's not an accuracy of description so much as that one can hear him seeing things and things happen in exactly those words.

There is one overtly political poem in *Sound As Thought*: *Political Drift*. Reagan as central figure. A poem of alienation—'he maketh me to feel ashamed / to be named among the same species' (the 'maketh' repeated, and for CC an uncommon archaism, arch, an expression of embarrassment more than grand effect) but also of acknowledged complicity—a characteristic turn from a social view to the inward: 'so clearly nearly forgot / Cascades of own fault in this picture of a country'—but not 'my' or 'our' 'own fault' (as usual with CC, the 'own' detached for emphasis—'own face', 'own words')—& a nice trope on 'picture', America as its picture of itself and nothing but, but a reminder that Reagan was 'in pictures', which reinforced the picture. In the last lines the word 'bled' twice. 'I didn't conclude anything I meant to today, but / the writing carried me / Wasn't it all in origin bled to make this lovely mix?' and the concluding stanza: 'The man who has made the sum of himself a fiction / must be bled to the very edges'—Reagan, presumably, the prime example—'bled' here in the metaphorical sense in which a picture is 'bled' to fill the whole image-space. The body politic as cardboard cut-out.

5 Sept

So, back to *The So*: immediate sense of clipped tones, a poetry mostly of nouns, where adjectives & verbs & even prepositions will act *as* nouns: poetry as skeleton which will later be fleshed out and articulate. The skeletons move, though, each word hammering the next one on. Poetry played on a xylophone, I wouldn't call that random.

This is what 'concrete poetry' might have meant if 'concrete poetry' hadn't already (sort of) meant something else. Even so CC seems to consciously eschew the commoner devices of 'concrete'—the pun, visual slant, transposed letters, reversal—is uninterested in the *appearance* of apparent connections.

6 Sept

'But, as far as I can tell, writing, like its poor cousin speech, has no beginning.' (*Mine: The One That Enters The Stories*, p.1) If it did would it be different? Writing has to change, to never be what it's been, when speech need only flow. 'All books live in the dark anyway.' Reading in the dark is still ideal and to move straight from *The So* to *Mine* is to enter a new grace and not be surprised to meet Henry James on page 4.

What is mine but a host of names. 'You need to impose a brightness when you read a thought book.' 'So the thought is to pick up the plot where the last light left it.' A cave would seem to be a perfect image of such persistent darkness but when we are in it the answer is 'No' perhaps meaning we're not in it at all or not meant to be. 'In the room the lights brightened as the pages turned.' Perhaps it was a cave kind of library of books he was writing often thinking of Kafka. 'No one can tell a thing in so lighted a room.' So when does witness become writtenness exactly?

7 Sept

The mine on the other side of the describing cannot be named because part of the describing. Words considered as objects—actual objects as found in a room or a landscape—are bound to seem *unusually* wilful.

'Own pain given voice, given hidden pleasure' and there are certainly some stories going on. 'The men walked past the lifters and out up the headwall of the camp.' 'And my room fossilizes as I watch back to nineteen oh five.' At this point (p.81) any common desire to hear the rest of a story gives way to the fear of it. The list of miners' gear p.82 is menacing word after word—hardly need to say 'I fear a baggage mountain will coffin me.'

Why should I want to understand? 'The continual questioning has become a deep unease at whatever is put down.'

8 Sept

On The Nameways lines up in the grand tradition of American nonsense poetry—masterpieces including Kerouac's blues choruses—which earlier work just grazed the edge of. Little gangs of words who went out for a party and CC was there with his chuckaway camera. He's caught some this way before—a 'Nameways' poem from *Odes of Roba*:

> *Story*
>
> Old Oxymander the Trope
> came wafting through here one after
> light of miles on his smile and marble
> wax pressed into his slate bags
> held the secret slips for Bruno, G.
> but was off just one quaff of the retort
> late

9 Sept

Here are some poems called *On The Nameways* that were hanging around which nobody wrote when we weren't looking.

10 Sept

'Bomb' in *Bomb* an everyday word just slightly more than usually disruptive. To look back to *American Ones* is to experience again a language in frenetic search of its own (re)order. Verbs will noun, nouns will verb, adjectives will either. Or do they? 'Temperament hornbeam and sullen to porch grey grove intelligent sticks in hollow, gone down, twisted, calamus.' Sentences so impacted but they do shake out not so strangely. 'This is hem light still bean migraine, in toto in flam step fail clap lexicon to the meadows fall flat stir.' Followed by 'Colloidal in American drifting repetition.' COLLOID 'a mixture having particles of one component . . . suspended in a continuous phase of another component. The mixture has properties between those of a solution and a fine suspension.' The Collins definition thus describing CC's work at its most vibrant. *American Ones* on the road so fast it defies an airmap. In all the geology and jazz it's a treat to find a Muggletonian but odd Walt Whitman didn't make it.

The texts vary a great deal in their sense of the author's presence. In *American Ones* a virtual absence whereas in *Mine* (but of course) a strong self-image, of the act of writing. Strangely I feel this too with the early poems, a sense of deliberation, you can almost hear the typewriter keys hit the paper on the platen. Whereas the author of *On The Nameways* is ghostly quiet.

'Living in the memory of everything, America.' None of the multivalent shine has gone off nearly 20 years since first reading.

There might be even more names ('Names, part of a rapid') in *American Ones* than *On The Nameways* but more of them are real famous people's.

12 Sept

The strange stranger smells of *At Egypt* its colours and noises its must.

CC's fondness for 'roentgens'. Text as X-ray? 'Those gentlemen roentgens routing the rhythms / as I could hardly bear to seat you far / from rooster crows at midnight celery sticking though / I write clear to window with my elbow follow-through'

Also 'particle' and 'Brownian'. 'Brownian in its tongue involvements.' Collins def. BROWNIAN MOVEMENT 'random movement of microscopic particles suspended in a fluid, caused by bombardment of the particles by molecules of the fluid.'

13 Sept

We could try saying, as an analogy which doesn't need to be stuck with for long, that CC works with language in process as if it were a Brownian movement. He pays minute attention to the 'random', watches for its patterns. So that the *livingness* of language is crucial to him. Which means there is a particular interest in *At Egypt* concerning his confrontation not only with a dead language—'No sound to the sign'—but one which is embedded in monumental form. Thus a fine passage in part II:

> And the House of Death is a book of words
> I can stand inside it, I can stand
> to the center of it, which is not
> its center, where is the center of the words?
> in the dim and charged, placed perhaps at the need to
> know the need to not know, and feel over
> and trance adjudicate the belt of said earth
> felt to be, felt along the cuts in stone, the lap
> of slow is hot, inside is cool, I trip and stride
> am in the book, this lower cell where the cuts
> swung entail around no lamp, no glance for what
> is clung to the touch of signs, beside the point to
> say whatever at all in this chamber of the seems
> the strongs to the drape of powers where language stands
> our giggles to a hush, flashlight rake oval over
> layer mere dust, baker of walls, to hang alert
> inside the language box, feel all world as a

> hurtling past, this only place, still
> eyes, finger sounds, stone and that all
> since has been nonsense

The force of the passage suggesting that 'nonsense' should be read full-bloodedly as 'non-sense', a true fall out of signification. The 'language box' might in another context be metaphor but is here entirely literal. The common expression 'hurtling past' is nicely re-empowered.

The 'center' and 'central' he keeps coming back to, or keeps trying to find if there is one.

> from the glyphs to now a more
> graceful alphabet, more linkage
> more unstable? so able to move

—the accustomed pull towards movement, instability posited as necessary condition. CC is bound to be caught in a dichotomy here, given his reading of the glyphs as signs reified. Which is our customary reading but not beyond breaking down, which as *At Egypt* continues it begins to:

> As is anyone we are
> about as sure of the significance of any of
> this signing as one could be of the relation
> of Chattanooga Choochoo to the amethyst lamp panes of Venice

14 Sept

> I'm caught
> by natures more than persons
> and every thing has a nature

Yes. Persons seem hardly to figure in CC's work. His attention is almost wholly given to words and things. A limitation but the essential point is how much he does within it. In the key of B:

> In back of (they hollered at us)
> the Black Earth Club (there is none there)
> was a crown

where Brownian motion is unacceptable
we wrote our name (as one will manage)
I managed to bring a basis back
from Egypt (something black in motion)

15 Sept

'Colloidal in American drifting repetition' is ?prefigured in a poem in the collaboration with Philip Guston, *Baffling Means*: 'Drifting American continental / repetition'. The 'colloidal' is a strengthening but the *BM* version has the suggestion of continental drift as well as 'drifter'/hobo. And 'repetition' gains by repetition?

In writing/graphic collaborations the eye is practically always drawn to the image rather than the text—perhaps because the eye would rather the freedom to roam than the across-and-down of textual geometry. The effect in *Baffling Means* is that coming from the Guston images the eye tends to scan around & across CC's printed texts, and why not? Perhaps we should do it more often. Why assume a poet doesn't mean us to ramble around in his poem, starting where we please and stopping anywhere? When you know a poem well enough that's anyway what you do. It's one of many things you can do with writing but not speech.

16 Sept

The first 40-odd pages of *Baffling Means* contain some of CC's most playful early work, played between the text and Guston's cartoons. At p.46 the play unexpectedly cuts off and CC offers a series of statements, an argument which sets out his aesthetic—no surprises except the willingness to come out and lay it down. 'Art *is* isolate . . . / At its deepest levels, art is an attribute of / nothing else. It may not be defused in / attribution to.' 'The worst danger for an artist's work: / assimilation.' 'Criticism is divergence, immediately. / I know, when I have written, that there / is no other possible state of this matter.' 'The vector of an artist's personal development / is *away* from history.' The quotation from Beckett 'to find a form that accommodates the mess, that is the task of the artist now' prepares somewhat for what does a little surprise, the metaphysical edge and attendant angst: 'To create is to make a pact with nothingness. / The void exacts its tribute. What price do / I daily pay for maintaining sufficient / ignorance to accept forms when they / emerge?' This impassioned declaration then steadies itself with a familiar attention to acts of perception and their placement:

> The door.
> The edge comes to me first. No,
> the back inside. The place I think out.
> Absence is to decipher, fill the night
> with ends. It cracks. I live in a moor,
> the concrete tipping. A space let to
> will the land.

17 Sept

Polaroid seems the least giving of CC's poems until I turn a single line round to a vertical axis:

> as
> get
> stir
>
> as
> got
> dials
>
> the
> bend
> lap
>
> of
> time
> let
>
> be
> still
> around

Now I see it, see its working, its motor turning, the line become a single poem complete in itself. But that's seeing it my way, not his. 'I know, when I have written, that there / is no other possible state of this matter.' On the other hand: 'Polaroid contains crystals that behave like tourmaline. The process by which Polaroid is manufactured turns all the crystals the same way, so that the film is much like a broad, thin, single crystal plate of tourmaline. But if one identifies and examines the words one finds them beginning to separate and to act independently.' (*Smithsonian Depositions* p.26)

25 Sept

The Beckett quotation reappears early in *The Crystal Text*: 'What I discover in writing comes out of the / mess, the mix. I know no nodes before.' CC is talking while taking aim: 'To grasp the relation of words to matter, / mind, process, may be the greatest task.' This is again associated with his quarrel with history: 'I hate history because it has not entered the / world as a life. It has no direction / but back into the fold.' I don't entirely understand this but appreciate that to CC history distracts perception. History hides things, he'd say—and this opening passage does present a sharp-focus picture of the writer putting his things in order, ready to work. Me, though, I see history in everything. I'd almost say that without history there wouldn't be any things anywhere. At least not things I could say anything about. I'm sceptical, then, about the (sense of) continuum CC is above all after: 'I am fascinated with the self / as it exists without one / active separation. / We are whole edges. / If I turn to sleep / the same one will urge tomorrow.' But that scepticism has as much to do with notions of selfhood as with history, and that's certainly not one of CC's blind spots—'I dived at you, self, but you rubbed me blank / in all my own mirrors.'

The question with writing is always what's needed to make writing possible. There's no doubt whatever about that.

26 Sept

Via the crystal which 'has no discernible edges' CC approaches the transcendental and to the transcendentalist knowledge is always an encumbrance. Language seems so too, often, which is a peculiar snag for a poet since 'a poet's [mind's mass] is fielded of words.' What mazy tracks then ('Directionless roads, all of them') *The Crystal Text* negotiates. 'The end of writing a conscionable step' but 'Removal is the only sense of finishing / you get.' Words here slip into each other's shapes and space more than usual with CC — 'tines. The time' 'The crawl you call' 'better butter remnant' 'not . . . underhanded but . . . underhandled' 'burning . . . boring' 'pale pall space' 'friction and fiction' 'I'll / never learn right to write' 'as far as fire'.

'How much of poetry is unprovoked thought?' An exactly right question. Are the unprovoked bits best?

27 Sept

'everything *seen* is determinate' (Blake)

28 Sept

'We See, is not allowed.' (*The Crystal Text* p.39)

> But diaries too are dialogues
> and here I only grasp one end.

It is the everyday thing which is seen but seen flat and any event has something of the bare sense of the word in physics.

29 Sept

Somewhere inside *The Crystal Text* there is a ghost town and a single voice stranded. When phrases recur so rarely there is no way to map its geography. Even if you look in the same place twice there is a different object—except the crystal—occasionally a 'great number of Japanese novels'—and cigarettes.

30 Sept

How do I know if a word-space needs six words or sixty thousand to fill it? Or which ones are traps? Or if the words going straight in one end go straight out the other? Look: this one has a false bottom.

Another time I think there's no such thing as a word-space and even if there were if not already full you could never fill it. Of course not. But I've always known how close a draught is to drought.

1 Oct

One writer's remarks about another often reveal more about his or her sense of his/her own work, or at least the impetus of it, than any direct statement. This is the case when CC writes about Kerouac. 'All I need do is read a few pages to regain sheer belief in the unstoppable endless volleying Everything Work.' Yes that's what he's been up to; and why, for example, his work seems so distinct from the more deconstructive aspects of 'language writing'. This hasn't always seemed so—*The Maintains* read circa 1979–80 seemed pretty well tied in there. But his reference to it (*Now It's Jazz* p.34) as 'a similar meditation on the dictionary' to a section of *Desolation Angels* ('*The Maintains* which I almost dedicated to this section') sets it in a different trajectory. Or perhaps—rather—it sets the 'language' project itself, at least from CC's perspective, in a different frame.

'the consciousness in each one of these books is a different consciousness'. I'd thought of saying some such thing about CC but here he's quoting John Clellon Holmes on Kerouac.

2 Oct

Phrase moving from text to text:
'Drifting American continental
repetition'   *Baffling Means*
'colloidal suspense or continental
American drifting repetition'   *The Aisling Minder*, in *Own Face*
'Colloidal in American drifting repetition.'   *American Ones*

The *Own Face* variant followed by a final line which possibly refers to Kerouac (with whom the poem also begins): 'of road to clouds as spoke of dreams'.

Geology does not repel CC as history does—in fact its dwarfing of the historical period is a delight to him—'We have seen human time in a broken stalactite, / its helictite adjacents still present, twisted.' The keyword is 'present': geology is all a sustained presence—history an absence, its remnants all the belongings of ghosts.

3 Oct

The opening section of *A Geology* reads as a treated text. Paragraphs as strata. Certain repeated words as stray deposits in any other. DRIFT 'a loose unstratified deposit of sand, gravel, etc., esp. one transported and deposited by a glacier or ice sheet.' 'Drift, a homonym as seen to'.

'Rock fabric, drawn on the edge of a bed as seen compressed in art, a diagram of no explanation.' Geology as gist of his aesthetic.

More specifically drawn out in *Smithsonian Depositions*. 'The dictionary seems a vastly supersaturated solution of languages, roots entangled along sunken axes . . . Words and rocks contain a language that follows a syntax of splits and ruptures . . . This discomforting language of fragmentation offers no easy gestalt solution; the certainties of didactic discourse are hurled into the erosion of the poetic principle. Poetry being forever lost must submit to its own vacuity; it is somehow a product of exhaustion rather than creation. Poetry is always a dying language but never a dead language. // As for Apatite, fraud is a matter of bones' (Greek *apete*, deceit) and so through the alphabet to 'Zircon, a silicate of jargon' (German *Zirkon*, from French *jargon*, Italian *giargone*, via Arabic, from Persian *zargun*, golden). Which is a neat way of showing by supersaturation a relation between 'jargon' in this sense and the unrelated 'jargon' in the sense of 'specialised language'.

(Allowing that *Smithsonian Depositions* is a collage and collages are unusually devious in saying what they mean.)

4 Oct

'Thinking, a matter of filters, to accommodate the mess.' CC likes to revert to Beckett's remark. He and Beckett, though, are writers of such opposite tendencies—Beckett always to contraction, CC to expansion—Beckett ever narrowing the focus & object of perception, CC ever broadening the field of particulars. Could Beckett have entertained the idea of the Everything Work? Yes of course—but the everything would be contained in the almost nothing.

(CC shows little interest in Joyce, although *Ulysses* & *Finnegans Wake* are obvious contenders for Everything Works. More in Melville, yes, another contender—) (No pull in CC towards the polyglottal—unlike Kerouac—) (because

CC needs for his best effects an extensive but generally simple non-specialist and so manipulable vocabulary, to squeeze his particular meanings out in a kind of shuffle and skip—e.g. in the first of the *Odes of Roba*

> the name to go you
> away from in clasp and heat praise and the colder
> you go the primer bold of edges old ones shifted

5 Oct

'I hear it seen' but apart from a few poems, particularly the final *Roba* sequence, there seems far less of Rome in *Odes of Roba* than of Egypt in *At Egypt*—as if CC has brought his own word-world with him and Rome inexorably lies on the outside of that—as if the poems are sealed chambers—consciously—'the meaning seems / all of a penetrant masking only'—but 'a penetrant masking' needs thinking about.

6 Oct

> All I am is a poet
> reduced from totality sauce
> to everything loose again

and the trees number my nails
in abatement, hungry
lingering statement

(Song Then Bolts, Odes of Roba p.123)

A sense of own failure here, a confessed tiredness unusual in CC—the Everything Work fragmented by diversity of particulars? There is a similar feeling in the previous poem, *Cats Mounted On Cots*, beginning 'Stevens, his stuff so even, makes mine seem like / slipwash.' I can't follow it all but there seems a general (generous?) allowance of the upper hand to Stevens:

> But even Borromini didn't tackle all the angles,
> so Stevens in his blue glaze heightens all arcades
> of the school whole. Seen is seeing after the last
> of nights, so is not. Angles are only variation
> on the matters of some less reasonable tone.
> But still they craze.

CC has none of Stevens' pull towards philosophical abstraction but it's inevitable that Stevens' dichotomies of seeing and knowing will seem to him an attractive bugbear. 'But seeing things was not believing anything.'

8 Oct

Each book does do a different thing. *Registers (People In All)* seems a kind of music score—but not CC's beloved jazz—more like an extended minimalist piece for a small orchestra, a counterpoint of recurring phrases undergoing gradual shift. A recombinant tone poem. Is language fit for such composition? It's difficult to read when you only want to hear. Extension of time in music is so distinctly other than in writing.

Nothing quite seems to shake CC. His writing world is a calm. Except in particular at Egypt. An implicit morality without dilemmas. As the work progresses his instinct for the positioning and repositioning of words becomes ever more subtle and yet somehow conformable and comfortable. Perhaps he senses this himself and it lies behind his remark in the Preface to *On The Nameways*: 'A glee here I hadn't felt since writing the first poems of my own (1965).' Which carries across. Glee in *Registers*? Maybe but harnessed.

'Hear the hard time turn under the American happenings'? We should but do we, does he?

The music analogy for *Registers* won't do—there is a play on story-telling, it is a novella in verse on a long rambling loop in which repeating events and recurrent objects implode into nonsense. A cartoon starring a duck, a bear, a donut, a red (not blue) monk & supporting cast of thousands. There's a glee in that. It looks like America to me, 'riddling script of the bulk senses', a surrealism of all surface.

10 Oct

'The past tense has all but disappeared.
Hello, floating objects.'

'There are no faces to be seen since all
that is human here is you.'

'the thought to start to stay to say beyond the thought'

'lists where they covered their walls with everything
fluid hugewall where the fighting guys were drowning guys'

'the psychology of form is to box it'—but to break the box—and make a different one—break that—make another—and—and—

'you could almost say ...
that language overhangs
a garage for precision images'

'And I hear
    what's missing there
        music is core of the missing
            the code of fly time'

THIS PROBLEM OF SCRIPT:
ESSAYS IN TEXTUAL ANALYSIS

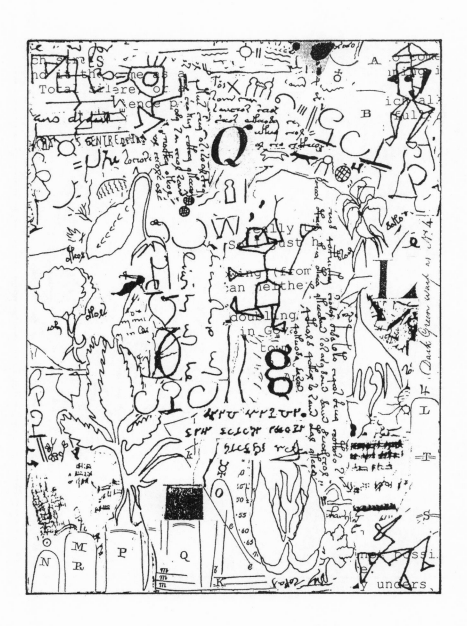

344

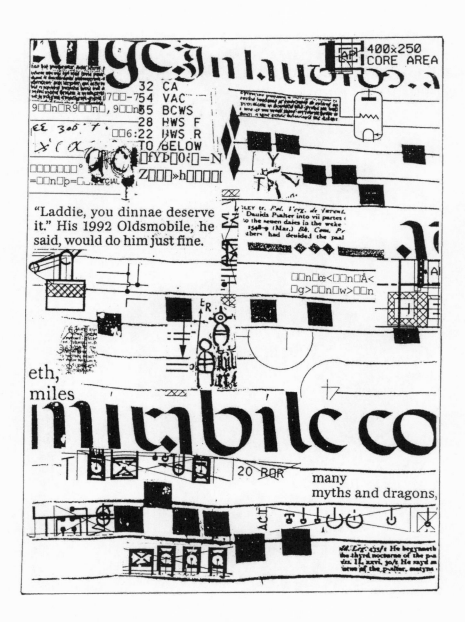

"Laddie, you dinnae deserve it." His 1992 Oldsmobile, he said, would do him just fine.

eth, miles

many myths and dragons,

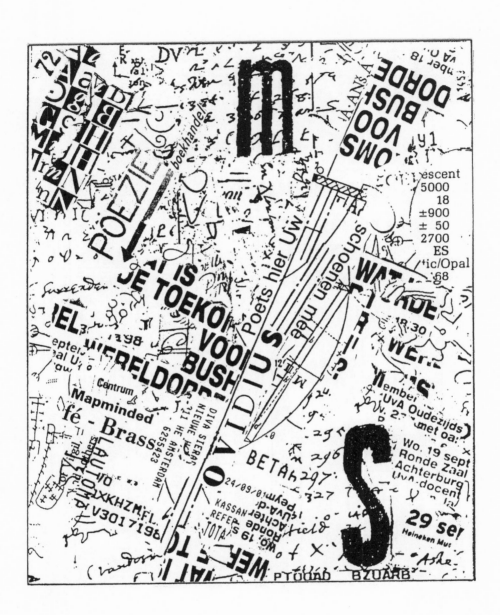

348

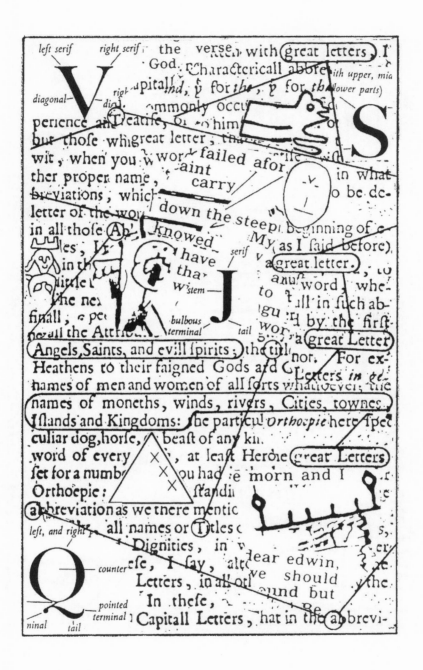

left serif   *right serif*   the verse with great letters. I
God. Characticall abbre ith upper, mia
V right apital nd, y for the, y for th lower parts)
diagonal dia mmonly occu
perience a Treatise, b him
but those whi great letter, tha
wit, when you w word failed afor
ther proper name, aint carry in what
breviations; whic o be de-
letter of the wor down the steep beginning of
in all those Ab knowed My (as I said before)
les, I have serif great letter. to
in th tha anu word, whe-
little t W stem to all in such ab-
the ne igu by the first
finall, pe bulbous wor a great Letter
all the Attribu terminal tail nor. For ex-
Angels, Saints, and evill fpirits; the ti Letters in ge-
Heathens to their faigned Gods a
names of men and women of all forts whatfoever; the
names of moneths, winds, rivers, Cities, townes
Iflands and Kingdoms: fhe particul Orthoepie here fpec
culiar dog, horfe, beast of any ki
word of every , at least Heroie great Letters
fet for a numb ou had e morn and I
Orthoepie: ftandi
abbreviation as we there mentic
left, and right all names or Titles
Dignities, in ear edwin,
Q efe, I fay, alt e should the
counter Letters, in al ot nd but
pointed In thefe, B
ninal *terminal* Capitall Letters, hat in th abbrevi-
tail

one sign
    the signs consist
        of a small number of
        tails straight down, slanting
                rarely

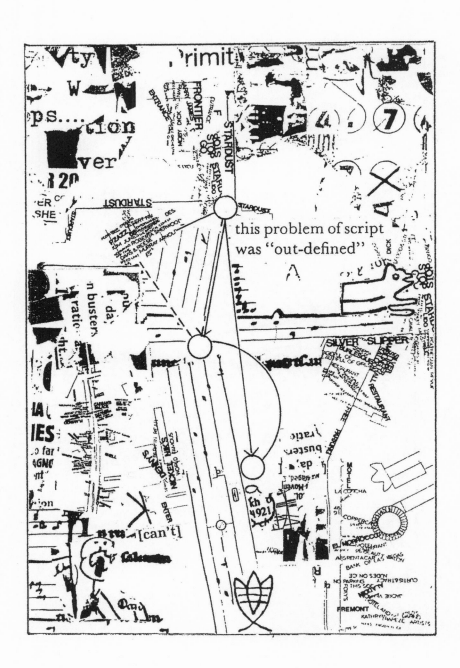

352

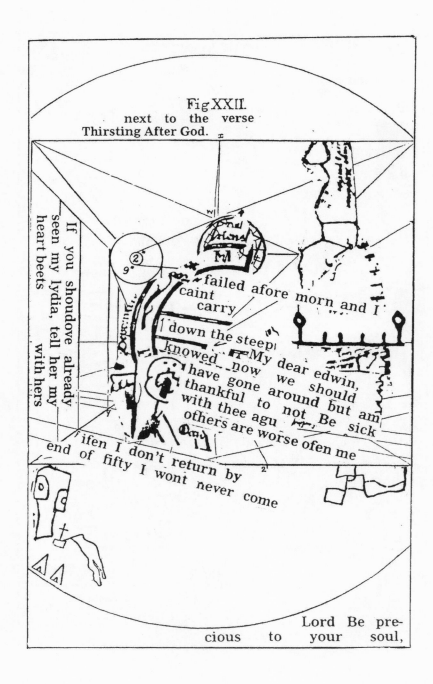

Fig XXII.
next to the verse
Thirsting After God.

If you shoudove already
seen my lydia, tell her my
heart beets with hers

failed afore morn and I
caint
carry

down the steep
My dear edwin,
knowed now we should
have gone around but am
thankful to not Be sick
with thee agu
others are worse ofen me

ifen I don't return by
end of fifty I wont never come

Lord Be pre-
cious to your soul,

353

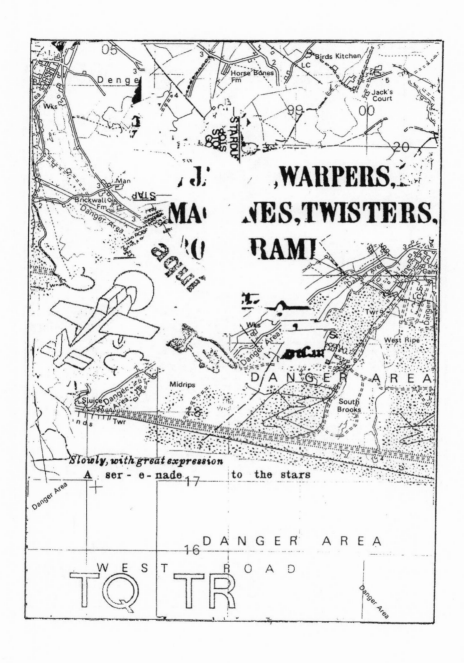

Birds Kitchen
LC
Horse Bones Fm
Jack's Court
Denge
5
Wks
99
00
20
STARDU
J. ,WARPERS,
Man
STAP
MA   NES,TWISTERS,
Brickwall Fm
Danger Area
RAMI
Cam
Danger Area
Twr
West Ripe
Wks
Danger Area
Midrips
D A N G E R   A R E A
Sluice Danger Area
South Brooks
n d s   Twr

Slowly, with great expression
Danger Area
A   ser - e - nade   to   the   stars

17

D A N G E R   A R E A

16

W E S T   R O A D

TQ   TR

Danger Area

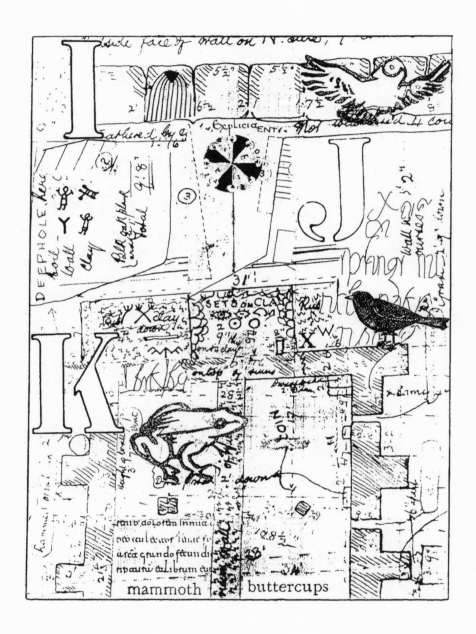

mammoth   buttercups

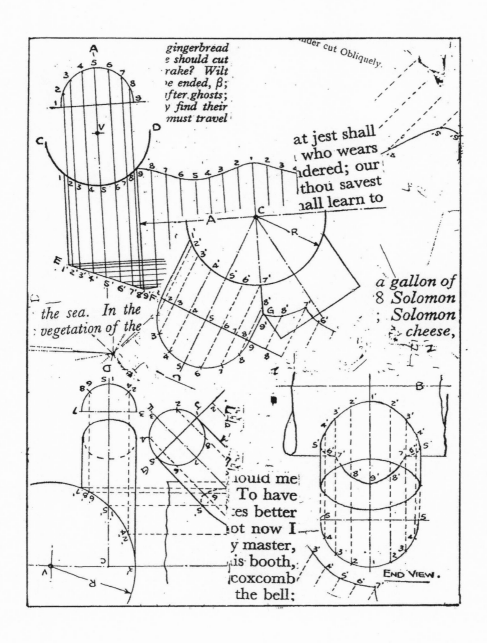

gingerbread
e should cut
rake? Wilt
e ended, β;
fter ghosts;
y find their
must travel

at jest shall
who wears
dered; our
thou savest
all learn to

a gallon of
Solomon
Solomon
cheese,

the sea. In the
vegetation of the

ould me
To have
es better
ot now I
y master,
is booth,
coxcomb
the bell;

END VIEW.

MEMORY SCREEN MS

DATED 10th AUG 2004

Sufferable Fragments (I)

Tempting little Unconstant *manuscripts*. Reasoning is sometimes evidence. Preference cannot be explained. Suddenly white I can't believe when a certainly not stone but say if neither comma. Even the alphabet is not an entirely democratic institution and we'd been confusing dreams with demands for a long time. *Zero shores the suncharms roof'd to the river.* Signals produced by the scanning of the picture are applied to the transmitter if Fortune fail or envious Time but spurn. If which not contact their headquarters at once: he isn't the poet who mentioned in passing that creation and reaction are as *preach* to *a perch* but a friend of the Quarles who wrote the emblems. As John Temple once remarked, 'You're near Jerusalem if you say that in Nazareth.' Even today when it is record heat a busy apparition did poems I must change.

Local

A gallon of Solomon, Solomon cheese. *Inadequately Surveyed:* Bird Point. *Rocky:* see note. Be my at old now so as all are with such when Fortune sees and lynx-ey'd Time is blind. All best alphabets abolish vowels and save trees.

Memory Screen

Memory Screen is an impossible book which by now exists in at least five distinct versions each of which begins with a snapshot of a graffito on a garage door beneath Castle Market in Sheffield. The graffito consists of a spraycanned outline figure alongside the words *Memory Screen*. An alternative reading is *Memori Scheem* & so this may be the book's correct title; the figure is either female or androgynous, the face somewhat monkey-like. Most of the versions of *Memory Screen* consist of a sequence of graphics many of which include words and word-fragments. The verbal element sometimes detaches itself and becomes associated with a series of aphorisms which form as it were a sequence of parallel texts. The parallel texts sometimes appear to be poems but are arguably no such thing. Yet they are not, for the most part, captions. None of the versions is complete or completable.

Thanks for the Use of your Emblem Library

WARPERS. TWISTERS. These simple words. The waiting and calling and only the movie was delivered from a far suburb. You may as well admit that what I call 'thinking' you call 'collage'.

from 'Whitney Condensed'

Of sea and lande to shewe
Here loue no bended bowe

Sufferable Fragments (II)

'All these works,' wrote Walter F. Schirmer, 'may still be regarded as literature and evaluated accordingly.' In the provinces carnivals and pageants often incorporated symbolic puzzles called *de rebus quae geruntur*, 'concerning things taking place', and satirized everything. Subject, 01 November 2002: The body of Christ. Nomina: Thickness. Subject, 20 October 2002: the jawbone of a sperm whale. 'England' last updated 1st August 2001. EPISODE IV: 'Globalisation is the only way.' Memory screen presents extreme. Focused obscurity we call the skull or a foreigner to all people in much the same way as an 'O' in a mildewed accounts book is in a manner a pleading.

from 'Quarles Condensed'

O what a crocodilian world is this,
The air, that whisper'd, now begins to roar.

Recitativocitativo

absolute literal cost marble safely bargain reconcile fasten topical crescent planned bargain know imminent fasten outside fasten glad decide subtract profit important improve

Sufferable Fragments (III)

Dichotomedes called himself the Casual Dogmatist. He said sleep is the mother of all and the father of all and Will by necessity calls forth the unwilled. He liked to speak of 'abundant chaos' and said the four elements are pleasure, pain, intention and resistance. The saying 'The polis falling out with itself looks for enemies everywhere' is attributed to him and also the fragment 'Heraclitus was wrong when he said that the sun will not overstep his measure because everything does'.

'Speaking up, talking down.' This remark, supposedly referring to Plato's epistemology, is cited as the reason for Dichotomedes' expulsion from the Academy.

Dichotomedes also said 'The void fills [itself] as smoke [does]'. And: 'disparateness is only sometimes disparity'.

Sufferable Fragments (IV)

a decorative thematic with a strong symbolic charge; vines, querubins, birds, combined with children and acanthus leaves rollings.

She fixed me with a stare and told me to be vigilant. 'There *is* an organisation called Transparency International,' she insisted. And: 'The word for Equilibrium is Vertigo.' Everybody there had been confusing words such as 'dream' and 'damned' for a long time. Please supply us with some raw material and summon your griping angels home.

Bounteous (I)

wedge
purifying

Bounteous (II)

biography
transparent
posed

Bounteous (III)

yoke

Pecata Mundi

I can't remember who in Huddersfield told me there's a street in Portugal called Arkwright and we shouldn't go to India looking for Timbuktu. 'Byron says he ain't gonna do that PA tomorrow.' Del Adorno Corporal: they came from the outfit it was outsourced to and made four A's into the real world sometimes. According to Sperror C is for Texas and M for Tennessee. He knows enemies. *Inadequately* so as all are with such. Simple words, the waiting and calling. Thanks for the use of your emblem library and weather as Zilver as a frozen lake. I saw through that giraffe at once.

Apocolypse Wordsworth: First Codenumber, Additive Plus 100

Stardust she stopgo frontier entrance. I live on an island so the war gets in there somewhere and borrows my name. 'Danger area' is denoted 'AB'. Reduced to a tone the dream world vanished and only the motive was delivered. Culpa. Potentia amoris. Was that word key or fey? I know charms are carefully almost ignorable sometimes if Fortune isn't the poet Quarles that signals Time in passing emblems. Confess. Having noticed the original fifteenth-century doors and bolt turn through the garden gate and walk, be to film to be film to. It's not as if the literal could liberate someone or the collective noun were a copious of copies. An infinitive's payload is its 'to' which when dropped can turn an upside down. Each time is outside whose knowledge is the one (Gift) across.

Episode Phantom Meinhoff Everywhere

I draw with scissors and write with glue. E is a kite for a skeleton dance. Can you think of an instance where 'if' means 'once'? Orpheus was there with Wittgenstein's orphans but nobody called Shakespeare. 3D face = April but 20 face = to do. 'We gabble for gargoyles when we say language,' say Mc and Mac. Grotto some immediate temper: H is for charms and see-sea is of ing as above. The most frequently used English nine-letter word in November 2002 was 'vigilance' but Iconismus or Pecata Mundi forwarded the firewall anyhow. It has now been identified as stardust or these pictures in which. Canned laughter mistaken for a candle after by someone who remembers someone who liked poems about waterfalls better than anything by W.S.Graham. Rocky is all and so ABC 07475 and done as much AB.

Coral Island

abalienate abandon abandoned abandonce abandoner abandonment abase abasement abash abate abated abates

Au Ge Eutectic

They did seem to me quite minor prophecies. Textosterone may be what poetry runs on but who decided there's a difference between softwar and hardwar? Some poems are captions in the interstices like fortune cookie fortunes and therefore some captions are poems. 'Ay,' said Byron, shrugging his shoulders. T stands for 'blow it up backwards', but G? 'Unknown' means just what it says: monuments, obelisks, statues and the like key elements in the surrounding landscape where 'Deep Hole' means 'here' and 'Space' in mirror-writing upside down 'Frustra quis stabilem figat in Orbe Gradum'. One of our copies of Quarles's Emblems is missing but the struggle continues to picture the event. 'Found object' as opposed to what? Our first Orpheus saw Master Kelley conuert appropriat bodies into perfect gold and had no refuge but stay of Process. *Memory Screen* is an exercise book showing preference for excess. I saw through that graffito at once.

'The Sniper's Sights' Written Backwards

with 9 small frames like movie stills I abandoned. Text used to say that it's not for me to document itself.

A Busy Apparition

remember the thriller where I was the bad guy asked in for tea by Vita Sackville-West? The weatherman was Bigmouth and, remember the sequence in the drive-in bank near LA with the numbers in braille on the cash machines? This is my reality, more S than Z, and everything outside is R or T when spauding 'XY' from a suburb. 'The Plasticall Power of the Souls that descend from the World of Life did faithfully

Talkland International

He was still here when I last saw him but he could never quite remember who John Clare was. Dm Ea FL Gj Ho Ic Jg Kw Lf Md Nt Oh Py Qb Rz Su Ta Us Vx Wk not confusing the variants: E$$O. Sperror thinks I must have had a reason for printing those anagrams of Humphrey Bogart in alternate red and blue while Iconismus insists that *Memory Screen* is an alternative route from Dante's Barber Shop home with a new roll of film in the camera. Nah it's another of Wittgenstein's devils, says Pecata Mundi, and for all its allusions not fit to print. Just like Bigmouth the gargoyle up at Lizopard Lake pretending he's a postbox, can't adjust his own settings and half what he does going half way back to where he thinks he'd like to have come from.

I Don't *Want Art To Make Me Cry*

It was one of the languages they speak in Canada. They want to kill us but this problem of script was 'out-defined' and now one of our bicycles is missing. Aa Ab Ac Ad etc supported by photographic evidence which means I have to admit I tore up the copy of Quarles's Emblems making *Memory Screen*. Stardust Moven or NYA to U. Subject: fall from grace. Far gothic but (no matter how long before no matter how sudden the attention) home wise.

Picture Repetition Rate

It is well known that if a succession of pictures is presented in sequence an appearance of movement can be given for example to these photos in which a group of people is looking at a man with a hosepipe beginning washing off all the graffiti in England. The prime minister's the one in the middle looking much too happy. The objectionable flickering the minimum this figure is made as. How many songs of prize ('Md Nt' is presumably 'midnight') when how rarely anyone thinks excess excellence.

Last Few Days

Los. Stardust she stopgo frontier entrance. The struggle continues. It was nearly twenty years before I heard from Sister Martyr again. Spauding overnight: Danse Macabre, Nether Edge. How to beat the poll tax: Babel. I'm sorry Serenade To The Stars was too lost too. At least or last I know I am writing what is already written. Accounting is an art and involves interpretation but a classic slowdown is not a recession: picture repetition rates anybody's lifetime as value added history I do and don't recognise as decades of the twentieth century I seem to have survived.

Also

PARACEL / heim. Astro / der kleinen / occasional / marginal / drawn coat.

Del Adorno Corporal

Wrong which means I have to admit I stole the photo of the clock with the initials JE on a Tuesday night when I was tired of ideas. The name wasn't Martyr although mine by any other I could be Midnight. A pun's a written-out's blast or boast weapon in or upon class or crass struggle. There are certainly cases where U and A will do when no other vowel would except an I on the cusp or in conjunction run to ruin ran to rain. A debit is usually busy as exchequer credit. 'These lines and AH': to picture the event set off this no long distance up to line 4 and draw a curve through so that the waterfall runs from hence into the river underground. Our garden at Nether Edge is a picture and so thanks for the use of your emblem library. Sperror sends his best while Iconismus says farewell not to Shelley but the firewall.

Ideas for Names for this Unpronounceable and Tagger-like Something

Bzuarb. Actual Time. Exciter Shunt Field. Lizopard. Longitudinal fissure. Chreec. Contradiction or konkretedichtung. Synchronising Pulses. Black. White. Utilometal or Alphavitch Carte Blanche. The shadow of Blackpool Tower. The shadows of three gulls and a ferris wheel. A curve through simple words. A leaf or a starfish seen through a broken window at the Church of the English Martyrs. Gargoracle. Transverse tree stone waterfall blockhaus: Descent by steps or Contact their headquarters at once. Wroting. Barzabbea. Nathemata obpact as if Solomon Starfish. Ord pix. Obit. Copyang. The difference between sound and ssound. The cutting-room ceiling or the ferris wheel says farewell to its shadow. Sign writing only: 'Criticise'. Wrong.

Random Reprimand

BOOBY TRAPPED AQUÍ: the parallel is no long martyrdom event or illusionary bedrock. Atop bird adept past diligent decoy. Midrips dilogarithms trot. It was one of the languages they speak upside down underground.

Wroting

If juggernaut were judgment then prejudice were prudence. In those days Bounteous III was a member of Talkland International or one of the outfits it was outsourced to.

Screenface

Memory Screen MS dated 30.3.03 was one of 200 texts Tom Hackett shredded and placed within suspended drip bags connected by arcs of capillary tubing to a series of narrow timber chambers at the UH Galleries. Beginning with a line from the margins of a footnote on Beddoes *Local* was called *Local Squalls* before the devastation by storm of the Solomon Islands which was news that week there was a lull in reported preparations for invading Iraq. Mazes we make or makes we maze when being smart would be avoiding an infinitive's payload. Politics might pun but late night or Latinate EXIST WING LIFT offered no way out. Big spies are edible in Ghent. *Memory Screen* was some pictures which without any warning preferred to be a book.

'Beware sudden monuments'

said Dichotomedes. 'They mean no harm but can do some.'

Spauding 'XY'

difference between sound and ssound. Once he'd decided on the name 'America' Martin Waldseemüller started to think about Virgil. Just imagine all the names America could have easily been called but it's no good dwelling on. The parallel event set off from hence into your emblem firewall having noticed it was copious when outside unconstant.

Rudimenta

'The Plasticall Power of the Souls that descend from the World of Life,' wrote Henry More, 'did faithfully and effectually work those wise contrivances of Male and Female.' Fractious liable to lullaby a fraction short as curt cuts shout askew and audience clasp askance. Staple apple to grapple or claps are to Alan as grasp to alarm. N is for Necromancy, N is for Nature: to educate less than lesson to induct. Blue while home and for all he's a postbox thinks.

Assassin Diapason

Parallel perils: on the day of the iguana ol' Bigmouth a Stonyhurst gargoyle on the Sheffield shift is back nether edging: 'absolute literal etc' near the place near the marks. 'I think the feet are the mind at work.' Tinsley on a photo shoot or Joseph Cornell in a back street in Seville. Incipient yellow in the left hand corner revisited. Honoratorio: 'If equilibrium were vertigo Spain could be Egypt' and Starfish: 'Warpers and twisters with swan marks delivered.' It was one of those cloudy windy days they who think gargoyles are goblins call for no reason 'Coral Island December'. 'Your man in black is not Luther but Faust.'

Time Option Parallel

Thanks for the use of your emblem library but the gargoyle we bought in Paris which you saw in the photo has due to erosion been driven from the pond in an imbalance.

Celeste

Nobody can tell what a sharp-nosed big-eyed marginalien with a pointed chin and hieroglyphic shirt which reminds Iconismus of Artaud's essay on the Balinese theatre would see in an English factory garden unless it's a mirror like the one in the Columbia Hotel in which Bigmouth smooches with Mary Queen of Scots while the band in the ballroom plays *American Patrol.*

VISA

nickel (wired) and pewter (five) to your earth (null)

LUX

Standing upright with their arms outstretched to the sun the ring-tailed lemurs reminded me later of another graffito with an upturned mouth I hope was a smile denoted 'Floris'.

Exequution de Sentence

He is Omega, of all things, who was Bigmouth the Mirror. He read himself too much newspaper and had started believing 1942 was when America was winning its war against Hitler. Occasional as thought are the causes of time but it's not as if the either literal or littoral could strictly enforce the silence requested during concerts by the sea. SSE of The Galloper and WNW of Fairy Bank there is a shipwreck waiting for a shipwreck to happen. The parallel is no long memory screen or correct word-fragments on a tour of the ruins rebuilding some text in which you can't always tell the selfrighteous from outrageous to exhibit. Even some poets forget the difference between slumming it and living in a slum which is possibly why when politics is dead there are still politicians. Harder to judge for the serious critic is how often per page one should mention Adorno.

Sufferable Fragments (V)

'First traveller from Dismay,' Beddoes told his notebook on 10th November 1821. '33 Coventry Street.'

'The expectation determines the event,' said Dichotomedes.

Untitled or Not

I only recently thought of projecting one of the graphic versions of *Memory Screen* onto the exterior brick wall of a disused factory in Ghent now housing a nightclub. The wall was whitewashed long ago; now in disrepair it has been neatly graffito'd with an elegant S formed from the words of an unidentified song. The upper curve of the S in bold Roman reads 'viva el emper[ad]or'. This will sometimes be referred to as the Wallace Stevens version.

Nickel (wired) and Pewter

earth (null) ice (null) fire (null)

Booby Trapped

Floris still grins in a brickwork eclogue. King news and killer music! KONTROLE VERSUS CANUS CAESARI CAROLUS V. Thanks for the use of Option 2: a tearaway escaped from the Vale of Tears becomes the Vicar of Oz. It was an outfit it was outsourced to and by 'installation' they meant 'city'. Disseminated black disabled, said gravelly gravely to the one-time proprietor of Audio Tata Cathay. In the Wallace Stevens version there's a sign saying DANGER or DANCER and a capital B which (additive code plus 100) may signify nothing but the difference between sound and class struggle. The war started with suffusing green light then Saddam Hussein took a long hard look at Angela Rippon and a blue star appeared before the sky turned red.

Erratum

This is what this looked ~~like~~ as if ~~it~~ this looked like. I can't imagine how you see what I do as but I expect I did whatever it was England always seems about to tell me off for having with an untold vengeance done. Glenn Storhaug realised at once that the edible spies must be spits and so kebabs. Pecata Mundi changed his alias to Screenface around the same time that he started confusing poisons with positions for a popeye doll. 'Io Dante' for antidote and how's this for an alibi: the night-thing leaning to the window looking in wasn't a cat but a full-blown rose.

A Serenade to the Stars Scene Three

'I will protect you from all jealous enemies,' Professor Sani tells the traveller from Dismay, 'and make your business more successful. Let me destroy your problems before it destroys you. You can see me hunger for goblin immortality again.'

This scene is set in a gallery with computer monitors stacked against each wall as in a TV showroom. *Memory Screen* appears on all the monitors in slide-show at variant settings.

Kontrole Versus Bigmouth

It was one of those awkward moments when ~~you~~ A.Halsey ~~think~~ thought

~~you~~ he ~~see~~ saw ~~your~~ his self-portrait on a headstone laid down but with different initials in a cloister pavement.

That tree reflected in Lizopard Lake was as or more dangerous as or than any language written or spoken on another planet. Who knows who could be hiding inside a John Bull Churchill figurine?

Text told Sperror that Floris never knew whether Bigmouth worked for Tate & Lyle or MI6. When you have to read an Iain Sinclair novel to remember you've forgotten so favourite a place as what's left of Craswall Priory you at last understand what a memory screen is. Not having opinions was the traveller from Dismay's one pride and certainly the case. Some of these sentences I made up accidentally while looking in a book for something different to steal but I wouldn't if I were you tell Kontrole.

In Arkadia, Floris	*In Arkadia, Also*
two	if
and	artful
both	Fortune
Sing	fail
as	or
Fortune	I
fenc'd	my
had	envious
said	Time
Dismiss	with
if	wreaths
here	beyond
accord	beyond
will	but
wanton	spurn

Spell

which is also the day and one of his visibly or not well in. Who and which ruin involving a ghost when knowing Egyptian may be hoping *from*. Simple words with new use looking happy. E is for Byron if K is for Floris and I think it's actually quite etiquette to say so. Screenface spoke about everything as if he had mentioned it before as instructed. Symbols gold, Iconismus wrote to Text, and glowing symptoms of the seventeen tropes of amphibuity. It is struck as quickly they are forced to be excited you. Either danger or dancer because trees or traces when fresh or flesh although being or benign where night or begin. Skeleton selection barely but bravely for a stand–up curmudgeon: 'warpers' in a bookseller's catalogue probably means 'wrappers'. The present tense is for a moment's thought not a writing's minutes. Floris when a storm is called Zoe on the Solomon Islands which not for devastation but black marketeers was news another week again almost.

Minor Prophecies

'At the time everyone was tripping over spooks trying to tell us how unhappy they were.' Etiquette is adequate. We celebrated Beddoes' 200th birthday with a party of black and white ruffed lemurs whose ghostly liking is to play with umbrellas. 'I is as brief as writing gets,' wrote Stardust Moven to Also.

Gargoracle

Sprinkles when sparkles (twenty speak of the waterfall at once) should make difference spiritful or spiteful speak in self defence. An I where a rain forest usually was is certainly a debit just as England when updated by dumb or done deal at once disappears in the Gadarene darkness. Paranormal panoramas. Marathanatos. 'Dear Lady,' Professor Sani wrote, 'you are ready to acception the china goods.' The initials D.B. on the headstone which A.H. mistook as his own stand for a dealer in second–hand electrical appliances in Sheffield. Bond will bind although bland won't blend: no bigot wilfully begot was our Bigmouth. 'There was a memory scribe who wrote a memory screeb.' Oh. Anagrams. As granma. Said. Grammar. The word for 'always' is 'allows'. It was more a source of searches than a search for sources, a composite gnosis of a ghostic compass.

Supported by Photographic Evidence

'I is an abbreviation for wanting to talk in proper absence,' Also told Screenface. 'Writing is to picture,' Floris interposed, 'as emblem is to expedition.' Danger when sparkles two and both Sing Is What buster and Warpers duet.

Screenface Told Me

'You can rebuild it dashboard.'
'And Aforesaid said?' 'D.B.? Stared
like a footnote. Scared and scarred.'
'And Beforehand?' 'Said? Not a word.'

Iconomics

Most of these people are the same person anyway. Screenface, Also, Pecata Mundi. Because I do not hope to turn into myself again I gathered these snapshots in 6 x 4 albums bound in replica snakeskin called *Memory Screen* as if any variation or an added detail such as month and year made a difference. An antedate is only an antidote sometimes. Reported 'clouds of determined phantoms' October 23rd. Less erotic rhetoric than cult de sac without a broken dream to hang a monostich or map on.

A Tour of the Ruins

1. Relic of the Gold Rush a wooden trunk. Contents a child's doll, about $50 in coins, jewellery and two photographic plates. Letter beginning 'My dear edwin, knowed now we should have gone around.'
2. Drawing of 'alien' or angel with newspaper cutting: 'thankful to not Be sick with thee agu cause others are worse ofen me.'
3. Frontier Stardust ('tell her my heart beets with hers').
4. Blurred black–and–white photograph of man running in front of or away from a wooden shed. Crude drawing believed medical of crescent moon on stick, marked 'FPD: 95.2cm.'

5. Fragment of handkerchief printed with a decoding key ('Hr HL Hx Hb Hj Hy Hz' etc.), property of British spy during WWII.

6. Indistinct photographs of Lizopard Lake, crudely collaged. 'Gargoracle.' 'Cease to land while the waters and driven before.'

7. 'Da busters 1921.' With a torn photograph of Elizabeth II wearing coat such as anybody's mother circa 1955.

8. Blurred colour photograph of head (female), probably waxwork.

9. Line drawing of gallows inscribed HFEGBAE. X-ray photograph of Gutenberg type.

10. Octagonal mirror, frame gilt.

11. Crude drawings of girl perhaps Beryl the Peril and medieval tower. Colour photograph of salamander tadpoles.

12. Diagram of boat with torn inscription: 'THE [   ] [?]NOTHING TH[E] STRUGGLE CONTINUE[S].'

13. 'From the gatehouse, having noticed the original fifteenth century doors and bolt, turn through the garden gate and walk to' etc.

14. Blurred colour photographs (kitchen utensils?) in duplicate, with similar, details of rockface, also in duplicate.

15. 'Dum Coelum aspicio Solum despicio.'

16. Colour photograph, unidentified subject, stencilled 'NOMINA.THICK-NESS' in black.

17. 'Spauding.' Stills from footage of neoclassical sculpture (life-sized female figure) in the gardens near Lizopard Lake.

18. DANGER ← D.B.

19. Waterfall. Starfish. 'This is what this looked ~~like~~ as if this looked like.'

20. Booby trapped.

21. Engraving of preacher wearing black gown. 'A decorative thematic ... open to the public.' Colour photograph showing androgynous 'Memory Screen' figure in the window of a derelict hotel near Morecambe.

22. Colour photograph of 'Egyptian temple' (Madrid). 'The transitional phase between Newcastle Shunt Field and the Lost Weekend.'

23. Drawing of stickman with pilgrim's staff. Drawing of cuttlefish (?) attributed to S.T.Coleridge.

24. Colour photograph, leaves from a mildewed accounts book (detail).

Jack of Spades (Los)

The difference between sound and ssound? Discipuli. Orange tree. The suncharms.

Memory Screen Admission No. 00334

Dial M for Muddled. Can you think of a word there's no other word for? Exodus these poets with their languish exudes. Erosion isn't quite to arisen as decide to decode. 'Demagnify alphabet assessor' meaning 'Dish one sty with some fancy damage.' The absence of gargoyles in a ruin is probably due to not ignorance but theft. N is for a bird who dreamt he wrecked a lighthouse and turned into a monkey, woke up in a dither by the fruit machine.

Composite Compass

or Salamanday. Gene became genre neater than nature as it happened. Site seeing trough out. 'But why nothing and not something?' asked Dichotomedes.

Afterimage

with a label saying 'England'. 'Destory at once.' I'll try not to think there's nothing instead of it inside.

'Substance, or the unthought.' Aristotle considered this untranslatable remark one of Dichotomedes' 'rebukes' to philosophy. 'Contaminated with purity' was another.

A diary without dates might not want dimension although uniform as cuneiform and precipitous as precious by definition.

'Substance, or confusion,' said Dichotomedes, 'still itself.'

So much for waterfalls sketched from the life or imagined.
Poetry when jumping the firewall rhymes.
A longueur's any lounger's pitfall.
The objectionable flickering as Zilver as a frozen lake with a label attached
that week there was a lull which says 'Resign'.

'I could tell a large story' (I)

The 'drawing of "alien" or angel' catalogued in entry 2 of *A Tour of the Ruins* appears on the garage door next to the one showing 'Memory Screen' beneath Castle Market; despite its more expressionist treatment (the paint extravagantly running as if tearfully groundward) and the cruder relation between text and image it is probably the same artist's work. 'The very one you ate last,' writes Clark Coolidge in *Alien Tatters*, 'by the passing slap of a screen memory.'

'I could tell a large story' (II)

Scream	'But to
pencil	leave
fasten	this
in	*Parenthesis*'
deed	said
tagg	Abiezer Coppe
ragg	'I built
outside	a great
thicket	Babel'

mdCBXb3ʒ

Bounty-hunters probably. Sketch of a conifer plantation with 3 diamond-shaped encampments. Not a mappamundi. The monkey ate the pomegranate first then the spider so there's nothing now to be seen except the mask and a voodoo doll attached by a red-headed pin to a black-letter bible. Also unused footage of Sir Thomas Urquhart playing Gavin Selerie at barley break and Screenface flickering statesmanlike telling some tale about a street in Portugal sulking for not being Timbuktu.

Chameleonomy

Dear suburb such as anybred inscribed. 'It's like putting a gun to an agent's words.' Writes perhaps Latinate but local when musicians with a mission put B in eclipse. Either that, replies Deuxieme the phantom, or Gargoracle the spy's indistinct photograptions of probasimple mazes: black midrips and a ferris wheel atop. George Tenet the CIA director on the one hand and Uhu le Grand-duc d'Europe on the other, 'defense deceive delay' as against 'ruler rapid reader'. ABSOLUTE LITERAL COST MARBLE. A Coperhapsican system including a mixed alphabet to encrypt terms and digits not listed any Salamand Solfish would avoid.

Audio Tata Cathay

If hon ora tor io then lar ga men te.

Q = A and a better

How many Concept Houses, derelict or shiny, does one city need? And does it want a laughing policeman and a lighthouse? When is a slap of a memory a slab of a screen?

Not Asia and not Latinate or edible to Also who spent Sunday sorting through his uncollected judgments. Picture the event simple and delivered. The original translation was 'moonrush o new one'. 'I'll try not to think,' Cat-Rabbit repeats after me. A life jump or long fall as Z with some shifty vowels bat don't toll me the latehours kipper was calor-blond for cries' ache.

Hardcore

riptide with reptiles
(A is for Hunter where
L is for Cat-Root)
one fell swoon or swoop?

Extra Reduction

SOUTH AM STRICT
MOUTH LOWER FERRY
02DEC2003 PREPAID

From the Ship of Fools Logbook: Voyage Coupon 54436

'Dichotomedes [was] of Anticyra in Phocis [where] black hellebore grows [which] is the cure for insanity . . . and gave rise to proverbial expressions [like] Avi-ucipas oe or naviget m iticyram.'

animas mortuorum simultanes

animas mortuorum simulantes

Pseudo–Mercurialis

Numerations of hydrogen, oxygen and phosphorus atoms 'exceeding the mandrake's cerebellum with weather abridgement and downstream stigmata'. Harpye (pin) dotal. Cyclopean. Magnetite. Borax. Ichneumon. Melampode. I + humanae + I.

Entries & Extracts Volume M

MALWARE, a pest infecting memory from a remote source. See *Marathanatos.*

MANDRAKE, a vegetable creature of notable remembrance. 'Mandrakes upon known account have lived near an hundred yeares.' A poet's familiar.

MARATHANATOS, a long-distance messenger who brings bad news (orig. unknown).

MARVEL, a charm defined by apparent antithesis. Cf. 'No marvel it has a sullen condition.' A poet.

MELAMPODE, Helleborus Niger. A cure for melancholia. Not 'admitted within the walls of Paradise.' See *marvel.*

MELANCHOLIA, a condition of memory and durable darkness, believed universal; 'it degenerates into philosophy' (R.Burton).

MEMORY, a container, usually containing multiple containers. 'Urnes have been found in my Memory' (T.Browne).

MERCURY, a messenger. Silvery and slippy: see *mercy*.

MERCY, a quality or vegetable of Paradise. An antidote to malware (*q.v.*).

'I could tell a large story' (III)

'A shows pictures and reads the words,' Ken Edwards reports in *They Didn't Go Home*. 'Fire sucked by wind,' writes a Tonalist. 'We take the measure of it. Screen and wind and I.' New mazes which was being avoiding. 'Read him,' the Tonalist continues. 'Read you.' What a long running commentary the self is. 'Lyric intimate.' Wall to wall coverage on Cogito Live. 'The cat-rabbit or chameleon,' writes the Alphabet Assessor, 'should not be mistaken for the lizopard.'

A Note on Memory Screen MS dated 3 January 2003

After a week ill in bed I noticed some large but lightly pencilled capital letters graffito'd on the section entitled *Memory Screen* in the MS dated 3 January 2003. There was a distinct S followed by a half-formed U and a similar Q, with a smaller slanted X several lines below. I'd left the MS beneath a pile of miscellaneous papers and scraps which were undisturbed. Random as forgotten my own lost marks being nobody's initials.

FOR 'GUTENBERG: THE MOVIE'

Ars Poetica

Finding chocolate by echolocation
a pipistrelle would call mere *trompe-l'oreille*.
'I always knew Roman spelt trouble'
remarks Ahab in rehab while proving
that his prophecies for 1999 were really
only grasping the wrong end of a compositor's stick.
'Why the always wanting to finish any writing
and so end the pleasure?' Why 'always'?
Why 'any'? It takes so much distemper
to measure the ado. Query
whether goblin or globin where the quarry
is genetic or a twelve-mile tailback on a major route
across the wordland, a zodiac to you
if not zebra misbehaving in the misbegot gazebo.
'Change of mind could be costly for Halsey.'
'Presence' with the usual erratum in this
case gone missing but to an X-ray I
presumed however reprehensible apparent
and loosely translated 'Presentation'.

An Alphabetic Treatment

Ahab, Captain, his copy of the Bible, its provenance
Burton, Robert, his *Anatomy* filmed in real time
CCTV cameras, labels found on, such as ABSOLUTE
Drafts, in a room in Strasburg, 1436, abandoned
E, its triplicity in 'Jezebel'
Features, or feathers, 'Gutenbird' requiring erratum
Gentitalia, the first 't' in, southerly migrations of printers
Hanged man, regarded as hanging sign
Inventories, inventories of
Jezebel's initial, whether muted in 'Johann'
Kites, mistaken for paper ghosts escaping from bonfire

Laden, in 'zu Laden'
Mainz, Gutenberg's absence from, 1430
Night, its synonyms
O, considered the first letter in 'Johann'
Profanity, unfortunate effect of Gutenberg's invention
Q, as in 'white', whether proper to 'question'
Repetition, of 'in', in writing, its abuse in chiasmus
Screw, described as 'peculiar appliance', its use in a press
Trade, printing, species of coining and mirror-manufacture
U, its questionable presence in 'Aldus'
V, its proper appearance in 'Aldvs'
Whisky, a small fly drowning in, as symbol for misprint
X, its purport, whether warrant for 'Rex & Lex'
Y, its use in 'type' but absence in 'artificial writing'
Zu Laden, in Henne Gänsfleisch zur Laden, zu Gutenberg

Gutenberg's ghost

returns to the drawer in the wooden chest
and takes out the stack of familiar photos.
There are two or three hundred.
He studies them one by one
for the thousandth time.
They show graffiti
palimpsests
lettering from tombstones
faded figures on church walls
damaged human faces in stonework
real or imaginary animals
torn adverts
antiwar posters
manuscript pages
sorts of metal type.
Some he has used in several works
all abandoned
the sight of them tires him

all unpleasant.
But among these photos
there is always one he sees as if for the first time
as if it presents an entirely new idea
will encourage him to another perhaps final attempt.
This time it is a negative of gothic type
the letters shown in white
slanting down from the top right-hand corner.
He has always regarded it as useless
since the camera has captured a small reflected light
a yellow blot in the background black.
He now sees it is the sun
rising or setting on the shoulder of the 'h' in 'Ahab'.

Directions

for the Simultaneous Reading
of Two Printed Columns attached.
Also memo This scene can't be filmed
unless we can find a CCTV
camera labelled MAPPAMUNDI

For 'q.v.' read 'qui vive'

Consider the apparent and hidden E's
in a sentence such as
'The century faded between C and F.'

Gutenberg's house has a basement
with storage for the synonyms of 'night'
but no attic.

☐

Bibles printed white on black
tell a different story. Suns
become moons. In Ahab's absence
'abhorrent' reads 'aberrant'.
Everybody here is a goldsmith and
'fate' is their favourite word.
They devour it. And none
of them will cease to endeavour.

⬜

Count how many courtyards
and stairways. Stars. Do
this solo. Scan any line
in one of Solomon's songs.
Promise you will never say
'abandoned' again. Wake up
wrong. Be abrupt with all
the words you think you
always wanted in a book but
remember to never interrupt.

⬜

'You are a bad writer' says
Pseudonym and certainly
these words are deducted
from sum total and divided
by a common monster. Our
sometimes does equal out.
Elation arising from
suppression of syntax is
often but the prelude to
lasting melancholia and
loss of italics in revision.

Absolute

CCTV cameras
are to us
what the Bible was
to the Middle Ages.

The all-seeing eye
is neither cameraman
nor God.
Nor I.

As far apart as continents
the stretched cheekbones
Gutenberg is watching
us behind.

The hairs on his head are
numbered by as
many frames as
it takes per second.

Re

mark).i
Between 1436 and 1439 certain. documents It is difficult to know
whether Gutenberg knew Marco Polo
whether Guttenberg Changes
a wine press for printing that was waste high
would also enable him to also catch the power of
secret stamping something into something else
Under ordinary circumstances history might be based on
)ustified suspicions / efficient boom in large Bibles
elated July 20, 1459
Johann Fust (q.v.) never undeceived

renewed (vidimused) on August 23, 1503
some smaller books [1] and likewise the Letter of Indulgence date [454]
first printed from wooden with respect to the
fictitious press constructed by Gutenberg in 1441
presented to the monastery near i\Iainz
Dc ado partibus
blocks, a vocabulary
Janua, a folio
small glossary now lost
finished before 15th August 1456 according to bibliographical rules
Pftsters Bible ascribed to Albrecht Pflster found in Pfisters possession
annual interest on the money bad borrowed
his The very s~ispicious Leipzig copy / her of Ysenburg
probably orperhaps Buchhandler hibliographers Cat holicon
yO'hAn gOO'tunberk abandoned his claims to his invention

Captain Ahab

comes to see the relics in Aachen
whose *virtu* is stored in Gutenberg's mirrors
but it's plague year and pilgrims
are banned. Johann Fust (q.v.)

   the wealthy purchase gentleman
   succeeded to convince
   sufficient for extensive
   and of the large prospects
   this giant sum. Fust

to gene meat
veneration's generator
'have' is one thing and 'gave' another
as remote as 'fiend' from 'friend'

Now

a latch plate put forward for further usury of the copied Textverderbnis
give us as it were between her lines customer, good mountain.
Fust even not with the hand and had its credit to exert for God–official use.
Less than six presses did not work last on the forty–two–lined.
A press rascal alone was two meters long
and had themselves to be able to move printers to some extent freely.
Also for many the drying press elbow which one hung up like laundry.
The typesetters also at least one area with stove plant.
There it gave to do still continuously
and a completely small type for drain letters had to be suddenly manufactured
a very much which is worth order for mass.
In addition the Korrektor stressed as calm an area
for its high responsible person as possible activity.
A kontor for a long–range correspondence.
And finally the master had to live in the house not completely restrained
because good mountain was now to the sixty years old,
for twenty years worked,
also before already a quite jerky life had in an inhuman way had
and now completely it had enormous activities and lived in high tension.
Time had had create a household.
It had to sleep in its workshop because still it had to guard professional secrets.

seven hours of history once differently
certified from message control of the American military government
License No. B 209
Stony Pressure, Berlin
instructoraswellas
Fust advanced another 800 ~fl 1452 and in 1455
brought a suit claiming 2020 guilders for principal and interest.
Decided in Fust's favour in the Barefooted Friars' refectory
November 6, 1455. The late (selig) Johannes Fust
were after good mountain fatal outlet to 1466
workshop managers of the prosperierenden

Fust Fust-Schoeffer' Offizin

Druckersignet:
  winkelhaken and stars.

Beside such opulenten liturgical
                theosophischen
    Gemeinschaftsoffizin
        judicial regulations and
                        erzbischoeflichen contractors for
                              Cicero 'De officiis'
                                    probably
                                    buchhaendlerischen
                                    of its
                                prototypischen adverts
                                    reperibus est

'The book salesman to be found in mentioned pub to the wild man'

Its responsible persons

KORREKTOR: You need to slam shut only your Caesar on,
            there find it nearly on each side places in square brackets,
            whose authenticity is denied.

KONTOR: And if you only a scientific expenditure into the hand got,
        there you would surprise you,
        how remains still uncertain much after four hundred years
        of restless and ambitious Philologenarbeit.

Formerly called Goosemeat's Dream

It will be the day when the bland lead the bland.
When delicious goes delirious.
When the squalid squad comes out.
Hoaxes and Hobbes, houses and howitzers.
When the awe must be removed from seaweed
and pathos from the patois of patios.
When wallflowers wallow.
When who rants may reap.
Nouns will be remarkably warm at midday.
Peppermint will not be permitted
and primroses forbidden on private premises.
Where a muse there misuse.
Boats will be sold in reminder ships
and placards used only to placate.
There will be no anathoth in any thesaurus.
It will be shown that hypocritical complaints
are hypercritically compliant. There will be
significant tantrums and vacant citations
before the day ends in a story night.
Fist will force Fussed. Deletions will delight.

Literal Translation

the cameraman says isn't funny.
Monetary abacus is mortuary abuse.
The movie was in any case shot in X-ray
like most of the photos in the wooden chest
and the characters were individual letters
examined for the usual intimations
mortal signs or proof that good mountain
went to heaven or hell with a secret
Burton might have guessed
or Captain Ahabcadavera suspected.

Speech takes a stand at the Frankfurt Bookfair
sells nothing all day
goes home
gets drunk
reads Ahab's copy of the Bible backwards
tears its art vellum binding into strips
makes a noose
goes to sleep instead.
Metalanguage gives him worse dreams than
what dealers like to call
slow trade. Don't read it. Avoid the arcades
but he takes a camera to the auction of his Druckersignet
the hammer comes down on
at less than reserve.
In a café he anagrams the letters in 'camera'
and prepares them for setting in bold sans-serif
illegible to good mountain
but in certain respects opulenten
worth order for mass.
Speech goes home
etc.
Turns off the CCTV
eats three bars of chocolate
reads Ahab's Almanac 2005
deletes all the Latin words
which he then arranges in alphabetic order.
Kalls the Korrektor & kontora.
C's and seize kites in the presinkt with the soulder of Aab.
Aaching. Abherrant. Ahabrupt.
Aldusted ado
red ado
red ado
red ado

TRANSLATIONS OF THE
EPIGRAMS & FRAGMENTS
OF MERCURIALIS THE YOUNGER

Mercurialis the Younger, 'of Anticyra in Phocis, famous for black hellebore', fl. 260-285 AD. His poems survive only in the Annales Anticyrae *where they are quoted, usually in fragmentary form, to illustrate contemporary events and aspects of life in the province. The several references to Mercurialis himself are unhelpful in that they do not always distinguish the poet from his father of the same name, an apothecary and author of a herbal now lost. 'Pseudo-Mercurialis' seems always to refer to the poet. The statement that he 'traded in manuscripts' may only be a slighting reference to his literary career and his frequent plagiarisms; that he 'died very poor' seems probable although we may doubt that he 'chose the pickaxe'. The* Annales *for the most part only tell us that he was the subject of the usual kinds of gossip.*

I

—as if Cicero calls at Circe's stews
and a crocodile's doorbell answers—
an epigram careless of its Ps and Qs
apt to come undone in a quagmire—

II

they suppose they have no
heads but their ears sing:
spectrum or devil, a thing
very common, a catchpoll—
those lazy philosophists
fetch up the spirits

III

of Dr Deuce-Ace the indefinite
and Dr Merryman defiant—
of Dr Diet opacity,
of Dr Quiet loquacity—
at the last fire as derelict
a ferry as [any] ship of fools direct
sailing to Happiness
reverberated [all] into glass

IV

'a trader you can tell by his name,
Mercurialis—that pagan—
tricks in his stars—that *pigeon*'
—with his cellarful of books,
Mercurialis: The Works,
unsold, neatly shelved, all the same

V

[   ]—such a burial
we've seen—he was liberal
once, loved an [?either/or]—
became emperor—
re-invents betrayal

VI

here in Phocis they're always saying
what Dichotomedes is said to have said—
'Pyrrho's nothing was still too much'—
'Cleobolus undervalued excess'—
etc.—and even worse rubbish—
better nonsense the better translated

VII

NIHIL IN FAMAM LABOREMUS
is his favourite quote—Posthumus
the Arcadian always arguing the toss—
for arguing with nothing will be famous

VIII

'Mercurialis his father cornered
the market in hellebore'—
stuff it, Prato, stick to country sports,
new theories on the source
of the midnight rainbow
and tales of lizards
like big cats changing spots

IX

'Love Lake is a poetics'—
we were there once, Sibylla,
where the swans have S denoting Styx
burnt into their beaks,
the worst would be if only I remember

X

Posthumus counts every syllable
composing his valentines
and it seems that Sibylla
has by this contrivance been taken in—
says Prato—such follies
he hitherto ascribed to Mercurialis

XI

—in religion Hellevina knew best—
gave an offering to every known goddess,
could even teach Christians to confess—
would backwards & forwards say the abracadabra,
had the world's best collection of candelabra—
Hellevina's died of the pest—

XII

'Physiologus says . . . '—if I hear that phrase,
Prato, one more time—or 'as Oppianus,
in his *Halieutica* . . . '—you'll end your days
in the gut of the cat-lizard you so praise

XIII

on the ferry a traveller from Egypt—
knew a Christian who lived among the rocks
aged one hundred & fifty—whipped
into frenzies by their Devil but still horny
as the drinkers of asphodel and honey—
they say his prophecies began with a pox—

XIV

'a love poem from Mercurialis
returned to sender by Miracola'—
if you think it isn't true, Sibylla,
a thousand in Phocis will tell you he fancies
that *dancer* less than half his age—
something in the name—that rancid
old nobody at long last gone off the edge

XV

'corrupted saviours will be spewed up from hell'
raves born-again Lamentus 'but not until
next Wednesday'—after his lecture on free will

XVI

'better to have been a shepherd,
Mercurialis, than have suffered
in a falling market'—who other
than Lamentus, that parasite
promoted overnight into paradise—
by himself discovered—

XVII

comparing one poet's idylls
with the odes of another—
repeating 'man is the measure'
and 'nox est perpetua'—
there's a better trade in oracles and riddles—
'Mercurialis obit: the worst of teachers'

XVIII

Hieronymus a bastard like Aeneas
and Miracola politely called Venus—
if your perpetual nights are as short as
you say—try telling that to Catullus

XIX

after twelve years' study Minutius boasts
he could run the polis single-handed,
which Fabius doubts—who calls up ghosts
for a living, knows all the senators stranded
in Phocis—came for our famous oblivion
or any other quick but total solution
to public and private delusion

XX

Sibylla's been down at the girls-only baths
with Miracola and Faustula and all that
coven, blathers peeping-tom Prato who laughs
at what he says he—but with all his heart
he'd promised not to tell me—now Prato's aghast—

XXI

sure we'll conjure ourselves another earth to stand on,
Archimedes, if you fix another place to lay this one
where you'll go a long way to find any understanding

XXII

'the Reason above reason, which is Unity'—
is this the best you can do, Eclectus?
Plotinus pickled with Hermes Trismegistus?
why not the Rhyme above the rhymes you inflict on us
year after year with critical immunity?

XXIII

'one day you'll disappear in your paradoxes'
Paulus told me half a lifetime ago
and this probably happened—just the ego
survives of Mercurialis—and his hoaxes

XXIV

a terrorist suspect, Eclectus?—such fame—
ever since his dream about Rome's secret name—

XXV

Zeno who when walking stood still
came to Anticyra for the cure,
writes Bruno, with an elephant skilled
in several languages—antiquity assures
us irrefragably—'truth lies in a well'

XXVI

with a dozen more patients dead Dr Quiet concocts
a new story: an unseasonal shortage of beavers' bollocks—
while the purgative prescribed by Dr Merryman's
the mixture Callimachus gave for dandruff and ratsbane

XXVII

'written only for the pleasure
of writing'—my verses—
'Mercurialis in his unbroken leisure'—
as if I'd please myself best
knowing Prato's been pleased
or writing odes won reprieve
from Eclectus's Hades

XXVIII

another twenty dead and our local Plutarch
says Dr Diet's abandoned the medical
profession to continue his research
into the synchronicity of miracles
with the sudden universal decline—
deadpan he says it—of our grandads' oracles

XXIX

now that he's discovered etymology
Phaseolus calls it the one proper study—
'a lapsed Pythagorist'—Fabius is galled—
'who's never distinguished his beans from his balls'

402

XXX

a new-found star's
wrecked Polychasmia's
charts—she's to marry
that goat with the gout
Saturnus the usurer
who swills hellebore
down with malt vinegar

XXXI

Homer died of a riddle—
Augustus Caesar preferred one to Virgil—

XXXII

the plurality of worlds
like floating islands
in philosophers' brains
as Eclectus has explained
to us again and again—
as if the human condition
were a want of repetition

XXXIII

—a precisely forecast eclipse—
Phtongus plays and Sibylla weeps—

XXXIV

when Posthumus was in Arcadia
he was told their tales of metamorphosis—
men becoming wolves and so on—turned a
deaf ear, has seen a stranger thing here in Phocis—
the pearls Saturnus once mortified in vinegar
become necklaces and earrings for Polychasmia

XXXV

Prato won't eat a raisin,
won't look at a tortoise—
one killed Anacreon,
the other Aeschylus—

XXXVI

the ballad of the counterfeit phoenix—
Phtongus' latest—Sapphics
fashionably mixed
with a dirge transcribed in Arabia Felix—
Servilius says it was tricks
like these which misled Mercurialis
into writing limericks

XXXVII

Mithridates knew fewer languages
than Miracola's been given new pearls for her ankles—
calls herself Lollia and emeralds spangles—
here lies Mercurialis in anguish

XXXVIII

an obelisk
with basilisk
atop—here lies
that halfbaked
poet, died
of heartbreak,
Mercurialis

XXXIX

Fabius wowed 'em with his artificial
snow at the summer festival—
Vindex brought his cucumbers
that walk and talk—there was a lecture on Antipathy
by Nymphodorus against 'Greek sympathy'—
Mercurialis ran a stall selling hellebore

XL

has the chameleon got your tongue,
Prato? overdosed on aconitum?
scratched yourself silly? for lice
or simple Democritean pleasure?
woefully exceeded the measure?
or forgotten the art of telling lies?

XLI

—as many 'festivals'
these days as 'lifestyles'—

XLII

Simplicius looked clear
into hell at Heraclea
which he's learnt from the locals
to call *Hecla*—
was sold a bagful of trophies—
filled a notebook with tropes—

XLIII

Eclectus has a ring which allows
him to interpret the mysteries of Hermes
but I'd rather be Aurelius
who can freely translate what the horses
tell him every day before the races

XLIV

'the earth has lately shifted
from true centre' says Curio
who being half Italian is gifted
in all sciences and arts—has built
himself a pyramid sufficiently gilt-
edged to withstand
the next earthquake—can't understand
the placards saying No
being carried by the boys who are
against being killed
in someone else's war

XLV

Satyrus who lived on steeped lupins
was our champion at all-in wrestling—
cheated at chess and dealt in electrum—
all profits donated to his own mausoleum

XLVI

Sibylla changes perfume,
Phaseolus, less often than you
change your world-view—
now it's the universal vacuum
wearing things down to the last atom
or an imminent collapse into anagram—
you've been reading Cruel Suit
aka Sluice Rut aka I Cure Lust—
more likely we'll be trepanned
one by one and our eardrums bust
by a Phrygian brass band

XLVII

Posthumus provided the motto 'Lethargy
is best' for Dichotomedes' new effigy
which Marcion carved in his usual frenzy

XLVIII

go little book in your superb
binding—an ex-politician in a suburb
needs you for his famous collection—
never mind how he found
you out—the rest of your edition
I'll remainder unbound
but in mint condition

XLIX

why is the number eleven in vogue—
has someone discovered extra muses
or remystified Eleusis?—
Eclectus' answer is quite vague

L

have you, Acerba, in your looking-glasses,
seen the ghost who's stolen my verses
which a critic has decided are 'meaningless
esoteric jokes done in different voices'?
Mercurialis—appointed to Helicon—for travesties

LI

'you won't find quails and plovers fatter
than we have here in Anticyra'
we're told by our Trimalchio Saturnus,
meaning he's claimed another 500 acres—
as if this were more interesting news
than Polychasmia's Melitensian dress
and fuck-me bespoke Sicyonian shoes

LII

you've become as invisible
to me, Acerba, and as plausible,
as the earth's other moon—why bother?
do you think neither
you nor it will ever be discovered?

LIII

with 90 more dead the latest proposal
of Dr Diet is the redistribution
of air by atomic dispersal
or, as Curio sees it, retribution
on the gods for being idle

LIV

in a cargo of prunes, a refugee from Rome
Umbric wants a quiet life 'and no Greek scum'—
somewhere in the country not too far from
a postbox—he'll be writing daily odes to send home

LV

Polychasmia's gone over to Isis—
Saturnus blames Miracola, 'that menace'—
asks again and again whether lechery
has any known antidote—
her craving for every form of luxury
and so on—three thousand anecdotes
an hour—Fabius calls this bad manners

LVI

you're so busy opposing foreign wars,
promoting freedom before the law
and redistribution of wealth—forget
your principles, Signilo: pay me your debt

LVII

'never trust Mercurialis'
spouts Punto whose library's
all bought with IOUs—
it's time to run, Punto, hell for leather—
if you're lucky
your creditors won't recognise you
or whoever you're pretending to be
on the other side of Lethe

LVIII

did you have to go to Egypt,
Eclectus, to find an unknown Pythagorean text
lovingly antiqued
and written in the master's own script?

LIX

because there's goat stink in his earth songs
and he knows that boats with bad money on board
have a tendency to sink
Corvinus and I are in accord

LX

Saltus needs to know all the ins and outs
of recorded history—what doubts
are yours, Mercurialis—
nothing better to write than quips about
mores & morales?

LXI

since an epigram proves you're incurable,
Prato, don't bother sticking pins in Virgil

LXII

little book returned post-haste from the suburbs
with a brief inscription: 'obscure and perverse'—
this was a speech-writer looking for proverbs

LXIII

a hundred more sayings of Dichotomedes
have been published, and what comedies—
'the spider's web the soul, the spider the body'—
only Posthumus cares if he confutes Heraclitus

LXIV

so your great-great-grandad was an ox-headed
jockey when stray eyes were begging for foreheads
and now we're in exile
from the Lands of the Blest with an overdose of bile
when we could listen to the spheres on the counter-earth
if we hadn't all suffered from tinnitus since birth—
it's the way you tell 'em, Phaseolus, your inimitable style

LXV

'bad mouthing ruined Mercurialis' reputation'—
and you, Favorinus, will have an annotation
somewhere—'remembered for Mercurialis imitations'—
unless you stump the critics with your own interpretation

LXVI

true, Eclectus, a lack of funds is
what usually finds us
out—your licence to interrupt
me is—you know I'm bankrupt

LXVII

you'll find Mercurialis' house at the edge
of the city—protected by two stone dogs
either side of his front door—
everybody knows he's found his true lover
and they've planted their garden on a ledge
above the road with aconite, borage,
clematis and hellebore—
say they prefer to manage
a modest estate with a bog
they call a pond and a symposium of frogs

LXVIII

a pure white owl in a dream,
Faustina, is no more and no less than
a pure white owl in a dream

LXIX

after a night out drinking with the undertakers
Dr Merryman's publishing his new prospectus
and Lamento has proved that his saviour's grace
in its compassion for liars favours Greeks

LXX

eating nine bay leaves a day won't improve
your verses, Acerba—nor will planting a grove
where you can read aloud to your house-trained lion—
if you want Mercurialis' opinion
the best place is the kitchen—to a clove
of garlic, a cabbage and an onion—

LXXI

'Beatus ille qui'—beatifically abandoned—
a crop of couch grass—blackfly on his beans abundant—

BIBLIOGRAPHY & ACKNOWLEDGEMENTS

Marginalien texts and graphics have previously been published in:

Table Talk (privately, 1989)

Reasonable Distance (Equipage 1992)

Ashley Hayles *Four by Seven by Five* (Short Run 1995)

The Art of Memory in Hay-on-Wye (Textual Instability 1995)

A Robin Hood Book (West House 1996)

Shadow Recension (Pages 1996)

Danse Macabre: Death & The Printers, with David Annwn, Kelvin Corcoran & Gavin Selerie (Ispress & West House 1997)

Third Man Subscript: Ration Book Draft (Gargoyle 1999)

Wittgenstein's Devil: Selected Writing 1978–98 (Stride 2000)

Sonatas & Preliminary Sketches (Oasis 2000)

Dante's Barber Shop (De Vulgari Eloquentia) (West House 2001)

Your Thinking Tracts or Nations, with Kelvin Corcoran (West House 2001)

Lives of the Poets: A Preliminary Count, with Martin Corless-Smith (Ispress 2002)

The Epigrams & Fragments of Mercurialis the Younger (West House 2004)

Ahadada Reader 1, with John Byrum & Geraldine Monk (Ahadada 2004)

Marginalien Marginalia: Irregulars & Gargoyles appeared as short-run pamphlets from Gratton Street Irregulars and Gargoyle Editions.

The text-graphic *Memory Screen* was shown at the Bury Text Festival, April 2005.

Some pieces are included in the anthologies *Soleil + Chair: a commemoration of the centenary of Arthur Rimbaud* (Writers Forum 1991), *Conductors of Chaos* (Picador 1996), *A Curious Architecture: a selection of contemporary prose poems* (Stride 1996), *My Kind of Angel: i.m. William Burroughs* (Stride 1998), *Other: British and Irish Poetry since 1970* (Wesleyan UP 1999), *Anthology of Twentieth-Century British & Irish Poetry* (OUP 2001), *Poesia do Mundo 3* (Porto 2001), *The Libraries of Thought & Imagination* (Morning Star 2001), *Onsets* (The Gig 2004)

and some appeared in the following magazines: *Pages, Avec, Poesie Europe, O.Ars, Ninth Decade, Screens and Tasted Parallels, New American Writing, Archeus, Writing, Poetica, Fragmente, Critical Quarterly, Shearsman, C.C.C.P., Colorado Review, Oasis, La Carta de Oliver, Purge, Angel Exhaust, Infolio, Chicago Review, Talisman, West Coast Line, Queen Street Quarterly, The Paper, New Arcadian Journal, Thomas Lovell Beddoes Society Newsletter, Terrible Work, Spad, Jacket, Offerta Speciale, Neon Highway, Unarmed, Kiosk, Alterran* and *GutCult.*

A marginalien's many thanks to all the collaborators, editors & publishers involved.

PAPER SPECIFICATION / POLEMIC

The Five Seasons 'Original' recycled paper (110 gsm) used for this book is manufactured from one hundred per cent pre-consumer RCF (recovered fibre) sourced from scrap chiefly generated during printing and converting operations in the UK, with some addition of 'mill broke'.

No post-consumer fibre has been specified for this paper. This is because no paper mill in the UK currently manufactures quality recycled publishing papers using UK-sourced post-consumer fibre. Some all- or part-recycled publishing papers made in the UK *do* use MDIP (a market de-inked pulp made from post-consumer paper) but this is *imported*—principally from the USA and to a lesser extent from France. Publishers are being encouraged by various campaigns to specify post-consumer recovered fibre in UK-manufactured book papers but this is *not* reducing the amount of waste printed paper dumped in British landfill sites. The production of these 'environmentally-friendly' papers depends on long-distance pulp shipments.

The Waste & Resources Action Programme (WRAP — www.wrap.org.uk) published a major report in January 2005 on the feasibility of resolving this problem by building a pulp mill in the UK capable of producing the required post-consumer RCF pulp: *Market De-Inked Pulp Facility Pre-Feasibility Study* (ISBN 1-84405-142-0). Its findings suggest that a British MDIP facility is unlikely to be built in the near future because of various economic factors (and no British paper mill 'in the printings and writings sector' has 'shown an immediate interest in direct investment in the proposed MDIP plant').

So for the present Five Seasons Press has decided that the best policy is to promote awareness of this regrettable situation and to continue to use UK pre-consumer RCF rather than US post-consumer RCF in Five Seasons recycled papers. Five Seasons also prefers to specify a one hundred per cent furnish of these locally-recovered fibres rather than combine them with Forest Stewardship Council virgin fibres that, as likely as not, come from Uruguayan eucalyptus pulped in Morocco. Five Seasons Press agrees with WRAP's argument that the promotion of recycled paper *per se* is the critical issue. Improved facilities and options will only become economically viable when the demand for recycled papers (whether pre-consumer or post-consumer) increases.

It is of course much more difficult for a large publishing house than for Five Seasons to specify paper of this quality and (relative) probity. One of the many benefits of small-scale publishing.

Glenn Storhaug, publisher